Maurice Blanchot

Maurice Blanchot is one of the key figures of post-war European thought. In both his fiction and his critical writings, Blanchot continually challenged traditional views of literature and philosophy. His texts on Hegel, Heidegger, Kafka, Bataille and Levinas, to name but a few, count among the most perceptive and penetrating essays on contemporary philosophical and literary culture; and both Foucault and Derrida are indebted to Blanchot's groundbreaking work.

This collection brings together the leading commentators on Blanchot from both sides of the Atlantic. It also addresses the controversial issue of Blanchot's political sympathies during the 1930s – an issue that Blanchot himself takes up in a letter to one of the contributors, which is published here for the first time.

Thanks to its combination of cutting-edge criticism and detailed analysis, this volume presents an ideal introduction to Blanchot's life, thought, politics and fiction; it will make fascinating reading for students of philosophy, literature and French studies.

Contributors
Simon Critchley, Paul Davies, Christopher Fynsk, Rodolphe Gasché, Leslie Hill, Michael Holland, Roger Laporte, Ian Maclachlan, Jeffrey Mehlman, Michael Newman, Marie-Claire Ropars-Wuilleumier, Gillian Rose, Ann Smock.

The editor
Carolyn Bailey Gill teaches critical theory at London University. She is the editor of *Bataille: Writing the Sacred* (Routledge, 1995).

Warwick Studies in European Philosophy

Edited by Andrew Benjamin
Senior Lecturer in Philosophy, University of Warwick

This series presents the best and most original work being done within the European philosophical tradition. The books included in the series seek not merely to reflect what is taking place within European philosophy, rather they will contribute to the growth and development of that plural tradition. Work written in the English language as well as translations into English are to be included, engaging the tradition at all levels – whether by introductions that show the contemporary philosophical force of certain works, or in collections that explore an important thinker or topic, as well as in significant contributions that call for their own critical evaluation.

Maurice Blanchot

The demand of writing

Edited by Carolyn Bailey Gill

London and New York

First published 1996
by Routledge
11 New Fetter Lane, London EC4P 4EE

Simultaneously published in the USA and Canada
by Routledge
29 West 35th Street, New York, NY 10001

Typeset in Times by
Harper Phototypesetters Ltd, Northampton

Printed and bound in Great Britain by
Clays Ltd, St Ives PLC

British Library Cataloguing in Publication Data
A catalogue record for this book is available from the British Library.

Library of Congress Cataloging in Publication Data
Maurice Blanchot: the demand of writing/edited by Carolyn Bailey Gill
    p. cm. – (Warwick studies in European philosophy)
    Includes bibliographical references and index.
    1. Blanchot, Maurice – Philosophy.   2. Literature – Philosophy.
    I. Gill Bailey, 1930–. II. Series.
    PQ2603.L3343Z78   1996
    843'.912–dc20

ISBN 0–415–12595–2 (hbk)
ISBN 0–415–12596–0 (pbk)

Contents

Contributors

Simon Critchley is Lecturer in Philosophy at the University of Essex. He is the author of *The Ethics of Deconstruction: Derrida and Levinas* (Blackwell, 1992) and *Very Little . . . Almost Nothing* (forthcoming from Routledge). He is the editor of, with Robert Bernasconi, *Re-Reading Levinas* (Routledge, forthcoming), with Peter Dews, *Deconstructive Subjectivities* (SUNY, 1995), and with Robert Bernasconi and Adriaan Peperzak, *Emmanuel Levinas: Basic Philosophical Writings* (Indiana, 1996).

Paul Davies teaches philosophy at the University of Sussex, having previously taught at Loyola University of Chicago and De Paul University of Chicago. He is the author of several articles on Levinas, Blanchot and related topics and of *Experience and Distance* (SUNY, forthcoming). He is currently working on material for a book on philosophy and the idea of a literary project.

Christopher Fynsk is Professor of Comparative Literature and Philosophy, and Chair of the Department of Comparative Literature, at the State University of New York at Binghamton. He is the author of *Heidegger: Thought and Historicity* (Cornell, 1994) and of *Language and Relation* (Stanford, 1996).

Rodolphe Gasché is Eugenio Donato Professor of Comparative Literature at the State University of New York at Buffalo. His books include *The Tain of the Mirror* (1986) and *Inventions of Difference: On Derrida* (1994). He is currently finishing a book-length study on the work of Paul de Man entitled *Wild Cards*.

Leslie Hill, Lecturer in French Studies at the University of Warwick, is the author of *Beckett's Fiction: In Different Words* (Cambridge

University Press, 1990), *Marguerite Duras: Apocalpytic Desires* (Routledge, 1993), and a forthcoming book entitled *Maurice Blanchot: Extreme Contemporary*.

Michael Holland teaches French literature at St Hugh's College, Oxford. He is one of the founders of *Paragraph*, a journal of modern critical theory, and currently one of its editors. He is the editor of *The Blanchot Reader* (Blackwell, 1995) and is now working on a full-length study of the work of Maurice Blanchot.

Roger Laporte was born in Lyons in 1925 and for many years taught philosophy in Montpellier. His major works were published as *Une Vie* (POL, 1986); most of his critical writings are collected in *Quinze variations sur un thème biographique* (Flammarion, 1975) and *Etudes* (POL, 1990). He was awarded the *Prix France-Culture* in 1978, and was in charge of seminars at the Collège de Philosophie from 1989 to 1991.

Ian Maclachlan is Lecturer in French at the University of Aberdeen. He is the author of *Roger Laporte: The Orphic Tezt* (Berg, forthcoming), and is currently working on a study of writing and time in recent French fiction and philosophy.

Jeffrey Mehlman is Professor of French Literature at Boston University and the author of *A Structural Study of Autobiography, Revolution and Repetition, Cataract: A Study of Diderot*, and *Legacies: Of Anti-Semitism in France;* and, most recently, *Geneologies of the Text: Literature, Psychoanalysis, and Politics in Modern France* (Cambridge University Press, 1995).

Michael Newman is Head of Theoretical Studies and Art History at the Slade School of Fine Art, University College London, and has held a Research Fellowship in Philosophy at the University of Louvain (Belgium) to complete a study of memory and forgetting in Heidegger, Levinas, Derrida and Blanchot. He is the author of many articles on art and philosophy.

Marie-Claire Ropars-Wuilleumier is Professor in the Département de littérature française of the University of Paris VIII. She has published several books on the theory of writing, notably *Le Texte divisé* (Presses Universitaires de France, 1981), *Ecraniques* (Presses Universitaires de Lille, 1990) and *L'Idée d'image* (Presses

Universitaires de Vincennes, 1995). Her research is situated at the frontier between literature, aesthetics and the cinema, examining the possible cross-overs between the notion of filmic writing and the work of the text in literary modernity.

Gillian Rose, who died last year, was Professor of Social and Political Thought in the Department of Sociology, University of Warwick. She is the author of *Dialectic of Nihilism: Post-Structuralism and Law, Hegel contra Sociology, The Melancholy Science: An Introduction to the Thought of Theodor W. Adorno, The Broken Middle, Judaism and Modernity: Philosophical Essays*; and, most recently, *Love's Work* (Chatto & Windus, 1995) and *Mourning Becomes the Law: Philosophy and Representation* (Cambridge University Press, 1996).

Ann Smock teaches French Literature at the University of California, Berkeley. She is the translator of *L'Espace Littéraire* and *L'Ecriture du désastre* (both University of Nebraska Press) and the author of numerous articles on Blanchot and other contemporary French writers. She is currently preparing a book-length study of texts by Blanchot, des Forêts, Melville and Beckett.

Acknowledgements

I wish to thank Malcolm Bowie, Marshal Foch Professor of French Literature and Fellow of All Souls College, Oxford, who was my co-organizer of the International Conference on Maurice Blanchot in London in January 1993, at which many of these chapters were first read. His support in bringing a group of papers on Blanchot to publication is acknowledged with gratitude. I should also like to thank the Institute of Romance Studies, London University, and the Institut Français du Royaume-Unie, who jointly sponsored the conference, as well as the Architectural Association, London, which provided the venue. Thanks also to my editor at Routledge, Adrian Driscoll, who steered the book to completion, and Andrew Benjamin, the editor of the Warwick Studies in European Philosophy series, who was enthusiastic about the project from the beginning. I am also grateful to Leslie Hill, who wrote the Introduction but also with whom most aspects of this book have been discussed: our friendly discussions made my task immeasurably easier.

A note on the translations

All French texts are quoted in English. Contributors have either quoted from the standard English translation, when one exists, or made their own translations. Readers who wish to consult the full texts of the published English translations of Blanchot's works referred to in the text and currently in print are directed to the following:

L'Arrêt du mort
Death Sentence, trans. Lydia Davis, Barrytown, N.Y.: Station Hill Press, 1978.

Au moment voulu
When the Time Comes, trans. Lydia Davis, Barrytown, N.Y.: Station Hill Press, 1985.

Celui qui ne m'accompagnait pas
The One Who Was Standing Apart from Me, trans. Lydia Davis, Barrytown, N.Y.: Station Hill Press, 1992.

'Le Chant des Sirènes'
In *The Sirens' Song*, trans. Sacha Rabinowitch, ed. and with Introduction by Gabriel Josipovici, Brighton: The Harvester Press, 1982.

La Communauté inavouable
The Unavowable Community, trans. Pierre Joris, Barrytown, N.Y.: Station Hill Press, 1988.

Le Dernier Homme
The Last Man, trans. Lydia Davis, New York: Columbia University Press, 1987.

L'Ecriture du désastre
The Writing of the Disaster, trans. Ann Smock, Lincoln and London: University of Nebraska Press, 1986.

L'Entretien infini
The Infinite Conversation, trans. with Foreword by Susan Hanson, Minneapolis and London: University of Minnesota Press, 1993.

L'Espace littéraire
The Space of Literature, trans. with Introduction by Ann Smock, Lincoln and London: University of Nebraska Press, 1982.

La Folie du jour
The Madness of the Day, trans. Lydia Davis, Barrytown, N.Y.: Station Hill Press, 1981.

'Les Intellectuels en question'
'Intellectuals under scrutiny', in *The Blanchot Reader*, ed. Michael Holland, Oxford: Blackwell, 1995.

'La Littérature et le droit à la mort'
'Literature and the right to death', in *The Gaze of Orpheus*, trans. Lydia Davis, ed. and Afterword by P. Adams Sitney, Barrytown, N.Y.: Station Hill Press, 1981 and in *The Work of Fire*, trans. Charlotte Mandell, Stanford: Stanford University Press, 1995.

'Michel Foucault tel que je l'imagine'
'Michel Foucault as I imagine him', trans. Jeffrey Mehlman in *Foucault/Blanchot*, New York: Zone Books, 1987.

'"N'oubliez pas"'
'"Do not forget"', in *The Blanchot Reader*, ed. Michael Holland, Oxford: Blackwell, 1995.

La Part du feu
The Work of Fire, trans. Charlotte Mandell, Stanford: Stanford University Press, 1995.

Le Pas au-delà
The Step Not Beyond, trans. and Introduction by Lycette Nelson, Albany: State University of New York Press, 1992.

Le Reassesement éternel
Vicious Circles, Two Fictions and 'After the Fact', trans. Paul Auster, Barrytown, N.Y.: Station Hill Press, 1985.

Thomas l'obscur (new version)
Thomas the Obscure, trans. Robert Lamberton, Barrytown, N.Y.: Station Hill Press, 1988.

Le Très-haut
The Most High, trans. Allan Stoekl, Lincoln and London: University of Nebraska Press, 1996.

Introduction

Leslie Hill

There can be little doubt today that Maurice Blanchot is one of the most challenging and influential literary and philosophical figures in the whole of the twentieth century. Published in the course of more than five decades, Blanchot's writings are numerous and extensive, and include countless critical essays on literary and philosophical topics as well as several novels and shorter narratives (known in French as *récits*). For all that, Blanchot is a writer whose exact place is difficult to determine. He approaches philosophy with the recalcitrant singularity of a writer of fictions; he reads literature with the urgency of a philosopher; and he writes fiction with the compelling authority that exists only at the extreme limit where the possible gives way to the impossible. Straddling the literary and the philosophical, his writing remains irreducible to both and asks fundamental questions of each, while also dramatizing the incommensurability that sets the two discourses apart yet thereby brings them into endless dialogue. In his writing, as a result, Blanchot has radically transformed the terms in which it is henceforth possible – indeed necessary – not only to think the question of literature, but also to think that deeper question of which Blanchot writes in *The Infinite Conversation* that it is the questioning that eludes and outstrips, precedes and exceeds the question of the all.[1]

Blanchot's intervention, then, touches the very heart of the matter. What changes, after Blanchot, is not just a localized part of the philosophical or literary critical landscape, but rather the very understanding we moderns and post-moderns may have of the relationship between literature and philosophy. Blanchot is one of the first writers of the age seriously to have demonstrated the radical philosophical import of literature, and thereby to have renewed the critical debate concerning the ontological and ethical questions raised by the very existence of the work of art; and he is also the thinker who has most consistently shown the crucial relevance of philosophy for literature: 'to write in ignorance of the philosophical horizon', he contends, '. . . is necessarily to write with facile complacency (the literature of elegance and good taste). Hölderlin, Mallarmé, so many others, do not permit this.'[2] Blanchot's remarkable achievement, then, is not only to have profoundly reinvented the language of literary criticism but also, one could say, echoing Derrida, to have – in a double gesture – both maintained the necessity of philosophy and questioned philosophy itself from a place – the place of literary or poetical thinking and writing – which has always resisted the endeavours of philosophy to assign to it its particular always already philosophical, truth.[3]

As a literary critic, Blanchot is the author of some of the most perceptive and penetrating essays of the last fifty years. His texts on Kafka, Sade, Hölderlin, Mallarmé, Rilke, Bataille, Beckett, Heidegger, Levinas and many others make him one of the most distinctive and cogent commentators of contemporary philosophical and literary culture. Blanchot is an incisive reader of many of the central philosophical texts of the last two hundred years; and he is perhaps one of the earliest and most rigorous proponents of some of the key insights in current literary critical theory. The concept of the death of the author, for instance, or the notion that literature affirms itself as a perpetual unworking of its inaugural stability according to a logic (or non-logic) of originary fragmentation, or the idea that writing carries an exacting, yet ever precarious ethical demand that cannot be founded on anything other than its own transgressive patience, these are arguments that receive their earliest and often most compelling elaboration in the work of Blanchot. Yet, even as he develops such themes, Blanchot remains decisively alert to the – constitutive – limitations, the necessary self-blindness and unavoidable partiality of any discourse that takes writing as its object and seeks to subordinate the language of literature to the theoretical rule of truth.

The experience of death, writes Blanchot, is simultaneously – yet without reconciliation or synthesis – the moment of life's most extreme possibility and the site of its most intimate impossibility. A similarly dramatic sense of incommensurability informs Blanchot's work as a writer of fiction; indeed, as a novelist, Blanchot is the author of some of the most trenchant – and intractable – of modern literary texts, some of which deserve to count among the most incisive and radically affirmative in the whole of twentieth-century fiction. In their limpid clarity yet irredeemable obscurity, what these texts do, as Georges Bataille once wrote, is to give voice to the vertiginous extremity of that which is itself without limits and which, as Derrida has shown, remains radically uncontainable within the bounds of discourse, even within the genre of narrative itself.

For all his exemplary centrality within twentieth-century thought, then, Blanchot is a figure of striking singularity. Throughout his writing life, just as his own work has resisted genre distinctions in order to problematize the borders that hold those genres in place, Blanchot has always written at some distance from the institutions and norms of academic philosophy or literary criticism. In some respects it would even be wrong to view Blanchot as an original thinker at all; for he produces few authentic philosophical or critical concepts of his own, unless one makes an exception for notions such as *désœuvrement* (diversely rendered into English as unworking or worklessness, or sometimes idleness), or the neuter, that crucial term of Blanchot's which, of course, is precisely not a crux, not a term, not even a concept, but rather a fragment of writing that is radically unstable and resistant to definition and belongs to philosophy only to the extent that it constantly slips beyond its control. Here, though, Blanchot is doing something arguably more important than producing a new concept or defining a new theoretical approach. It is rather that Blanchot tends instead, in his writing, to occupy the discourses of others, tiring them out, pushing them to the limit, overwhelming and transforming them. And what then comes to be inscribed in Blanchot's writing, both within and beyond philosophy, within and beyond literature, is the radically ineliminable character of that which – without origin or identity, beyond memory and meaning – enables and disables the totality of thought as its paradoxically simultaneous condition of both possibility and impossibility.

Blanchot himself is a writer who, for many years now, has consistently and single-mindedly resisted the creeping appropriation of literature (especially in France) by the mass media, and has maintained an anonymity and a reserve of quite exceptional discretion. There are few photographs of the writer and no biographical accounts. Yet in recent years, here and there, in letters, in fictional asides and a few fragmentary narratives of his own, Blanchot, in unforeseen and unexpected ways, has slowly yielded to his readers, in a seemingly deliberate yet necessarily piecemeal fashion, some of the key events in his writing life; and it is these that now make it possible to begin to assemble something resembling the story of an intellectual itinerary and to understand the particular – always complex – course that Blanchot has followed through some of the most telling intellectual and political events of the last sixty-five years.

Already in 1973, in *The Step Not Beyond*, Blanchot reflected, in covertly autobiographical mode, on his own beginnings as a novelist during the 1930s and on the distance that separated his daily writings as a journalist from his – literally – night-time activities as a writer of fiction.[4] In 1983, in *The Unavowable Community*, some months after republishing with a new postface the two early stories of *Vicious Circles*, first written in the 1930s but published only in 1947, and in part by way of defending Bataille against the belated charge of sympathy with fascism, Blanchot undertook to retrace part of what he describes in that book as 'our history' ('notre histoire'), referring to the parallel life pursued by Bataille and himself – still strangers to one another at the time – in their common yet separate search for community against the background of a world divided between communism and fascism, between the threat of war and the anxious quest for alternative spaces.[5] The following year, as part of a more topical debate about the tasks of the intellectual in France, Blanchot gave his own personalized account of the challenges facing the intellectual from the Dreyfus Affair to the Algerian War. Also in 1984, in a rare autobiographical sketch entitled 'Les Rencontres', published in the left-wing weekly *Le Nouvel Observateur*, Blanchot described the course of his own life in terms of its encounters, its meetings with a series of seminal literary and philosophical figures whose names recur in his intellectual life with insistent regularity: Emmanuel Levinas (through whom he read Heidegger and Husserl), Georges Bataille, René Char and Robert Antelme.[6] The following month, in an unpublished letter to Roger Laporte, Blanchot began recounting in more detail what the preceding texts had alluded to only implicitly, his own political itinerary from pre-war revolutionary nationalism to post-war radical communism. More recently, too, on the occasion of the London conference of January 1993, he voiced, in another letter to Laporte that is published for the first time in this volume, something of his own reaction upon re-reading a largely forgotten book review of 10 March 1942 devoted to the politics of France's great nineteenth-century critic, Sainte-Beuve. And in 1994, in a short third-person autobiographical narrative entitled *L'Instant de ma mort*, readers were given the story of how, fifty years previously, in July 1944, a young man – the 36-year-old Blanchot – faced a German military firing squad, and inexplicably, unpredictably, unaccountably, escaped, and thus survived, so to speak, the very moment of his own dying.[7]

The story these texts tell, discontinuous as it is, is necessarily an incomplete story; and in some respects, as Blanchot would no doubt readily concede, it is just as important for what it fails to say as for what it does say. The names it cites to punctuate the writer's intellectual itinerary are nonetheless crucial ones. Indeed, of all Blanchot's encounters the first was perhaps the most important. For it was in 1925 (possibly 1926) in Strasbourg, at the age of 18, that Blanchot first met Emmanuel Levinas, his elder by nearly two years, recently arrived from Lithuania. Both were students of philosophy; and despite their many differences, they quickly formed a long-lasting bond of friendship: 'it happened', wrote Blanchot in 1993, 'not because we were both young, but by a deliberate decision, a pact I hope never to break'.[8] Levinas it was who in 1927 or 1928 introduced Blanchot to the Heidegger of *Being and Time*; and sixty years later Blanchot was still able to describe that first encounter as a veritable intellectual shock.[9]

The shock, however, though profound, was not without its complications; and, like Levinas, Blanchot was to spend considerable time during the coming years pondering the implications of Heidegger's philosophical legacy and facing the challenge of thinking beyond it. To this extent Heidegger represents an important reference point for Blanchot's own philosophical and literary beginnings in the 1920s. This is clear, for instance, from Blanchot's enthusiastic reaction, given in a review of Sartre's *Nausea* in 1938, to Heidegger's celebrated Rome lecture of 1936, 'Hölderlin and the essence of poetry', which had recently appeared in French translation.[10] Blanchot refers to the lecture admiringly in the years that follow and, re-reading the early fictional texts such as the stories collected in *Vicious Circles* or the 1941 version of *Thomas l'Obscur*, it is easy to imagine how Blanchot at the time, like Heidegger, might feel persuaded by the concept of the work of art as an inaugural, foundational act intervening in history like an irresistible call and illuminating the world in its epochal historical reality. Indeed, poetic language, or *Dichtung*, Heidegger had argued in the lecture, is what founds Being and makes history possible. Poetry inaugurates and determines every new historical epoch; as such, writes Heidegger, it is like 'the original language of a historical people'.[11] Or as Blanchot phrased it in 1941, in words of his own, glossing Jean Paulhan's essay, *Les Fleurs de Tarbes*, 'all that is necessary is to think that *true* commonplaces are words traversed by lightning and that the rigours of the laws found the absolute world of expression beyond which chance is but slumber'.[12]

Heidegger's phrase – unlike Blanchot's – resounds, of course, as do many similar statements by the philosopher made in the 1930s, with all the sinister political overtones of his deeply held convictions regarding the historical destiny of the German people. It is therefore worth emphasizing at this point the extent to which, despite the philosophical similarities between aspects of his own thinking and that of Heidegger, Blanchot remained resolutely hostile to the appeal of National Socialism, to which Heidegger, for his part, so notoriously succumbed from 1933. Indeed, one can perhaps even argue that Blanchot's own early non-conformist nationalism – shocking though it often is to Blanchot's readers today – functioned less as a French equivalent to Heidegger's embrace of authoritarianism than as a radical counterpoint to it (and Blanchot suggests as much of Georges Bataille – who was not a nationalist – in *The Unavowable Community*). One could similarly contend that Blanchot's surprisingly slow coming to fictional writing (his first fictional text was not published till 1941) was the result of a gradual realization on his part of the extent to which literature, though it may seem to found community, is in fact – *pace* Heidegger – without founding anything other than itself. Literature, by that token, becomes for Blanchot in principle inseparable from the unworking of its own possibility. What it does is to issue a radical challenge both to the world it negates and to the work it founds; by the very paradox of its own authority, it turns into an impossible act that is perpetually in want of authority, forever at odds with the prospect of power, irreconcilably antagonistic, as Blanchot was later repeatedly to assert, to the idea of national – nationalist – destiny.

It is now known that after leaving Strasbourg, Blanchot was mainly active as a political journalist. As early as 1932 he was writing leader articles for the long-established conservative nationalist daily the *Journal des débats*, and he soon became its *rédacteur en chef*. But Blanchot's journalism was not confined to the mainstream press, and he was soon contributing articles to a number of extreme right-wing journals. Blanchot's position was one of radical refusal: refusal of parliamentary democracy, capitalism, Marxism, internationalism, much else besides. 'Refusal', he wrote in 1933, 'tolerates no conditions, except that of never going back on itself.'[13] From April till August 1933, Blanchot was also editor of the shortlived daily *Le Rempart*, which, under the ownership of Paul Lévy, pursued an editorial line (inspired by Georges Mandel) that was fiercely nationalist and vehemently anti-Nazi; and in the years that followed, alongside his work for the *Journal des débats*, Blanchot was a frequent contributor to a series of other revolutionary nationalist ventures, including notably the monthly *Combat* (edited by Jean de Fabrègues and Thierry Maulnier) and the short-lived weekly *L'Insurgé* (run by a loose grouping of Maulnier, Jean-Pierre Maxence, Blanchot and several others). And by 1937, if not indeed earlier, Blanchot was also editing Paul Lévy's nationalist and anti-German satirical weekly, *Aux écoutes*, which repeatedly came under attack from its avowedly anti-Semitic rival, *Je suis partout*, later one of the principal vehicles of collaborationist opinion during the Occupation.

In all these different publications, Blanchot pursued many similar concerns. Like numerous other right-wing commentators, he was deeply exercised during the 1930s by the threat of German expansionism and the apparent indecisiveness of the French government. He was particularly scathing in his condemnation of the foreign policy pursued by successive French governments since the Treaty of Versailles. French foreign policy, he argued, was essentially founded on an – illusory – contractual, legalistic view of relations between states, and this is something he denounces repeatedly. For Blanchot, it seems, the realm of politics was necessarily always already the realm of violent conflict and of force; the only secure policy for France therefore was one founded on the material and moral strength of the nation. Hence Blanchot's vehement attacks on the woolly internationalism of the League of Nations and on the policy of appeasement adopted by the French government when it allowed Hitler's troops to reoccupy the Rhineland in March 1936, thus setting the scene for the Munich accords of October 1938 and the invasion of Poland in September 1939. For similar reasons Blanchot was an unremitting critic of Léon Blum's Popular Front, that government coalition of socialists, communists and radicals which, from May 1936 till April 1938, pursued a foreign policy of friendship towards the Soviet Union while also failing to make good its initial promise to intervene in Spain on the side of the republican government; and it was for reasons such as these that in a notorious series of articles in 1936 and 1937, Blanchot called for its violent overthrow. Yet, at the same time, Blanchot was a consistent and energetic opponent of both Italian fascism and German Nazism, which he had attacked, as early as May 1933, as relying on an entirely mystical idea of nationhood.[14]

It is true that Blanchot himself has been much criticized in recent years for his pre-war involvement with the nationalist right; and in particular the question of Blanchot's alleged anti-Semitism during the 1930s has given rise to considerable polemical debate.[15] In response to the charges raised by various critics, three points are worth making. First, one has to say that there is no evidence whatsoever to support the view that, during the 1930s, Blanchot was the proponent of anti-Semitic views. However, second, it still has to be acknowledged that, during the 1930s, anti-Semitism was (as it still is) endemic in the French extreme right, and it is clear that for some readers the apparent proximity of Blanchot within the pages of *Combat* with, say, an anti-Semitic writer such as Robert Brasillach (from whom Blanchot in fact vigorously dissociated himself) will be enough to compromise the whole of Blanchot's journalism of that period. Third, it would nonetheless still seem to be the case that, in a small but significant group of perhaps no more than half a dozen articles published in *Combat* and *L'Insurgé* during 1936 and 1937, Blanchot does have recourse to a form of invective that may appear to be damagingly close to the anti-Semitic diatribes of the time, and it is indeed on the evidence of these articles that the charge of anti-Semitism rests.

The main purpose of these articles by Blanchot, all of which are couched in the most vitriolic of terms, was to draw attention to the impending threat of a major conflict with Germany; as war seemed ever more inevitable, it appeared ever more likely that France would be overrun. In this context, the main target of Blanchot's attack was the socialist prime minister, Léon Blum, the very embodiment of what, in typically nationalist vein, Blanchot dubbed France's current state of 'degradation'; and it is indisputable that here Blanchot, if only implicitly, seems to be relying on at least some of the anti-Semitic language that was common currency in right-wing circles as part of the campaign to discredit Blum. And on at least two occasions, Blanchot does appear to go further, broadening his attack on those claimed to be propelling France into war to include various sections of the Jewish émigré community, if not indeed the Jewish émigré community as a whole.

Blanchot himself, it must be said, has since the 1930s never sought to justify such remarks, and, when the occasion has arisen, as his letter to Laporte in this volume shows, he has been an unforgiving critic of some of his own earlier published texts. If literature necessarily entails the question of the community to which it gives rise, Blanchot argues, it is because writing as such is inseparable from the complex responsibilities it imposes. As he puts it, for instance, in the unpublished letter to Laporte of 9 December 1984 to which I have already referred: 'vous connaissez mon principe. Laissez chacun s'exprimer selon sa responsabilité' ('You know my principle. Let each express himself according to his own responsibility').[16] Yet as Blanchot is well aware, what has been written cannot be unwritten; and while he has abandoned these polemical texts to the oblivion they best deserve, it is clear that he has also taken responsibility for them to that extent that, explicitly or implicitly, all his subsequent writing has acknowledged everything that is intolerable about them and sought to draw the necessary philosophical and political conclusions from them. It is for this reason, at any rate in part, that Blanchot has inscribed at the heart of many of his texts of the 1970s and 1980s the watchword, addressed as much to himself as to his contemporaries: 'N'oubliez pas' ('Do not forget').[17]

More generally, Blanchot's main – and often private – concern has been to maintain, as he sees it, the accuracy of the historical record. So it is, for instance, that he writes as follows, in the same letter of 9 December 1984, with regard to his relationship with Paul Lévy:

Il faut dire que l'émigration qui trouvait auprès de Paul Lévy un appui constant, constituait alors presque mon milieu naturel; la vérité sur l'extrême danger que représentait Hitler se faisait jour là clairement, mais parmi aussi des rumeurs fantaisistes (que Hitler était gravement malade, qu'il était fou – et comment ne pas assimiler à une sorte de folie ses desseins politiques horrifiants: l'incendie du Reichstag, la Nuit de Cristal, l'annihilation de ses proches compagnons). D'autres, les plus nombreux, disaient au contraire: n'exagérons rien, il faut être prudent, réservé, mettre en garde les Juifs contre eux-mêmes. C'est de là que sont venus les textes que, avec raison, on me reproche. Mais il serait odieux de rejeter sur d'autres une responsabilité qui est la mienne. A cela s'ajoutait la méfiance des Juifs français assimilés à l'égard du sionisme. Levinas m'avait appris l'importance et la signification de la Diaspora, l'errance malheureuse qui avait comme contrepartie la 'dissémination' de la singularité juive, son exclusion de tout nationalisme comme vérité dernière, sa participation à l'histoire sous une forme tout à fait autre. C'est pourquoi j'ai été amené à dire un mot (un mot de trop) sur la 'doctrine nouvelle' d'Israël.

(It must be said that the émigré community which found in Paul Lévy a constant source of support constituted at the time almost my natural environment; the truth about the extreme danger represented by Hitler was plain to see there, but amidst other, fanciful rumours (that Hitler was seriously ill, or mad – and how could one avoid thinking that some kind of madness was behind his horrifying political projects: the Reichstag fire, the *Kristallnacht*, or the annihilation of his close companions). Others, who were more numerous, kept saying on the other hand: let's not exaggerate, it's essential to be careful, reserved, and to warn the Jews against themselves. This is how those texts came about for which I am reproached today, and rightly so. But it would be odious to displace on to others the responsibility which is mine. In addition, there was the distrust felt by assimilated French Jews towards Zionism. Levinas had taught me the importance and the meaning of the Diaspora, that unfortunate wandering which had as its counterpart the 'dissemination' of Jewish singularity, its exclusion from any form of nationalism as final truth, its participation in history in an entirely other manner. This is what caused me to say something – too much – about the 'new doctrine' of Israel.)

By the beginning of 1938, Blanchot had ceased publishing articles in the extremist press. He continued, however, writing for the *Journal des débats*. After the outbreak of war, and as defeat loomed in the summer of 1940, Blanchot was vigorous in his calls upon the government to reject the offer of the armistice and thereby refuse what was shortly to become the policy of collaboration. Many of his editorials were subject to censorship by the authorities; and when finally, in June 1940, Blanchot was witness to the self-dissolution of the French Third Republic, this marked the end of his political involvement with the nationalist right.

Towards the end of 1940 occurred the second major encounter of Blanchot's writing life: his meeting with Georges Bataille. The two men were from very different political and intellectual backgrounds, but an immediate friendship bound them together; this was to prove an important turning point for both writers. One of the fruits of the relationship was Bataille's *Inner Experience* of 1943, sections of which drew on discussions held with Blanchot and others during the early period of the war. In October 1941 Blanchot finally embarked upon his own career as a novelist with the first version of *Thomas l'Obscur*, a text he had been working on since 1932. This was closely followed in 1942 by *Aminadab*, a novel which – surely by design – bore the unusual name of Emmanuel Levinas's brother.[18] One year later, *Faux pas* appeared; this was a collection of literary essays which drew for the most part on the book reviews that, since April 1941, Blanchot had been contributing – primarily, it seems, to earn a living – to the *Journal des débats*, which, now based in Clermont-Ferrand and surviving economically with the help of a government subsidy, was carrying on under Vichy as a staunch supporter of Pétain's collaborationist regime. (In July 1940, Blanchot had attempted, it seems, albeit without success, to persuade the paper to suspend publication altogether.)

The end of the war found Blanchot about to begin the most prolific period of his literary and philosophical career. He contributed extensively to a wide range of different literary journals, such as *L'Arche*, one of the first to appear after the war, *Critique*, edited by Georges Bataille, the *Cahiers de la Pléiade*, edited by Jean Paulhan, and *Les Temps modernes* of Sartre and Simone de Beauvoir. By 1950, Blanchot had brought out a second collection of literary essays under the title *La Part du feu* (*The Work of Fire*, 1949). Two years earlier, his third and final novel appeared, entitled *Le Très-haut*, together with the first of what was to be a series of short *récits*. *L'Arrêt de mort* (*Death Sentence*, 1948); he had also completed a second, revised – severely truncated – version of *Thomas l'Obscur* (*Thomas the Obscure*, 1950), which conserved little more than a third of the original text. In January 1953, the *Nouvelle Revue française* recommenced publication under Paulhan's editorship, and it was there that Blanchot published the first of the famous regular monthly articles that for the next fifteen years or so were to be one of the most significant features of the journal and which, in turn, provided Blanchot with the main substance of the ground-breaking volumes of essays that appeared over the following two decades and on which Blanchot's philosophical and literary reputation now rests: *L'Espace littéraire* (*The Space of Literature*, 1955), *Le Livre à venir* (1959), *L'Entretien infini* (*The Infinite Conversation*, 1969) and *L'Amitié* (1971). During the 1950s and early 1960s, Blanchot also published four further *récits: Au moment voulu* (*When the Time Comes*, 1951), *Celui qui ne m'accompagnait pas* (*The One who was Standing Apart from Me*, 1953), *Le Dernier Homme* (*The Last Man*, 1957), and *L'Attente L'Oubli* (1962). But already *L'Attente L'Oubli*, like – in its own way – *The Infinite Conversation*, had begun to dispense with attributions of mode or genre. Indeed, both books, by their recourse to complex techniques of fragmentation, effect what amounts to a radical refiguring of textuality in general; and the process is pursued further in *Le Pas au-delà* (*The Step Not Beyond*, 1973), a book that lies both beyond and between essay and narrative, and in the similarly unclassifiable text *L'Ecriture du désastre* (*The Writing of the Disaster*, 1980).

From 1947 until 1957, as he outlines in 'Les Rencontres', Blanchot withdrew to the village of Eze in the south of France. Yet in 1958, upon his return to Paris, he was quickly mobilized by the political concerns that had so monopolized his attention in the past. Gone, though, was any commitment to nationalism. Indeed, on his arrival in Paris one of Blanchot's first acts was to contact Dionys Mascolo and join with him in resistance to General de Gaulle's coup d'état of May 1958; and in de Gaulle it was as though what Blanchot was combating was also the spectre of Pétain and the memory of dictatorial military rule. Three years later, together with Mascolo, Antelme, Maurice Nadeau and various others, Blanchot was a key figure in drafting the celebrated Manifesto of the 121, which called for the right of French conscripts to refuse the draft, and had a major impact in challenging the legitimacy of the government's pursuit of the Algerian War, a war that was, of course, never declared as such. The experience on Blanchot's part was the point of departure for the (abortive) initiative, during the years that followed, to set up an international journal which would have brought together in a common endeavour writers from at least four different languages, four different countries, and four different literatures.[19] Finally, during the *événements* of May 1968, Blanchot was an active member of the joint committee of revolutionary students and writers, the 'Comité d'action étudiants-écrivains', and the – anonymous – author of many of the texts printed in the group's broadsheet, which, under the title *Comité*, had only one issue, dated October 1968. Here, Blanchot was fully committed on the side of a revolutionary movement fiercely opposed to the *status quo* in whatever shape or form. Of communism, Blanchot now wrote that it could be defined only as 'that which excludes (and is excluded by) any already constituted community'.[20] Shortly afterwards, however, in the wake of the Six Day War, perturbed at the extreme left's hostility towards the State of Israel, a hostility born (Blanchot conceded) not of anti-Semitism as such, but of ignorance and disregard for the real vulnerability of Israel, yet for that very reason all the more culpable and responsible, Blanchot suddenly withdrew from radical politics, maintaining nevertheless for himself, as for others, what in 1984 he described as 'the right to the unexpected word'.[21]

Despite the undoubted power of his essays and fiction, Blanchot is not an easy writer to approach. Some of the reasons why this is so are explained, in an admirably succinct overview of Blanchot's work, by Roger Laporte – himself, as Ian Maclachlan describes, one of France's foremost novelists as well as one of Blanchot's most patient readers. Blanchot, Laporte suggests, is a writer of complex paradoxes and dizzying displacements. For Blanchot, as for Heidegger, the question of the essence of art is inseparable from the question of its origin. As Laporte argues, however, that origin can only be thought in terms of a radical absence of origin; and even the literary work that seeks to found itself and locate its own origin within itself has necessarily therefore to yield to this prior logic of the absence of the origin, without which, of course, paradoxically, the work would have no chance at all of appearing as an inaugural artifact obeying its own rules or laws. But if one can say that the absence of the origin is what enables the work to appear, this must also mean that the work cannot find its origin in itself but only in the absence of origin to which it is thereby indebted; and if this is the case, it is hard to see how the work can come into being at all. What at one moment functions as a condition of possibility turns round at the next to be more nearly a condition of impossibility, and the search for the origin becomes at one and the same time that which is most essential for the work and the site of its ultimate ruination.

Such paradoxes are a constant and deliberate feature of all Blanchot's writing. As Rodolphe Gasché argues in a remarkable and powerful analysis of 'Literature and the right to death', one of Blanchot's longest, most programmatic essays, which first appeared in 1947 and 1948, paradox in Blanchot is essential; it is, writes Gasché, 'the necessary but insufficient condition for the happening, of the chance of literature'. The question of the possibility of literature for Blanchot, Gasché suggests, is neither a self-reflexive nor a transcendental question; for literature is what necessarily eludes the canonic (Sartrean) question: what is literature? Literature is understandable only as its own question, its own refusal, its own ambiguity. In this respect, Blanchot's recourse in 'Literature and the right to death' to the language of Hegel's *Phenomenology of Spirit*, prompted no doubt in part by Bataille's interest in the work of Kojève (whose *Introduction to the Reading of Hegel* had appeared some months earlier), is, as Gasché demonstrates, entirely deceptive. In Blanchot's text, unlike Hegel's, nothing is ever sublated or eliminated; none of the many contradictions staged by Blanchot is ever resolved. In Hegel's sense, therefore, they are not contradictions at all; what literature does is to introduce into the progressive movement of dialectical thought all the symptoms of radical paralysis.

If Blanchot uses philosophy, then, it is for non-philosophical ends. But this does not imply cavalier neglect; on the contrary, Blanchot's more exacting purpose in that early essay was to exhaust the dialectic not by contradicting it (at best a self-defeating enterprise) but by pushing it to that extreme limit where, losing its grip on itself, it founders of its own accord. The implications are far-reaching. The work of art forfeits all self-identity and unity; the author too is turned into another, an Other who, Gasché writes, is 'someone strange, foreign to himself, unable to master himself dialectically'. In the place of the Hegelian dialectic, there emerges from Blanchot's account of the work of art, then, a conception of alterity that is radically irreducible to a logic of the Same. What writing uncovers, in Gasché's words, is 'an absolutely dissymmetrical Other whose address is unpredictable'.

This thinking of Otherness is no doubt what motivates, in the course of Blanchot's essay, the turn from Hegel to Levinas, and from the former's insistence on the possibility of death to the latter's account, in *Existence and Existents*, of the impossibility of dying. What Blanchot draws on here, as several chapters in this book make clear, is Levinas's notion of *il y a*, that affirmation of being prior to (or beyond) negation that, Levinas explains, is what both enables and pre-empts the possibility of negation and language as such. The *il y a*, as Simon Critchley terms it, is Levinas's 'appropriation and ruination of the [Heideggerian] *Seinsfrage*'; and it is also, Critchley contends, the very origin of the artwork in Blanchot's sense. Indeed, as Christopher Fynsk goes on to suggest in the course of his own illuminating discussion of the same essay by Blanchot, it is in the very logic of the *il y a* that the essential ambiguity of literature has its ground, or rather its absence of ground. The *il y a*, Fynsk suggests, is the moment when language becomes a site of relation (or non-relation) with the Other; constantly underscoring the fatality of the day, it formulates the obscure necessity that gives rise to the day and which cannot be negated, since to negate it is already to affirm the prior possibility of the day itself. This giving of the day, Fynsk suggests, needs to be treated therefore as a 'giving prior to the law that is the birth of the law.' The call it enacts, he adds, 'is wholly anonymous, wholly other'.

What Blanchot does in these texts, then, is less to engage purposefully with philosophy than to traverse it, in the constant attempt to uncover that which is always already other. It is true, as Paul Davies reminds us in a probing discussion of Blanchot's use of the terms 'work' (*œuvre*) and 'worklessness' (*désœuvrement*), that Blanchot's opening questions are undoubtedly those of philosophy. But as Davies goes on to show, Blanchot constantly displaces philosophy both in the sense that his own itinerary as a writer refuses the teleology associated with all linear narratives of evolution or progression and to the extent that philosophy, too, by his intervention, finds itself perpetually confronted with the irreducible singularity of that which resists stable and definitive conceptualization.

This question of singularity or irreducibility is, in much of Blanchot's writing, inseparable from the question of death, or it is death, as Simon Critchley affirms, that gives rise in the texts of both Blanchot and Levinas to the most radical questioning of all. Heidegger, in *Being and Time*, it will be remembered, describes death, famously, as *Dasein*'s ownmost possibility, as that possibility which is the possibility of *Dasein*'s own impending impossibility. Death, however, for Levinas and Blanchot, is what the logic of *il y a* explicitly excludes; not being available as experience at all, it belongs to the realm not of possibility, but rather impossibility; death, in this respect, is more importantly thematized as the impossibility of possibility. Death, then, is not self-relation but a relation (without relation) with Otherness, and the community to which death gives rise, as Blanchot argues in *The Unavowable Community*, is not a community that embodies propriety and truth, but a community, in so far as it is founded at all, that is necessarily traversed by impossibility and irreducible heteronomy. Yet, as Critchley goes on to argue, the philosophical relationship between Blanchot and Levinas, despite the close friendship between the two men, is itself complex and tense. They adopt divergent stances in their critique of Heidegger; and Blanchot, for his part, rejects peremptorily the thought of God, on which a number of Levinas's central philosophical theses arguably depend. Yet it is precisely these divergences that allow Critchley to embark on a radical re-reading of Levinas, and envisage an account of Levinas that would resist the – theological – recourse to the transcendence of the Good beyond Being, and insist instead, after Blanchot, on the atheological, neutral transcendence – the *pas au-delà* – of the *il y a*.

Interestingly, when Levinas draws attention to the presence of *il y a* in Blanchot's writing, it is largely from Blanchot's fictional work that he takes his examples. This indicates perhaps that the structure of *il y a* is not for Blanchot merely of philosophical interest, but rather that it has to do, as Fynsk proposes, with the possibility of fiction itself. As such, it provides Blanchot's novels and *récits* with their most characteristic rhythms: of narrative sequences suspended or dispersed, of extreme events suddenly giving way to the non-arrival of something other. This is particularly clear in *L'Attente L'Oubli*, the subject of Ann Smock's meticulously executed homage to Blanchot's art of paradoxical fiction-making. In her chapter, Smock dramatizes powerfully the perpetually unresolved question of the relation between the one and the other in the story; and as her own reading follows the proliferating disjunctions of the text across the incommensurable space between the two protagonists, one male, one female, one is aware that reading Blanchot's fiction is also an experience of relation and non-relation, communication and separation.

One of Blanchot's most famous essays from *The Infinite Conversation* is entitled 'Speaking is not seeing'.[22] The title has often led to the belief that Blanchot is an author committed to denigrating vision. However, in a brilliantly searching and painstaking investigation into the relation between worklessness (*désœuvrement*) and the image, Marie-Claire Ropars-Wuilleumier shows how, contrary to what is sometimes suggested, the image in Blanchot functions as means of disturbing the unitary nature of theoretical discourse. She shows how, in Blanchot, the image is no longer derived mimetically from an object seen; rather, escaping mimesis, what it manifests is an activity of originary doubling no longer subject to the Platonic logic of original and copy. The image in Blanchot has a paradoxical structure here; what is essential about it is its spectrality, and what spectrality offers is a possibility of inscribing Otherness within the orbit of the Same.

As Michael Newman goes on to illustrate in his turn, citing many of the same texts, the extensive chain of motifs deriving from the theme of vision in Blanchot is subject to innumerable shifts and transformations. Newman begins his discussion with Blanchot's rewriting of the myth of Narcissus, a Narcissus who, in a bold inversion, is characterized by Blanchot as lacking that very self-reflexive presence that the figure is usually held to embody. Once more the logic is one of paradox, and in his suggestive analysis Newman explores in detail the function of that blind spot of invisibility that operates in Blanchot's writing as a transcendental or quasi-transcendental motif. Newman's purpose, however, drawing on Lacanian psychoanalysis, is to probe further into the two stories of vision and blinding – given in *The Madness of the Day* and *The Writing of the Disaster* – that are a central crux with regard to the motif of sight. The point here is to suggest how, for Newman, despite evident similarities, Blanchot's project differs from that of Derrida; whereas the latter is concerned with the failure of the transcendental-sacrificial logic of vision, the work of the former turns more on the relationship between the law and desire or enjoyment.

Much of Blanchot's work of the 1970s and 1980s is concerned directly or indirectly with the simultaneous necessity and impossibility of thinking the event of the Holocaust. Responding to this, Michael Holland, in a remarkable piece of historical textual analysis, examines the changing emphasis of Blanchot's own philosophical and political thinking with regard to the question of violence from the 1930s to the 1970s. A key index here, as Holland argues, is that provided by the shifts in Blanchot's reading of Heidegger. In a close comparison between the two versions of Blanchot's paper 'Nietzsche, today', first published in August 1958 and reproduced, with revisions, in *The Infinite Conversation*, Holland shows how it is possible to uncover in Blanchot's writing the traces of a complex coming to terms with his own largely unmentioned but nonetheless pressing political past. Even though it is not explicitly articulated as such, Holland concludes, Blanchot's own responsibility towards the past in this chapter is nonetheless clear to see, as, too, is the measure of his fundamental commitment to justice.

At this stage in the discussion, Gillian Rose, in the chapter that follows, protests; and in the course of a powerfully moving account of private grief, which is also framed as a vigorous critique of Blanchot's reading of Hegel, she argues that the impossibility of dying and of mourning, as Blanchot figures them in his texts, must finally lead to a retreat from the possibility of justice. She staunchly refuses Blanchot's invitation to think responsibility by way of the notion of passivity beyond passivity, a passivity that, according to Blanchot and Levinas, needs to be thought outside the opposition between active and passive; in its place Rose argues in favour of what she describes, reinscribing the opposition, as activity beyond activity. A different reading of Blanchot might object that justice is a topic crucially at stake in Blanchot's own thinking and that, in questioning the complicity of knowledge and oppression, what he is attempting is to formulate a response to the complex question of the relationship that exists today between justice and power. And it is worth recalling in this connection that for Blanchot, too, the thinking of justice is inseparable from the need for specific, local modes of active intervention (whence, for instance, his involvement in the struggle against the Algerian War and, more recently, his texts in support of the imprisoned Nelson Mandela and Salman Rushdie[23]). In this respect, there is perhaps less of an unreconciled difference than there may seem between Blanchot and Rose; the debate engaged in here between the two positions remains, at any rate, unresolved, and it is to be hoped that it will give rise to a more extended discussion in some other place.

This volume closes with a remarkable exchange between Blanchot and one of his most persistent recent critics, Jeffrey Mehlman. Mehlman's project, in a variety of texts, has been to display in the work of various key figures in the development of what is now generally known as deconstruction – specifically Blanchot and Paul de Man – the damaging, unacknowledged legacy of European anti-Semitism and fascism. Already, in an earlier controversial essay, Mehlman had raised the issue of Blanchot's alleged involvement, as secretary, with the collaborationist *Nouvelle Revue française*, a charge vigorously rebuffed at the time by Blanchot on grounds of historical fact.[24] Even today, there is no conclusive evidence to indicate that Blanchot's role went any further than lending initial support to Paulhan in his necessarily devious negotiations to retain effective control of the journal even as editorial responsibility had already been ceded to Drieu La Rochelle in his role as collaborationist proxy. In any case, the enterprise failed, and the *Nouvelle Revue française*, lacking both credibility and contributors, folded in the summer of 1943.

Readers of Mehlman's earlier work will be familiar with the distinctive critical approach that he has developed. In a series of brilliantly written analyses, his main strategy has been to consider texts as performing a kind of allegorical or figurative mise-en-scène of their own ideological circumstances of production. To read, for Mehlman, is to scrutinize the margins of texts for the other potential discourses that any piece of writing arguably enfolds within it; and it is to extract from those margins a series of recurrent, myth-like scenarios which are then superimposed upon the text to explicate its hidden meanings. Each text, for Mehlman, proves to be traversed by a chain of analogical or allegorical self-reflexive figures. Here, for instance, in this new contribution to the debate, overlaying Sainte-Beauve's political career with that of Blanchot, Mehlman reads Blanchot's review of Maxime Leroy's *La Politique de Sainte-Beauve*, from the *Journal des débats* for 10 March 1942, as a transposed, cryptic account of Blanchot's own position in 1942 with regard to his recent political itinerary and the current politics of the newspaper he was writing for and the Vichy regime it enthusiastically supported. Mehlman raises in his chapter a number of important questions having to do with Blanchot's political and philosophical itinerary; what he describes with persuasive insight is the complex fashion in which Blanchot, seemingly misreading

Leroy's book, sends a clear signal to the editors of the *Journal des débats* and his own readership, indicating his complete rejection of the politics of collaboration. As far as Blanchot's own response to a re-reading of the review is concerned, this is given in the letter to Laporte that appears in this volume.

Writing, Blanchot argues, is an act sustained only by its own emptiness, by a radical excess or nullity that is irrecuperable by any totalizing dialectic and inassimilable within the founding unity of Being. Writing lies before us as a challenge, an extreme exigency that bears witness to the irreducible futurity of that which is still to come. It is Blanchot's achievement to have given in writing the promise of that future; and on the evidence of the chapters in this volume it is that writing that it has now become both possible and indeed urgent to begin to read, as though perhaps for the first time.

NOTES

1 See Maurice Blanchot, *The Infinite Conversation*, trans. Susan Hanson (Minneapolis and London: University of Minnesota Press, 1993), pp. 11–24.
2 Maurice Blanchot, *The Writing of the Disaster*, trans. Ann Smock (Lincoln and London: University of Nebraska Press, 1986), p. 103.
3 See Derrida's contribution to Didier Cahen and Jean-Claude Loiseau, *Sur les traces de Maurice Blanchot*, France-Culture, 17 September 1994.
4 Maurice Blanchot, *The Step Not Beyond*, trans. Lycette Nelson (Albany: State University of New York Press, 1992), pp. 1–2.
5 Maurice Blanchot, *The Unavowable Community*, trans. Pierre Joris (Barrytown, N.Y.: Station Hill Press, 1988), p. 5.
6 Maurice Blanchot, 'Les Intellectuels en question', *Le Débat*, 29 (March 1984), pp. 3–24; and 'Les Rencontres', *Le Nouvel Observateur*, 1045, special issue (November 1984), p. 84.
7 Maurice Blanchot, *L'Instant de ma mort* (Montpellier: Fata Morgana, 1994).
8 Maurice Blanchot, 'Pour l'amitié', in Dionys Mascolo, *A la recherche d'un communisme de pensée, entêtements* (Paris: Editions fourbis, 1993), pp. 5–16 (p. 16); translation mine.
9 See Maurice Blanchot, 'Penser l'apocalypse', *Le Nouvel Observateur*, 22–28 January 1988, pp. 77–9 (p. 79).
10 See Maurice Blanchot, 'L'Ebauche d'un roman', *Aux écoutes*, 30 July 1938, p. 31.
11 Martin Heidegger, *Erläuterungen zu Hölderlins Dichtung* (Frankfurt-am-Main: Klostermann, 1981), p. 43; translation mine.
12 Maurice Blanchot, *Faux pas* (Paris: Gallimard, 1943), p. 101; translation mine.
13 Maurice Blanchot, 'Le Marxisme contre la révolution', *La Revue*

française, 28ᵉ année, 4, 25 April 1993, pp. 506–17 (p. 516); the article is reprinted in *Gramma*, 5 (1976), pp. 53–61 (p. 59); translation mine.

14 See Maurice Blanchot, 'M. de Monzie, émule de Mussolini et de Hitler', *Le Rempart*, 32, 23 May 1933, pp. 1–2.

15 See, for instance, Jeffrey Mehlman, *Legacies: Of Anti-Semitism in France* (Minneapolis: University of Minneapolis Press, 1983).

16 Letter from Maurice Blanchot to Roger Laporte, 9 December 1984. I am grateful to Maurice Blanchot for permission to cite both this passage from the letter and the longer extract that follows; I wish also to thank Roger Laporte and Jean-Luc Nancy for their assistance and advice. Translations from the letter are my own. The text of the letter was originally to have been published in a special Blanchot issue of the *Cahiers de l'Herne*, edited by Philippe Lacoue-Labarthe and Jean-Luc Nancy, which unfortunately never appeared.

17 See, for instance, Maurice Blanchot, 'N'oubliez pas!', *La Quinzaine littéraire*, 459, 16–31 March 1986, pp. 11–12; and ' "N'oubliez pas" ', letter to Salomon Malka, *L'Arche* (May 1988), pp. 68–71.

18 See Marie-Anne Lescourret, *Emmanuel Levinas* (Paris: Flammarion, 1994), p. 68. Aminadab Levinas – whose name is translated 'my people is generous' – died, according to Lescourret, in Lithuania at the hands of the Nazis; on the circumstances in which Blanchot was instrumental in finding a safe haven for Levinas's immediate family during the Occupation, see pp. 121–2.

19 On the project for the 'Revue internationale', see the documents collected in *Lignes*, 11 (September 1990), pp. 159–301.

20 Maurice Blanchot, 'Le Communisme sans héritage', *Comité*, 1 (October 1968), p. 13; translation mine.

21 On the reasoning behind Blanchot's withdrawal, see the letter from Blanchot to Levinas cited in Emmanuel Levinas, *Du sacré au saint* (Paris: Minuit, 1977), pp. 48–9. The phrase from 1984 appears in 'Les Intellectuels en question', *Le Débat*, 29 (March 1984), p. 17.

22 Blanchot, *The Infinite Conversation*, pp. 25–32.

23 See Maurice Blanchot, 'Notre responsabilité', in *Pour Nelson Mandela* (Paris: Gallimard, 1986), pp. 215–17; and 'Adresses', response to a questionnaire on Salman Rushdie, *La Règle du jeu*, 10 (May 1993), p. 206.

24 See Mehlman, *Legacies: Of Anti-Semitism in France*, pp. 6–22. Blanchot has recently offered a more detailed account of the events concerned; see 'Pour l'amitié', in Mascolo, *A la recherche d'un communisme de pensée, entêtements*, pp. 5–16.

1 Roger Laporte, reader of Blanchot

Ian Maclachlan

In recent years, the work of Derrida, Lacan and others has reminded us that thought and writing of compelling originality may go hand in hand with the scrupulous reading of the work of others. Indeed, such work has given rise to a revision of the very notion of reading, a revision in which the work of Maurice Blanchot holds a privileged place. One might say, summarily, that this is a notion of reading which involves an infinite attention to the *Dire*, the Saying of the other which resists the homogeneity of the Said. To put it in such terms is, of course, to evoke the figure of Emmanuel Levinas, who may be said to participate with Blanchot and others – such as Bataille, Derrida, Jabès, Lacoue-Labarthe, Nancy – in a heteronomous community, the sort of community described at various times by Bataille, Nancy, and of course by Blanchot.[1]

Despite attracting the admiration of Blanchot himself, as well as that of Levinas, Derrida, Lacoue-Labarthe, Nancy and others, Roger Laporte's work has yet to receive the wider recognition it deserves. Laporte's lifelong creative relationship with the work of Blanchot, in particular, is of exemplary significance for anyone who would seek to understand the nature of this community of voices. Taking the lead from Laporte's own distinction between the different *plumes* (pens) which characterize his writing, we can briefly outline the manifestation of this relationship under two headings.

Firstly, there is Laporte's own contribution to the critical reception of Blanchot's work, a contribution which itself occupies an important position in Blanchot criticism. It was Laporte who, in collaboration with Michel Foucault, prepared the special issue of *Critique* devoted to Blanchot in 1966 at a time when, as Laporte has subsequently remarked, there were few who were prepared to offer critical comment on Blanchot's work. Laporte's contribution to this field has to date taken the form of four articles and two longer studies, and, in 1989, the organization of a colloquium *Autour de Maurice Blanchot* under the auspices of the Collège International de Philosophie.[2]

This contribution may itself be further subdivided between studies such as 'Le oui, le non, le neutre', which remain broadly within the realm of conventional literary criticism, and essays such as 'Une passion' and 'L'ancien, l'effroyablement ancien', which are accounts of a singular experience of reading, an experience which, for Laporte, must in turn give rise to writing. In a gesture which is itself indicative of the scrupulousness of his reading of Blanchot, Laporte's subsequent dissatisfaction with 'Une passion' has led him not only to repudiate it but to forbid further printing or partial reproduction of it. The later study, 'L'ancien, l'effroyablement ancien' has been reprinted in a collection of Laporte's recent critical writings entitled *Etudes*; it is a remarkable exploration of writing, death and the 'disaster' in Blanchot which, in common with Blanchot's own critical work, is characterized by an unsettling limpidity which eschews any oversimplification of the intractably difficult domain which it examines.

Exceptional as this critical work is, readers of Laporte would, if need be, readily sacrifice it for the sake of that other manifestation of Laporte's involvement with Blanchot, his own creative output. The importance of Laporte's reading of Blanchot for his own writing is signalled in the studies already mentioned, as well as in the published extracts of his *Carnets*,[3] which between them trace the beginnings of this involvement to Laporte's reading of *Faux pas* in 1943 and of Blanchot's regular contributions to the *Nouvelle Revue française* in the 1940s and 1950s, followed by his discovery of Blanchot's fictional work in the 1950s. It was also at this time that Laporte published his first *récits*, *Souvenir de Reims*, first published in 1954, and *Une Migration* and *Le Partenaire*, published in 1959 and 1960 respectively.[4] The last two in particular attest to the impact on Laporte of Blanchot's work, the first being dedicated to him and the second bearing an epigraph from *The One who was Standing Apart from Me*.

Laporte's subsequent work, from *La Veille*, first published in 1963, to *Moriendo*, of 1983, is collected as *Une Vie*, published in 1986.[5] This collected volume bears the designation *biographie*, first employed in 1970 for *Fugue*. It is a designation which marks the ambition of this generically unclassifiable writing, an ambition described hesitantly by Blanchot, in his 'Post-face' to Laporte's *Lettre à personne*, as being 'to write writing and, thereby, to create life or to subvert it, by accepting from life what does away with it, in other words, what pushes life to the limit where it bursts open – to infinity'.[6] In the course of Laporte's extraordinary attempt not to write *on* writing but to write writing itself, we may at times read the trace of Levinas or, particularly in the *Fugue* series, of Derrida, or of others in the community which I mentioned earlier, but the impact of Laporte's reading of Blanchot remains discernible throughout, returning with particular force in the two final volumes, *Suite*, which is once again dedicated to Blanchot, and *Moriendo*, which bears an epigraph from *The Step Not Beyond*. These two volumes, which Laporte has said together constitute the work – or perhaps the nearest approach to the work – towards which he had been striving over the years, are the culmination, the suspended termination of an interminable adventure of writing, of a biography which is haunted throughout by thanatography, of an *œuvre* whose accomplishment is deferred by an endless *désœuvrement*. The singular opening to reading effected by this necessarily incomplete work marks a relation to the other which is analogous to the relations which obtain in the heteronomous community, relations which the work of Blanchot and of Laporte allows us to begin to think.[7]

NOTES

1 Cf. Maurice Blanchot, *La Communauté inavouable* (Paris: Minuit, 1983); Jean-Luc Nancy, *La Communauté désœuvrée* (Paris: Christian Bourgois, 1986). For Bataille's conception of community, see, for example, the chapter 'Principes d'une méthode et d'une communauté' in *L'Expérience intérieure* (Paris: Gallimard, collection 'Tel', 1978), pp. 22–42. A recent English discussion of the heteronomous community may be found in Timothy Clark's *Derrida, Heidegger, Blanchot* (Cambridge: Cambridge University Press, 1992), pp. 139–42.
2 Laporte's studies of Blanchot are: 'Le oui, le non, le neutre', first published in *Critique*, 229 (1966), pp. 579–90, reprinted in *Quinze variations sur un thème biographique* (Paris: Flammarion, 1975), pp. 17–30; 'Une passion', in Laporte and Noël, *Deux lectures de Maurice Blanchot* (Montpellier: Fata Morgana, 1973), pp. 53–155; 'Nuit blanche', in *Critique*, 358 (1977), pp. 208–18; *Maurice Blanchot: l'ancien, l'effroyablement ancien* (Montpellier: Fata Morgana, 1987), reprinted in *Etudes* (Paris: POL, 1990), pp. 9–50; ' "Tout doit s'effacer, tout s'effacera" ', first published in *Lignes*, 11 (1990), pp. 13–21, reprinted in *Etudes*, pp. 51–62; 'Vers "L'absence de livre" ', in *Revue des sciences humaines*, 221 (1991), pp. 33–4. Since the writing of this piece, Laporte has also published *A l'extrême point: Bataille et Blanchot* (Montpellier: Fata Morgana, 1994).
3 *Carnets (extraits)* (Paris: Hachette, 1979).

4 These are collected in *Souvenir de Reims et autres récits* (Paris: Hachette, 1979).

5 *Une Vie* (Paris: POL, 1986) comprises *La Veille* (1963), *Une Voix de fin silence* (1966), *Pourquoi?* (1967), *Fugue* (1970), *Supplément* (1973), *Fugue 3* (1975), *Suite* (1979) and *Moriendo* (1983).

6 *Lettre à personne* (Paris: Plon, 1989), pp. 94–5; my translation.

7 There is, to date, only one brief study of *Une Vie* available in English, but fortunately it is one which can be warmly recommended: Andrew Benjamin's 'The redemption of value: Laporte, writing as *Abkürzung*', in his *Art, Mimesis and the Avant-Garde* (London and New York: Routledge, 1991), pp. 197–211. My own study *Roger Laporte: The Orphic Text* is to be published by Berg in 1996.

2   Maurice Blanchot today

Roger Laporte

I have been reading Blanchot for precisely half a century, since the appearance of *Faux pas* in 1943, the year in which Sartre's *Being and Nothingness* and Bataille's *Inner Experience* were published. Perhaps it would be helpful to give a comprehensive outline of his work – specifically, his work as a *writer*, not his journalistic output, about which other contributors to this volume will write. Blanchot's books fall into three genres: the critical work, the fiction, and finally two books for which there is no generic term, *The Step Not Beyond* and *The Writing of the Disaster*, which appeared in 1973 and 1980 respectively.[1]

The critical work comprises *Faux pas, The Work of Fire, The Space of Literature, Le Livre à venir, The Infinite Conversation* and *L'Amitié*. To this list may be added some more recent short studies, of which I shall just cite *The Unavowable Community* and *Michel Foucault as I Imagine Him*. Blanchot's latest book *Une Voix venue d'ailleurs*, devoted to the poetry of Louis-René des Forêts, appeared in September 1992.

How can one do justice in a few words to this critical work? Blanchot owes much to Mallarmé, Kafka, Artaud and many others, but it should immediately be added that Mallarmé, Kafka, Bataille, Char, Levinas and many others owe much to Blanchot. How would we read Kafka today if Blanchot had not devoted ten studies to the author of *The Castle*? It is impossible to answer this question: we read Kafka through Blanchot's commentary. When we read the text entitled 'The "sacred" speech of Hölderlin' in *The Work of Fire*, we are reading, not Hölderlin, but Blanchot, who reads Heidegger, who reads Hölderlin, who reads the Greeks; and yet, contrary to any egocentricity, Blanchot not only turns, and turns us, towards Hölderlin, clearing a path for us to his work, but above all elicits the faint resonance of that fascinating, incessant call of the remote to which 'literature' tries to respond. Blanchot makes us contemporary with the works he discusses; he draws them together in the same present moment, even if they belong to different periods, or to different genres, some pertaining to literature, others to philosophy or to mysticism.

Blanchot is not simply one great commentator amongst others, for the unique character, the principal feature of his work consists in disengaging works from their past and from their present by opening them to their outside, by taking it that all 'writing' is oriented towards a book-to-come which, according to Blanchot, will only ever be conspicuous by its absence.

The fictional work falls into two periods: that of the great novels, *Thomas the Obscure*, *Aminadab* and *The Most High*, followed by that of the *récits*, *Death Sentence*, *The Madness of the Day*, *Thomas the Obscure* (new version), *When the Time Comes*, *The One who was Standing Apart from Me*, *The Last Man*. *L'Attente L'Oubli*, the final work of this second period, published in 1962, does not bear the designation *récit*. In the various new editions of his works, Blanchot has eliminated any indication of genre.

Blanchot has published no further novels or *récits* for over thirty years; barring an unlikely indication to the contrary, we can therefore consider the fictional work, in the strict sense, to be concluded. The importance of this renouncement cannot be stressed too greatly: Blanchot has abandoned fiction precisely because it was no longer compatible with his enterprise. The place of the *récits* has been taken by a new style, a new genre represented by just two books, but major ones: *The Step Not Beyond* and *The Writing of the Disaster*. If one insists on labelling these works, one could call them *fragmentary*, as, on reading them, one cannot help but think of German romanticism, and more precisely of the Athenaeum. Blanchot's fragmentary works, like the fragments of Schlegel or Novalis, neither set apart nor merge philosophy and literature, but seek what is beyond them: the unmediated experience of thought. In *The Step Not Beyond* and *The Writing of the Disaster*, 'writing', with its stakes, its enigmas, its ruptures, its abysses, lays itself bare and tries to say itself. Blanchot puts Nietzsche's watchword, 'One must shatter the universe', to literal effect, but, for Blanchot, fragmentary writing is not the consequence of a choice, but the result of an experience of dislocation, to which we shall return. Blanchot has long sought the origin of writing, of the work of art, the point where inspiration and lack of inspiration coincide, but this pursuit of a centre has foundered, or has been halted by an opposing force, and thus it is that, in

Blanchot's words, 'the idea of an origin has faded into itself, as it were, leaving behind as a sign the idea of difference, of divergence as the primary centre . . ., a centre which is the absence of any centre, since it is there that any unity is dashed; in a sense, the non-centre of non-unity'; but is it not precisely in this initial break (*brisure*) that the fragments find their 'origin', if we may put it in these terms?

* * *

I shall endeavour to set out the main features of Blanchot's work, but shall be unable to do so exhaustively. My discussion will comprise three parts, each referring to a myth, a narrative, an emblematic figure, let us say. I shall discuss, then, in the following order, the Sirens' Song, the Hunter Gracchus, and Orpheus and Eurydice.

Let us begin with the Sirens' Song, of which Blanchot gives us a version very different from Homer's: 'The central point of the work', writes Blanchot, 'is the work as origin, the point which one cannot reach, but the only one worth reaching.' Blanchot also writes (one could add many more quotations): 'The work draws whoever devotes himself to it towards the point where it undergoes the ordeal of impossibility: an experience which is precisely nocturnal, which is that of the night.' Are we not the victims – and Blanchot, first of all – of a strange fascination? Undoubtedly so, but to maintain that Blanchot's work is linked with fascination is only to say that it responds, that it tries to respond to the call of the origin. 'The sirens', writes Blanchot,

> with their imperfect songs which were only a song yet to come, were drawing the ship towards the space in which singing would really begin. What happened once this place was reached? What was this place? It was a place where the only thing left to do was to disappear, because the music in this region of source and of origin had disappeared more completely than in any other place in the world . . . as if the mother region of music were the only place entirely devoid of music, a place of aridity and drought where silence scorched any means of access to singing.

In approaching the origin, one therefore draws away from any beginning: the book, indefinitely deferred, forever future, gives way to an absence of book, and so it is that, in *The One who was Standing Apart from Me*, when one of the two characters asks the other 'with a strange voracity', 'Are you writing? Are you writing *at the moment*?', the other can never say 'Yes', as the elusive origin makes any 'Now I am writing' impossible. What, then, is the goal of 'writing'? The work, the *chef d'œuvre*, the BOOK of which Mallarmé dreamed? Not at all, as 'to write', says Blanchot, 'is to produce an absence of work (worklessness (*désœuvrement*)). Or else, writing is an absence of work such as it *produces itself* through the work and across the work.' One understands, even if one finds the phrase saddening, dismaying indeed, why Blanchot could say: 'Literature is perhaps designed essentially to disappoint.' How could it be otherwise when 'the book is only a ruse by which writing goes towards an absence of book'! What, then, becomes of one who, for the sake of the work, of the origin, responds to the sovereign demand? 'A wretched, feeble being' at the mercy of an 'incomprehensible torment'. Blanchot also writes: 'Man speaks in the work, but the work gives voice in man to that which does not speak, to the unnamable, the inhuman, to what is without truth, without justice and without legitimacy.'

Have we been led to ruin by allowing ourselves to be seduced by the call of the origin, the Sirens' Song? Even that is not so! Led to disaster, yes, but not to outright ruination. There is in Blanchot a nostalgia for genuine ruination, as one may observe in the way in which he comments on Balzac's *Chef-d'Œuvre inconnu*. Anyone can sympathize with the failure of Frenhofer, who kills himself after burning his painting 'La Belle Noiseuse', but Blanchot remarks that Frenhofer's ruination is not absolute, and is not therefore ruination. Literally, Blanchot is certainly correct. The two people permitted to look at Frenhofer's masterpiece see nothing at first, but they draw closer and, writes Balzac,

> the two men noticed, in one corner of the canvas, the tip of a bare foot emerging from this chaos of colour . . . a delightful foot, a living foot. They remained frozen in admiration before this fragment which had escaped a slow, progressive destruction.

In *Le Chef-d'Œuvre inconnu*, Balzac effects the *mise en abîme* of his own phobia: that his vast *œuvre* should come down to nothing, or almost nothing; perhaps this 'delightful foot' reassures Balzac, but Blanchot has something quite different in mind:

> In *Le Chef-d'Œuvre inconnu* one can still see, in one corner, the tip of a charming foot, and this delightful foot prevents the work from being completed, but it also prevents the painter from saying, with the utmost peace of mind, before his empty canvas: 'Nothing, nothing! At last there is nothing.'[2]

Why, then, should there be disaster, but not ruination? Why has not

Blanchot, or anyone, ever been able to say: 'Nothing! At last there is nothing'? Because in this place of origin, the mother region, there is a complete lack of music: it is as if a form of speech (*une parole*), but blank speech, an unheard murmuring, were addressing us. 'The strangeness of this speech', writes Blanchot,

> is that it seems to be saying something, when perhaps it is saying nothing. Much more than this, it seems as if, in this speech, the depths speak and the unheard-of may be heard . . . [but] it is the speaking silence which has become this false speech which one does not hear, this secret speech without a secret.

In *When the Time Comes*, Judith says to Claudia the singer, 'you sang in your pauper's voice', or 'you sang blankly (*en blanc*)', which brings to mind the meagre, unadorned 'singing' of Kafka's 'Josephine the Singer'. This blank, feeble voice, this speaking silence, that is what persists, what precludes ruination, what prevents any 'Nothing! Nothing! At last there is nothing!' It is certainly the case that Blanchot's wish is to take another step beyond, beyond the absence of the book, as is indicated by this formula which has come increasingly often from his pen, 'Everything must be erased (*s'effacer*), everything will be erased', but this Nothing is impossible, this void inaccessible, for even if 'writing is destined not to leave any traces, but rather to erase all traces with its traces, to disappear more definitively than one disappears in the grave', this sentence had to be written and will have to be erased, and so one will have to write again, write endlessly, a ceaseless movement which makes it impossible to step beyond the absence of the book.

Let us turn now to the emblematic figure of the Hunter Gracchus, firstly allowing ourselves the pleasure of reading a few lines by Kafka:

> 'Are you dead?'
> 'Yes', said the Hunter, 'as you see. Many years ago, yes, it must be a great many years ago, I fell from a precipice in the Black Forest . . . when I was hunting a chamois. Since then I have been dead.'
> 'But you are alive too', said the Burgomaster.
> 'In a certain sense', said the Hunter, 'in a certain sense I am alive too. My death ship lost its way; a wrong turn of the wheel . . . the distraction of my lovely native country, I cannot tell what it was; I only know this, that I remained on earth and that ever since my ship has sailed earthly waters. So I, who asked for nothing better

than to live among my mountains, travel after my death through all the lands of the earth.[3]

What, then, has happened to this hunter who was killed falling from a rock, but who has not entered the kingdom of the dead? His ship, with neither pilot nor wheel, cannot cross the Acheron: it sails 'with the wind which blows in the nethermost regions of death'. 'I cannot tell what it was', declares the Hunter Gracchus, but as readers of Blanchot, of *Thomas the Obscure*, of *Death Sentence*, of that exemplary *récit The Last Man*, we know that a 'monumental, abject event' has severed all connections, disordered time, transformed the dying man into an 'eternal man', 'dreadfully gentle and weak', 'absolutely wretched', for, even though he is 'on the point of death', he will nonetheless never manage to exhaust what little strength remains in his weakness. How could one fail to feel compassion for this Last Man who is filled with 'an unknown suffering, clearer than the clearest day . . . more terrible than that of a child'? Since 'he eternally asks for help without being able to indicate where he is', since we feel friendship for him, we should find the courage, if not to approach, then at least not to turn away from an 'immeasurable weakness', from an immense 'weakness which fills us with terror'. There is nothing we can do for him: such is essential solitude. What, then, is the everlasting torment of the Last Man? 'He is unable to die for want of a future.'

Levinas wrote, with regard to Blanchot, that 'death is not the end, it is *never-ending ending*'. Certain expressions, which are paradoxical, or even absurd if taken out of context, underline this impossibility of dying; Blanchot goes so far as to write, 'The dead revived dying.' In the dark heart of the *récits*, it is as if an 'ancient accident' had made death impossible, an event which took place in the past, long, long ago, in an immemorial, 'fearfully ancient' past, an event which spans the passage of time without ever becoming present, and this is why the dead man can only approach his death indefinitely. The Last Man is sick, dying, dead perhaps (the narrator says, 'I am convinced I knew him first of all dead, then dying'), but he returns among the living, although a little weaker than before, 'a being whose life, one would have said, consisted in growing more and more rarefied', until he once again becomes very ill, 'terribly poorly'. The narrator entertains the most irreconcilable hypotheses: 'I now think', he says, 'that perhaps he did not always exist, or did not yet exist', but also asks, 'What if he were already dead, or if what I took for him were only the silent, surviving presence of an infinite suffering which remained with us, and with which we would have to live, work, die endlessly?'

In the second part of *The Last Man*, the 'scene' is set in the kingdom of the dead, where the shades wander in search of an impossible burial. The narrator evokes a 'grave of light', 'a very white light in which he is immersed', but he cannot find eternal rest, as he is pursued by a 'murmuring' which is not a noise, yet which he cannot silence: 'This murmuring was intoxicating me, perhaps driving me insane.' Can he not hope for a moment of calm? Will the silence not grow? No doubt it will, but 'the more silence there is, the more it changes into murmuring', a quotation which continues with the sentence which will conclude the second part of my discussion: 'Silence, a silence which makes so much noise, a constant disruption of the peace and quiet, is this what is called dreadful, the eternal heart?'

We may finally consider the myth of Orpheus. 'These words are obscure, nothing can make them clear': this is Georges Bataille's judgement of the final lines of *Death Sentence*. It is true that Blanchot is a difficult, profoundly obscure writer, but would it not be naïvety, a mistake – one which is hard to avoid – to believe that this obscurity can and must purely and simply be dissipated, that day must succeed the Night, that Thomas the Obscure must give way to a solar Thomas? The obscure must be cherished as such and therefore safeguarded: this is one of the fundamental, doubtless disconcerting points of Blanchot's thinking. Let us follow his absolutely original commentary on the myth of Orpheus, a commentary to which Blanchot himself draws our attention, as, in the Preface of *The Space of Literature*, he points out that the – admittedly elusive – centre of this work is the text entitled 'Orpheus' gaze'.

In a straightforward interpretation of the myth, Orpheus is normally taken to be guilty of impatience, forgetting the imperative 'Do not turn around', wishing to live with Eurydice without delay and first of all to see her in her true, diurnal nature, her everyday charm. Blanchot takes quite the opposite view, writing that

> Orpheus wants Eurydice in her nocturnal obscurity, in her remoteness, her body inaccessible and her face inscrutable; he wants to see her, not when she is visible, but when she is invisible, and not as in the intimacy of normal life, but as in the strangeness of that which excludes any intimacy, not to make her live, but to have in her the fullness of her death.

'It is as if', adds Blanchot, 'in disobeying the law, in looking at

Eurydice, Orpheus were only obeying the underlying demand (*exigence*) of the work.' This is doubtless so, but is it not also a way of acknowledging that there is an insurmountable contradiction between the demand of the work and concern for the obscure? How, then, may one approach the obscure, allow the obscure to approach, but without making the same mistake as Orpheus? Blanchot has never ceased to ponder this problem, writing, for instance, 'How may one uncover the obscure, bring it into the open? What would be an experience of the obscure in which the obscure yielded itself in its obscurity?' In a text first published thirty years ago, entitled 'René Char and the thought of the neutral', Blanchot returns to this question. Let us relish the richness, the clarity of these lines devoted to the obscure, the unknown, terms which must always be understood in the neuter:

> The pursuit [which poetry and thought constitute] relates to the unknown as unknown. A disconcerting expression, it has to be said, since it proposes to 'relate' the unknown in so far as it is unknown. In other words, we are postulating a relation in which the unknown would be displayed, manifested, uncovered, and from which perspective? – from the very perspective of what keeps it unknown. The unknown, in this relation, would therefore uncover itself in the light of what keeps it under cover.

Reading this text today, one cannot help but think of the philosophy of Heidegger. Is it not, in fact, as if the hypothesis put forward by Blanchot answered a major concern of Heidegger's thought? We know that Heidegger, in his reflections on truth, on *aletheia*, on *Unverborgenheit*, stressed first of all unveiling, unconcealment, disclosedness, the clearing, the open. Later, Heidegger gave increasing importance to Heraclitus' famous fragment, 'Phusis kruptesthai philei.' Nature – emergence, the dawn – likes to hide. Being likes to withdraw into its crypt. To employ the terminology used by Heidegger when he was writing *The Origin of the Work of Art*, let us say that Being destines itself, destines us for unveiling, the World, the light, but at the same time it turns back towards the Earth, its shelter. Can we not say, as no more than a working hypothesis, that in so far as 'the unknown', in Blanchot's words, 'would uncover itself in the light of what keeps it under cover', Being would no longer be rent apart by the struggle – which, of course, makes the work of art – between the World and the Earth, the clearing and non-disclosedness, since Being would come forward to the daylight whilst still remaining under cover?

We may now return to Blanchot and to Char, who is also considered obscure, but is this not in fact because Char's poetry is devoted to the unknown, which neither speaks nor keeps silent, but presents itself to us just as it is: apart, unfamiliar, unknown indeed? To embrace the unknown whilst leaving it unknown means refusing to identify it, leaving it in its obscurity, in a secrecy never to be dispelled. We may recall that Char thought of Heraclitus the Obscure as a 'substantial ally', admiring his famous fragment: 'The Lord whose oracle is in Delphi neither speaks out nor conceals, but gives a sign.' Char translates this fragment with a violent metaphor when he refers to poetry, devoted to the unknown, as an 'index finger whose nail has been torn off'.

Devoting oneself to Blanchot's work is hardly a soft option: there is always the fear that, after fifty years of work, one may be no further forward than on the first day, at least if one measures possible progress in terms of clarity. But what have we learnt? What proposition can we put forward? In fact, we might suggest, Blanchot fulfils what he presents as a hypothesis. Can we not say, indeed, that Blanchot's work, taken as a whole, uncovers the unknown whilst leaving it unknown, this work which attracts us like no other, which captivates us with its obscurity, a transparent Night in which the transparency is at heart more opaque than opacity itself, a wild Night in which we cannot make our way, the succourless solitude of the Disaster, and yet can we not hear a ceaseless murmuring? Do we not think that we can hear 'the streaming of the eternal Outside'?

Translated by Ian Maclachlan

NOTES

1 Translator's note: references are given to the titles of English translations of Blanchot's work where available. However, all translations from Blanchot are my own.
2 Maurice Blanchot, *Faux pas* (Paris: Gallimard, 1943), p. 126.
3 Translator's note: translation by Tania and James Stern, *The Penguin Complete Short Stories of Franz Kafka* (Harmondsworth: Penguin, 1983), p. 228.

3 The felicities of paradox
Blanchot on the null-space of literature

Rodolphe Gasché

At the beginning of 'Literature and the right to death' Blanchot remarks that all answers to the question 'What is literature?' have proved to be meaningless. Further, to the astonishment of all whose approach to literature has been guided by this very question, its answers have underrated and disparaged literature. Even more, the 'what is' question, whose form ('the form of the question') assumes an essence or substratum for its object, becomes spurious when applied to literature. The question 'What is literature?' is a reflective and cognitive question (pp.22–3).[1] Such a question and the reflective attitude that it presupposes immediately disintegrate in the face of poetry or the novel, Blanchot holds. However, having thus failed to understand literature does not mean that understanding would be altogether out of the question. Quite the contrary. The lack of essence that the meaningless and belittling answers to the essential-izing thrust of the 'what is' question imply, as well as the tendency of the reflective approach to consume itself in the presence of litera-ture, or rather of literature's lack of an essence present to itself, might well provide auspicious conditions for an understanding of literature whose questioning form would be distinct both from the cognitive question addressed by the philosopher about the nature of literature and from the writer's self-questioning, his own doubts and scruples.

The denigration of literature that springs from the question's concern with the essence of literature is, of course, not accidental. It does not result from the narrowness of the questioner, but is rather rooted in 'the form of the question' itself. Hence arises the necessity of understanding why the reflective approach comes to grips with literature only by disparaging it. But such an inquiry may well locate this failure in the insufficient degree to which literature has become disparaged. Might it not be that literature offers itself to understanding only where it is radically put into question, seen as a nullity? Certainly, in 'Literature and the right to death', Blanchot suggests that reflection, with its gravity and seriousness, with the importance that it attributes to itself and its object, must withdraw in the face of literature. The retreat of the reflective and essentializing attitude signals that 'literature once again becomes something important, essential, more important than philosophy, the religion or the life of the world which it embraces' (p.23), he writes. Throughout his essay, Blanchot seeks to hold the philosophical question, and hence philosophy as a whole, at bay so that literature can make itself manifest in all its force and importance. When it comes to literature, although one cannot avoid asking the philosophical question, it is, to cite Roger Laporte, 'la question de trop'.[2] But oddly enough, the distancing of the philosophical gesture in the hope of doing justice to literature also belittles it. Literature reveals itself as something vain, vague and impure. Refusing the essentializing approach, literature becomes its own self-negation. It denounces itself as deceitful, as illegitimate. But this movement of self-negation does not stop here: 'literature is not only illegitimate, it is also null' (p.22), Blanchot adds. It is hard to imagine what could be more devastating to literature, and yet this is the radical consequence of Blanchot's concern with literature itself, of his attempt to understand it by holding 'the form of the question' in check.

Putting aside the question in order that literature may manifest itself from itself thus means that literature presents itself as a nullity, or more precisely, as its own absence. In other words, as soon as the question regarding the essence of literature is put on hold, literature re-emerges as the question itself, and of itself. The nullity of literature has in fact allowed literature to appear, to manifest itself, as the question of its own possibility. This is a question entirely different from that of Jean-Paul Sartre, for example. Indeed, it is a question that the nullity of literature addresses to itself and with which it itself coincides. It is nothing but that question, a 'pure' question, as it were, one whose subject is as much a nullity as its object, a question that presumes no self-present essence of what it questions.

'Let us suppose that literature begins at the moment when literature becomes a question' (p.21), Blanchot writes. The question, rigorously to be demarcated from the writer's self-questioning, with which literature is said to begin, is literature's own question about 'the possibility of writing' (p.21). The becoming question of literature occurs in the act of writing in which the writer's pen, without asking why it writes, will always have passively performed that question. 'Now you have done what you did not do; what you did not write has been written: you are condemned to be indelible' (p.21), a writer tells his pen. This question is 'present on the page' once writing has taken place. It is not asked by the writer and perhaps even without his knowledge, incessantly addresses itself to him as he writes. And once the writing is done, it speaks to the reader. This quasi-objective question addresses itself questioningly above all not to the writer and the reader, but 'to language, behind the person who is writing and the person who is reading, by language which has become literature' (p.21). From this it follows that this question that is the beginning of literature is not a self-reflexive question. For at the beginning there is nothing yet to reflect upon in the hope of achieving self-identity. The question is addressed to Others – the writer, the reader, common language. Moreover, since literature begins only as literature becomes a question, the question on the page asks questioningly about the possibility of becoming a question as well. Addressed to Others, the question is in question as well.

Left to itself, free from the impositions of the reflective and essentializing question, literature comes into being as being nothing but the question of its own possibility, begins where it becomes such a question. It reveals itself in its beginning, beginning to exist as the question, and continuing to exist only as its incessant beginning. If literature, then, is constituted by the question of its possibility, is this question perhaps a transcendental question in a philosophical sense? But since the question is all that literature is, it would seem not to be so. If the question that is literature were in a position to enable anything, it would only be itself, or what amounts to the same, literature, 'this concern that literature has with itself' (p.21). What is more, remaining suspended from the response of the Other to whom it is addressed, this question, rather than constituting literature in a technical sense, voids it. The question about the possibility of writing or literature coincides with literature's own self-negation. It is the latter's 'own negation' (p.22). If literature begins with the question concerning its possibility, then literature is not, has not yet been, and has no essence as yet. It exists as this absence of itself, as the question of its possibility. In the absence of the reflective gesture and 'the form of the question', literature presents itself as a mere nullity.

The question, to quote Blanchot, is 'the secrecy of works loath to emerge into broad daylight' ('au sein de l'œuvre . . . repose silencieusement la même interrogation'). Moreover, 'the meaning of this question is . . . difficult to discover'. It tends to disguise itself under all the appearances it takes, especially, by turning into art's self-indictment, into 'the prosecution of art and art's capacities and goals' (p.21). Since it concerns the possibility of literature, the work, or writing, we shall have to ask whether this silent question at the heart of literature does not derive from what Blanchot establishes about the involvement of literature with the whole. He notes, in *La Part du feu*, that 'this Whole with which poetry now finds itself tied up draws it also into an extreme intensity of mysteries, interrogations and oppositions'.[3] Is it because of literature's ambition to be the whole that it cannot but begin and take shape as a question? As will become clear later, this concern with the whole is a concern with meaning, with meaning itself, and as such. Putting off a discussion of literature's claim to totality until later, the following remark on Kafka's thinking already provides a clue. It is, says Blanchot, 'a thinking that plays at being general, but is thinking only to the extent that it is caught in the thickness of the world reduced to uniqueness'. Kafka's thought concerns the general; more precisely, it plays at thinking the general, but, at the same time, 'it is singular, that is, precisely, the thought of one person only. Even though it uses abstract terms . . . it resembles more a strictly individual history.' Because of this embeddedness of the thought of generality in the thickness of the world, or in an individual history, Kafka's thinking 'is not quite a thinking' (n'est pas non plus tout à fait une pensée'). It is *not quite* thinking since it is unable to 'to find a rest in the general' with which thought is intrinsically tied up. And yet, while occurring only as a singular shape, it remains thinking, for it is not confined to incommunicable absolute solitude.[4] Not quite thinking, but thinking nevertheless, literature and poetry make, as Blanchot notes in his essay on René Char, the 'general dependent on what is unique'. But such dependence and its lack of rest cause literary thinking to amount to essentially nothing but 'unrest of a movement without beginning or end'. To understand that in a poem the general depends on what is unique 'is to understand as well why the poem is division, contrariety, torment'.[5] In other words, if the generality constitutive of thinking in literature is intrinsically dependent on uniqueness and singularity, this thinking, unable to ground itself in a higher truth, is tortured by a dependence on something that stands in a relation of contradiction to it. It is a thinking that, called into question by singularity, is tormented by the question of what underwrites it. It puts itself into question and becomes the question of itself. In literary thinking, thinking is then reduced to 'nothing' but a question concerning itself. The shape that thinking takes when its entirety has shrunk to an interrogation about itself is nothing other than the question concerning its possibility.

When thus allowed to negate itself, become a nullity, and be reduced to the condition of its possibility, literature works a marvel. Alluding to the surrealists, Blanchot remarks that 'if literature coincides with nothing for just an instant, it is immediately everything, and this everything begins to exist: what a miracle (*grande merveille*)' (p.22). Sheltered from the reflective question, left free to be a nullity, literature reveals, in lieu of an essence, the opposite pulls of paradox. Its *existence* coincides with the marvellous movement by which an absence, emptiness or nullity turns into everything, the existing totality of the whole. Pushed to its extreme in a literature that assumes the nullity in question – where literature becomes 'the exposure of this emptiness inside . . . open[ed] up completely to its nothingness, realiz[ing] its own unreality' (p.22) – this nullity becomes an extraordinary force, the force of everything, of the whole (*le tout*). Blanchot writes: 'as long as this nullity is isolated in a state of purity, it may constitute an extraordinary force, a marvellous force' (p.22). The aim of what follows – an analysis of Blanchot's essay in the light of this marvel – is not simply to argue that Blanchot delights or even revels in paradox, but rather that paradox is the necessary but insufficient condition for the happening, of the chance of literature. If paradox plays such a role in Blanchot's understanding of literature, if he celebrates it as a marvellous force, it is because in contrast to the prevailing opinion of paradox as logical antinomy, and hence having been fully accounted for, Blanchot takes such antinomy to be the fortunate condition for a possible (yet not for that matter, necessary) happening of literature.

Given the dominating presence of Hegel's *Phenomenology of Spirit* in 'Literature and the right to death' – one that is visible not only in the numerous themes borrowed from Hegel, but especially in the order in which Blanchot develops his arguments – one could be tempted to classify the movement from nullity to everything as a Hegelian dialectical inversion, and paradox as merely a speculative proposition and leap (*Satz*). Undoubtedly, this temptation is not fortuitous, or entirely unjustified. It would even seem to impose itself, for does not Blanchot's own mode of exposition and argumentation in the essay have all the characteristics of dialectic? But although Blanchot has recourse to *this* man who had lived some 150 years before to substantiate his contention that 'the volatizing and volatile force which literature seems to have become' (p.23) today is not the result of passing historical conditions but coextensive with literature itself, after having put philosophical reflection and its essentializing question at a remove, it would be difficult to reduce his subsequent description and analysis of all the contradictions faced by the writer, the work and literary language to a display of the contradictory moments of literature's dialectical self-manifestation.[6] Are not precisely all these Hegelian references, whether thematic or formal, part of the movement by which literature, once philosophical reflection has retreated, 'once again becomes something important, essential, more important than . . . philosophy' (p.22)? Of Mallarmé, Blanchot holds in *The Space of Literature* that 'his Hegelian vocabulary would merit no attention, were it not animated by an authentic experience'.[7] The same is true of Blanchot's own borrowings from Hegel. Right from the start, he acknowledges that his remarks on Hegel 'are quite remote from the text of the *Phenomenology* and make no attempt to illuminate it' (p.23). These remarks serve non-philosophical, non-reflective purposes.[8]

Blanchot sketches out the main features of his conception of paradox and its 'constitutive' role in a series of developments that call on a number of (often consecutive) passages in Hegel's *Phenomenology*. The first passages to be invoked are from the section 'Individuality which takes itself to be real in and for itself', or more precisely from its first chapter, 'The spiritual animal kingdom and deceit or the "matter in hand" itself', an analysis, according to Blanchot, of 'human work in general' in which Hegel is also said to describe the contradictions 'in which someone who has chosen to be a man of letters' becomes entangled (p.23). The writer, he notes, from 'his very first step . . . [is] stopped by a contradiction': to write, a writer needs talent, but he has no talent until he has proved it by writing. In this first account of what Blanchot terms the 'anomaly' constitutive of 'the essence of literary activity' (pp.23–4), Blanchot faithfully seems to reproduce the Hegelian dialectic between the individual and his effective reality as work, including the final solution of this contradiction by means of the individual's beforehand consciousness of his work 'as *entirely his* own, i.e. as an End' (p.24). Yet Blanchot concludes the rendering of this contradiction with the remark that 'the same [i.e. contradictory situation] is true for each new work, because everything begins again from nothing' (p.24). In short, now that the contradiction in question has been sublated, rather than following Hegel to another, and higher one, Blanchot hangs on to what Hegel leaves behind. Blanchot continues to insist on the necessity that the writer go endlessly through the same contradictory motion without respite. What is more, he complicates the initial dilemma of the writer, deepening it, making it ever more hopeless, by asking, first, why the writer who has his future work present as an End should still translate it into words; second, by remarking that if the writer is aware that his work has value only as a realized work, 'he will begin to write, but starting from nothing and with nothing in mind – like a nothingness working in nothingness' (p.24). The requisites considered by Hegel for the dialectical solution of the writer's contradiction are thus shown only to aggravate his situation. As should already be evident, Blanchot's emphasis in these descriptions is the insolubleness of the contradiction. He notes that the problem of talent and work 'could never be overcome if the person writing expected its solution to give him the right to begin writing' (p.24). The contradiction we are dealing with is thus not to be solved, dialectically or otherwise. 'The writer both must and must not overcome' it, we are told (p.23). In other words, to overcome it, he must not overcome it. To be a writer, and to bring forth a work, he must hold out the contradiction in all its insolubility. While Blanchot appeals to Hegel's authority to claim that the writer must 'start immediately, and, whatever the circumstances, without further scruples about beginning, means or End, proceed to action' (p.24), the immediacy of the act of writing which Blanchot has in mind is indicative of the insolubility of the problem, not the beginning of the solution of the contradiction itself in the actual work. For, indeed, the work in which the contradiction is overcome is logically, or dialectically, underivable from the contradiction. For a work to arise from it, a work that merits that name, the contradiction must be unsolvable. The unsolvability of the contradiction and its 'immediacy', that is, the irreducibleness of what springs from it, are thus the first traits of paradox that we need to refine further.

Let us now suppose with Blanchot that the work has taken shape and that with it the writer has been born. This situation exhibits a new set of contradictions which Blanchot couches again in Hegelian language, drawing on the dialectics of exteriorization as developed in the second half of the chapter on 'The spiritual animal kingdom'. Still, one must not lose sight of what has been established so far about the work. The work, supposed to have come into existence ('let us suppose'), can only be a work that stands in no causal or dialectical relation to the contradictory conditions of its production. In addition, the new set of contradictions that arises once the writer has shown his talent in producing a work is incommensurate with the first set. It is not derivative from the first set, nor is it made up of higher contradictions. It is just one more set. What, then, do these additional contradictions amount to? Although the work makes the writer a writer, it does so only to the extent that it is not exclusively his work, but 'belongs to other people, people who can read it'. But the interest other people have in his work differs from his own interest in it and 'transforms it into something different, something in which he does not recognize the original perfection' (p.26). None of the possible solutions to this 'disconcerting ordeal (*épreuve déconcertante*)' (p.26) – that the writer suppress the work as a public institution by insisting on individual authorship, or that he suppress himself as a writer by letting the reader be the true author of the work – have any chance of succeeding. Valéry's answer to this dilemma, based on a reflection on the technique involved in the creation of an artwork, fails as well, Blanchot argues. But what of the claim that this disconcerting ordeal reveals something objective about the work, something of the order of 'the truth of the work, where the individual who writes – a force of creative negation – seems to join with the work in motion through which this force of negation and surpassing asserts itself' (p.28)? This idea of a synthesis of work and individual, in Hegel's terms, the 'Thing itself' ('the matter in hand itself', Miller translates), plays, Blanchot admits, 'a vital role in the literary undertaking' (p.28). Yet what Hegel understood to be a (still abstract) Concept gained by self-consciousness in the process of its self-realization through the work, and hence a (first) solution to the contradictions in question, is immediately shown to engender yet another set of contradictions.

It is already necessary, particularly in anticipation of what Blanchot will establish about the new set of contradictions, to broach the question about the notion of contradiction itself as used in 'Literature and the right to death'. Are the exigencies between which the writer and his work find themselves contradictions in a strict sense? First, what is one to make of the fact that while elaborating on the conflict a writer encounters when attempting to write, Blanchot describes as contradictions moments that for Hegel mutually call upon one another? Although Hegel speaks of contradiction when he begins his discussion of the dialectical relations between work and individual (*der Grundwiderspruch des Werks*), the analysis of the moments of talent and action serves only to show that the individual, eager to bring about a work, is caught in a (non-vicious) circle. He writes:

> The individual who is going to act seems, therefore, to find himself in a circle in which each moment already presupposes

the other, and thus he seems unable to find a beginning, because he only gets to know his original nature, which must be his End, *from the deed*, while, in order to act, he must have that End beforehand.

He emphasizes that the individual 'is beginning, means, and End, all in one'. Talent, action and end, being intimately interconnected (*verknüpft*) as his own moments, are sublated contradictions from the start. The contradictions between them are only contradictions on the face of it. Hegel even speaks in this context of the 'illusory appearance of an antithesis'.⁹ It is thus apparent that Blanchot's understanding of contradiction is not identical to Hegel's. Hence, a satisfactory answer to how one is to take 'contradiction' in Blanchot's text will depend on a deeper understanding of the conflictual nature of the positions outlined. But this much should already be clear: they are not contradictions in the formal logical sense. Indeed, as Blanchot remarks, they do not represent a 'problem [that] could never be overcome' (p.24); they are not 'an insurmountable problem, [that is] nothing more than the impossibility of writing' (p.25). But despite the pervasive references to Hegel, nor are they dialectical contradictions capable of reconciliation. Blanchot writes:

> There is no reconciliation of opposites: oppositions, contradictions do not find rest in a superior synthesis. Rather, they stick together in a growing tension, in a choice that is at once a choice of exclusion and a choice of contrariety.¹⁰

Like logical contradictions, they are absolutely unsolvable, but in contradistinction, the hopeless situation to which they give rise can be overcome, as what has been shown about the 'work' illustrates. The opposite pulls between which writer and work find themselves do not lend themselves to a reconciliation. No causal, mechanical, logical or dialectical solution can be conceived. And yet, the work *is*, in its very underivableness from the insurmountable ordeal, the *impossible solution* of that conflictual situation.

If Hegel's 'Thing itself' plays a crucial role in the literary undertaking, it is because through all the various meanings it may take, it stands for 'everything which, above the work that is constantly dissolved in things, maintains the model, the essence and the spiritual truth of that work just as the writer's freedom wanted to manifest it and can recognize it as its own'. As the idea of the work (in distinction from the actual worldly work), the 'Thing itself' is at the origin of 'a perpetual enticement, an extraordinary game of hide-and-seek'. Blanchot distinguishes two such games in which the writer takes both himself and his reader in and which make up opposite sides of a divide. In the first, recourse to the ideal of the work allows the writer to claim that 'what he has in mind is not the ephemeral work but the spirit of that work and of every work' (p.28), and thus to fool not only others about the nature of his work, but himself as well. Every failed work can be declared a success since failure must be the essence of the work which can never be adequate to its ideal. But should the writer opt for the second game, and relinquish this claim, pretending to write for the reader alone, he again fools himself and the reader as well. 'Were [he] not concerned with literature as his own action, he could not even write' (p.29). Blanchot offers the politically engaged writer as an illustration of the mechanics of the second game. The example, neither arbitrary nor a veiled reference to Blanchot's political involvement with the far right, comes from the same chapter of the *Phenomenology* that Blanchot has been following through its consecutive moves.[11] Although the engaged writer claims to be on the side of a Cause, as soon as the Cause claims him, he shows himself to be 'only on his own side' (pp.29–30). The analysis of the politically engaged writer allows Blanchot to indicate yet another 'equivocation', as he now calls it. If the writer disengages himself from worldly causes, turning himself rather to the wall, he transforms that wall into the world, not a solitary universe but a space which 'contains within itself a point of view which concerns everyone' (p.30). The writer who withdraws into pure self-intimacy fools himself and his readers in the same way as the engaged writer. Playing off Hegel's ruminations in 'The spiritual animal kingdom' regarding the honest consciousness – the consciousness whose truth is the 'Thing itself' or 'the true work' – in which he concludes that the honest consciousness owes its honesty to its own thoughtlessness and thus is caught up in a number of deceptions of both self and others, Blanchot draws the much less dialectical conclusion that, paradoxically, deceit is the necessary condition of the writer's honesty. Blanchot writes: 'What is striking is that in literature, deceit and mystification are not only inevitable but constitute the writer's honesty, whatever hope and truth are in him' (p.30). There is no escaping the contradictions that the writer faces when he approaches the task of writing, nor, when the work is complete, is there any escape from the equivocations just mentioned. Self-deception and the deception of others are the writer's inescapable condition. But this mystification and deceit are not simply negative, for they represent the conditions in which a writer can be a writer, that is, honest and truthful. Without the equivocalities in question, the writer would be absolutely unable to realize the truth that is in him.

To throw this 'logic' of contradiction and equivocality more clearly into relief, Blanchot opens a discussion of the so-called sickness of words, only to conclude that

> this sickness is also the words' health. They may be torn apart by equivocation, but this equivocation is a good thing (*heureuse équivoque*) – without it there would be no dialogue. They may be falsified by misunderstanding – but this misunderstanding is the possibility of our understanding. They may be imbued with emptiness – but this emptiness is their very meaning.
>
> (p.30)

Like contradiction, equivocation is good and felicitous, provided that the tear, here, within words themselves, is absolute. In Blanchot's own terms, the contradiction, the equivocality, the paradox, must be 'rigorously contradictory'.[12] Only where there is no possible solution, no way out, that is, where 'each aspect [of the contradiction] requires that it be fully seen', and where 'each aspect demands that it be shown to advantage, strengthened, and rendered extremely visible',[13] can the equivocation of words become the possibility of dialogue, understanding and meaning. More generally, the positive insolubility of contradictions or equivocalities, the impossibility of their reconciliation, can turn into the very condition under which a 'solution' of sorts becomes possible. Contradiction, equivocality, paradox, are forces 'at once friendly and hostile' (p.61), that if completely hopeless, offer a chance for their solution. Speaking of rigorously contradictory attempts that cannot lead anywhere, Blanchot remarks: 'And yet, it [the contradictory attempt] has value only in so far as it is impossible; it is only possible as an impossible effort.'[14] But this solution would not obtain if the contradictions and equivocalities were inherently to lend *themselves* to their resolution. A solution to a rigorous contradiction, or a positively unsolvable paradox, must be 'made possible by what makes it impossible'.[15] The condition for any solution worth the name must be the condition that makes it rigorously impossible. A felicitous equivocality may not contain within itself the means of its possible overcoming. For Blanchot, a 'solution' is only a solution where it is neither pre-programmed by nor capable of anticipation by the contradictory elements.

Literature, writing, the wor'<, are solutions to the positively irreconcilable contradictions and equivocations. Poetry, Blanchot writes,
is 'the realization, or carrying out, of a total irrealization, such that
once it is completed . . . the original absence from which arise all our
gestures, all our acts, and even the very possibility of our words, is
affirmed in it'.[16] Now, although literature *is* the solution to unresolvable paradoxes, it cannot be a logical or dialectical one. It must
remain a solution that, even though it occurs, is impossible. Blanchot,
after having evoked the hopeless challenge of poetry, writes:

> At first sight such an attempt appears to be contradictory, unrealiz-
> able, and, as Mallarmé says, merely a delusion. One must,
> however, remark that real poetry is the effort towards what is thus
> unrealizable, and that it has . . . this impossibility and this contra-
> diction that it seeks to realize in vain, for its foundation.[17]

Literature or poetry, then, are positively this solution to the extent
that they are the effort and aspiration to carry through the unrealizable attempt. Yet, even though such a solution perpetuates its impossibility, it is irreducible to the impossibility that makes it possible in
the first place. The possibility of literature or poetry, irreducible to
and underivable from the felicitous conditions from which they have
sprung forth, thus becomes a pressing question. It is indeed the silent
question that lies at the core of all works of literature. If literature is
a marvel, a wonder (*une merveille*), as Blanchot holds, it is so
precisely because its origin is a mystery. It occurs in ways that are
not predictable. It happens as if it had no antecedents, each time new
and singular. The contradictory conditions that give rise to literature
are felicitous, precisely because it remains mysterious how literature
depends on them. The wonder of literature is nothing but the silent
wonder about its existence.

Before further exploring the felicity of equivocation and contradiction, it is imperative to follow Blanchot's analysis step by step.
Imposture is an inevitable characteristic of the writer, first, because
'literature is made up of different stages (*moments*) which are
distinct from one another and in opposition to one another'. Since
the writer is 'the action (*mouvement*) that brings them together and
unifies them,' another series of contradictions arises. Given that he
is the gathering movement of the different moments in question,
when 'challenged under one of his aspects,' he cannot but 'present
himself as someone else' (p.31). He constantly shifts, or glides
between all the aspects of the writerly activity and the work. 'This
shifting (*glissement*) on the part of the writer makes him into

someone who is perpetually absent, an irresponsible character without conscience, but this shifting also forms the extent of his presence, of his risks and his responsibility' (pp.31–2). Asserting one aspect when approached about another, he eludes being ever pinned down, avoiding any responsible response to the demand to identify himself. But this irresponsibility that derives inevitably from the status of the writer as the gathering movement of all the contradictory aspects is also the sole condition under which he can be truly present and responsible. How is one to understand this? The difficulty that the writer faces is that he is

> not only several people in one, but each stage (*moment*) of himself denies all the others, demands everything for itself alone and does not tolerate any conciliation or compromise. The writer must respond to several absolute and absolutely different commands at once, and his morality is made up of the confrontation and opposition of implacably hostile rules.
>
> (p.32)

However, what would seem the tragic situation par excellence is in fact not tragic. The rules that face the writer are absolutely incompatible, not merely the moments of an underlying substance that would embrace them, and hence tolerate no mediation or reconciliation. Consequently, as the writer takes (momentary) refuge in one anchored as he escapes the immobilizing identificatory power of another, never does the writer identify himself with a whole substance through a single one of its moments. The way out open to the tragic hero is thus not open to the writer, nor does he call upon himself the wrath of the excluded rule. Even though at one point Blanchot will use the term 'tragic' to describe the conflictual nature of literature, the conflict of the writer is not tragic in a strict sense. Indeed, it is even more difficult. Whereas the tragic hero must respond to one rule, and through it to the whole that has divided into opposite rules, the writer must respond to several 'implacably hostile rules' at once. His is an impossible task, and yet his work is and is only a response to these uncompromisingly conflictual demands to the extent that it responds to this impossible challenge. Through his work, the writer will have succeeded in providing an answer, one that, because of the impossibility of the task, is inevitably singular and unique. There is no general rule for the 'solution' that such a work provides to the unsurmountable conflict. The rule that presides over an answer to the 'implacably hostile rules' can only be an irreducibly singular rule which hence cannot serve as a model for future responses. Such a response on the part of the writer and his work thus always runs the risk of failing. Without this danger, however, there would be no chance of responsibly succeeding. A responsible response to contradictory commandments, that is, to an impossible task, literature's response pivots upon itself, and becomes the questioning of its own possibility.

Yet although the hostile rules' demands on the writer are such that one might think literature to be merely the dream of a response, literature is not nothing. Literature is not a passive manifestation on the surface of the world, but a concrete intervention in the world, Blanchot claims. Closely following Alexandre Kojève's rendering of the master/slave chapter in the *Phenomenology*, in which work is defined 'as the force of history, the force that transforms man while it transforms the world' (p.33), he ascertains that 'a writer's activity must be recognized as the highest form of work' (p.33), and that his work is one 'to an outstanding degree' (p.33). However, in spite of these new references to Hegel, a concept of work emerges from these developments concerning the book as a work that does not easily square with the Hegelian concept. Blanchot writes:

> For me, the written volume is an extraordinary, unforeseeable innovation – such that it is impossible for me to conceive what it is capable of being without writing it. This is why it seems to me to be an experiment whose effects I cannot grasp, no matter how consciously they were produced, and in the face of which I shall be unable to remain the same. For this reason: in the presence of something other, I become other. But there is an even more decisive reason: this other thing – the book – of which I had only an idea and which I could not possibly have known in advance, is precisely myself become other.

> (p.34)

The work, according to Blanchot, as a response to a positively insoluble contradiction, must be absolutely unpredictable. With work that meets an impossible challenge, something entirely new comes into existence. Although Hegel might admit that for the finite consciousness of the writer, his book may appear as 'an extraordinary, unforeseeable innovation', it is an illusion to be overcome in the dialectical process. For Blanchot, in contrast, the quality of unpredictability and extraordinary novelty is an objective aspect of a work. Strictly speaking, it is a work – 'a work in the highest sense of the word' (p.34) – only if it has been unforeseeable, and if, in addition, its effects also escape the writer. The work is an Other in that it is unpredictable, unmasterable in its effect, and escapes reappropriation. It is not an Other in the Hegelian sense of being the Other of self. Its Otherness is not that of the alienated self, but of something that refuses derivation from self and hence remains irrecuperable. The book, indeed, is 'this *other* thing [my italic]'. If it changes the writer, it is a change in a radical sense. It others its creator. Rather than triggering a self-consciousness through the dialectical reappropriation of one's alienated self, the work that represents 'myself become other', that is, myself become unpredictable to myself, hence no longer assimilable to myself, turns the author of the work into an Other as well, into someone strange, foreign to himself, unable to master himself dialectically.

But let us return to the question of the history-making writer. Undoubtedly, the writer is free to negate all there is and to transform the existing world into a world of freedom. 'In this sense, his work is a prodigious act, the greatest and most important there is' (p.35). But however incomparable, this world-transforming feat of the work must instantly be put into question by its opposite determination. Indeed, since the writer achieves such a transformation of the world immediately, that is, through an abstract negation of the real and of all limits, his action discredits all action, and merely remains at the margins of history. Literature thus represents a danger to any possible active intervention in the world, yet not so much because it distracts us from the problems of real life by luring us into an *imaginary* world, but rather because it puts the *world* as a *whole* at our disposal. The writer 'makes all reality available to us. Unreality begins with the whole. The realm of the imaginary is not a strange region situated beyond the world; it is the world itself, but the world as entire, manifold, the world as a whole' (p.36), Blanchot remarks. What kind of world or whole is it that literature puts at our disposal? It is whole in the sense that all its particular realities are negated. The whole that literature offers us through a global negation is the world itself as the absence of everything that is in the world, from which absence everything in the world is to be re-created. Literary creation, Blanchot specifies, begins

> by the realization of that absence itself . . . when literary creation goes back over each thing and each being . . . [in] the illusion that it is creating them, because now it is seeing and naming them from the starting point of *everything*, from the starting point of the *absence* of everything, that is, from nothing.
>
> (p.36)

These diametrically opposite and mutually exclusive determinations of the literary – as action par excellence in, or as escape from, the world – explain the three temptations faced by the writer which Blanchot develops in conformity with the three ways in which self-consciousness shapes itself before being sublated by Reason. In the chapter immediately following the one on the master/slave dialectic, Hegel distinguishes these shapes as stoicism, scepticism and unhappy consciousness.[18] But there is a fourth temptation, a temptation unlike the previous three, to which Blanchot devotes a lengthier analysis. This additional temptation arises from the 'movement which proceeds almost without transition, from nothing to everything' (p.37), seen at work in the two determinations of the literary. The immediate reason for considering this fourth temptation is once again Blanchot's reading of the *Phenomenology*, more precisely, of Hegel's account of the French Revolution, in particular of Jacobinism, in the chapter, in *On Spirit*, entitled 'Absolute freedom and terror'.[19] The fourth temptation consists of the wish to realize *in practice*, rather than merely through the unreality of words, the whole abstracted from all there is, from which the writer as writer could re-create everything in the form of the literary work. It is thus a wish that conflicts both with what the work qua *literary* work achieves and with the status of its creator. For, indeed, in the fourth temptation it is a question of re-creating the concrete world in the name of the whole and of the writer becoming a public, historical person. The temptation of 'the writer [to] see himself in the Revolution' is not just any temptation. It is an unavoidable temptation, coextensive with writing itself. 'Any writer who is not induced by the very fact of writing to think, "I am the revolution, only freedom allows me to write" is not really writing', Blanchot writes (p.40). But, if he lingers on this fourth temptation, it is not only because it is coextensive with writing, but because it comprises the maximum of contradictions. Of Sade, who exemplifies this temptation, Blanchot contends: 'Sade is the writer par excellence: he combines all the writer's contradictions' (p.40). Whereas the stoic, the nihilistic writer and the writer of unhappy consciousness are caught in a limited number of contradictions, the writer of the fourth temptation enacts them all. His literature is hence also literature in a paradigmatic fashion. It is the mirror image of the revolution. Evoking a famous passage from the Preface of the *Phenomenology*, Blanchot writes:

> Literature contemplates itself in revolution, it finds its justification in revolution, and if it has been called the Reign of the Terror, this is because its ideal is indeed that moment in history, that

moment when 'life endures death and maintains itself in it' in order to gain from death the possibility of speaking and the truth of speech.[20]

And he concludes: 'This is the "question" that seeks to pose itself (*à s'accomplir*) in literature, the "question" that is its essence (*être*)' (p.41). As already seen, the question of the possibility of literature is the silent question at the heart of literature. But in what sense can the fact that the revolution is that historical moment in which '"life endures death and maintains itself in it" in order (for whom? life or literature?) to gain from death the possibility of speaking and the truth of speech' be called a question? Blanchot himself puts 'question' between inverted commas. The 'question' that makes up the heart of literature is not simply a question. It is not an essence; it only seeks to pose itself, or rather, to carry itself out, to formulate itself as a question. This 'question' seeks to become the question, to cross the threshold of silence and to articulate itself as literature. But what is the question that literature, after having spoken to the writer, reader and common language, addresses to the revolution in which it mirrors itself? Undoubtedly, it is one concerning its possibility as well. The question is addressed to the revolution in the first place because 'revolutionary action is in every respect analogous to action as embodied in literature: the passage from nothing to everything, the affirmation of the absolute event and of every event as absolute' (p.38). Undoubtedly, the question concerns the paradox that there is only life in death, and that speech and its truth are rooted in the human being's mortality. In these decisive moments of history 'when everything seems put into question' (p.38), the question is, first, active negation. It creates an emptiness, but, second, this emptiness is the immediate realization that '*everything* is possible' (p.38). As Blanchot's account of the Reign of Terror demonstrates, the passage from nothing to everything is achieved in the revolution by holding out a maximum of contradictions. For our purposes let us only point out that in the Reign of Terror, the first act, the act of negation, is also the final act; that the individual is universal freedom itself; that to be alive is to be dead; that to die is to be alive and to achieve absolute freedom; that death has no importance but is also 'the richest moment of meaning' (p.40); that there is nothing more to be done since all has been done, etc. The task of literature is to emulate this infinite power to endure contradiction, and thus to allow the 'question' to manifest itself. In literature such emulation takes the form of the question – the question of how it is that it can be everything, in short, the question of its own possibility. From the revolution it also seeks to learn something about the 'question' itself that is its most intimate being. From the revolution it desires to learn not only how to realize the question, but also what this 'question' *is*. Addressing itself to the revolution, literature inquires into how 'to gain from death the possibility of speaking and the truth of speech'. Put in general terms, this silent question concerns the possibility of possibility, of how possibility arises from impossibility. In the last resort, it is a question about the possibility of the 'question'.

Blanchot sets out to describe the fourth temptation as follows: 'Let us acknowledge that in a writer there is a movement which proceeds without pause, and almost without transition (*presque sans intermédiare*), from nothing to everything' (p.37). In the pages that follow his discussion of this last temptation – pages that deal with language in general, and the language of literature in particular – we must now investigate further how the passage in question should be read. These pages discuss the object of literature's manifold inquiries and addresses. How is negation to be understood here, first and foremost? This is, of course, a question about the silent question at the heart of literature, marvelling at the wonder that literature *is*.

Claiming that 'all . . . poets whose theme is the essence of poetry' have felt that 'the act of naming is disquieting and marvellous (*une merveille inquiétante*) (pp.41–2) – he mentions Hölderlin and Mallarmé – Blanchot begins his reflections on language by elaborating on naming. Understood from the perspective of naming, language is 'life's ease and security' (p.41) because names put things into our possession and allow us to control and manipulate them. But such naming presupposes a prior, and profoundly disquieting, annihilation and suppression of what is named, Blanchot holds. What naming annihilates is the particularity of things, their status as uniquely real things, or as *existants*, as Blanchot also writes, thus pointing towards the Levinasian distinction between *existence* and *existant*. But this approach to language in terms of appropriation and annihilation is Hegelian in origin. After citing a text by Hegel on Adam's naming of the animals, Blanchot writes: 'The meaning of speech . . . requires that before any word is spoken there must be a sort of immense hecatomb, a preliminary flood plunging all creation into a total sea' (p.42). Things enter language only as universal and ideal things, deprived of the singularity of their being, without their 'flesh and blood reality' (p.42). Language is the medium of universality, Hegel says at the beginning of the *Phenomenology*. In the daylight of language, in its never-ending light, to use Blanchot's words, beings dissolve in their here and now, to resuscitate in the universal signification that is Being.

For Blanchot, the annihilation through which signification comes about in language is in the last resort a function of the human being's mortality. It announces real death: 'my language means that this person, who is right here now, can be detached from herself, removed from her existence and her presence and suddenly plunged into a nothingness in which there is no existence or presence' (p.42). But more important is the fact that it is real death, the inevitable possibility of real destruction, that makes language possible as an idealizing and universal medium of signification. More precisely, language is the mode in which the factuality of death as acquired universality and the ontological status of ideality. Language is the thought of death, death as thought. According to 'Literature and the right to death':

> My language does not kill anyone. But if this woman were not really capable of dying, if she were not threatened by death at every moment of her life, bound and joined to death by an essential bond, I would not be able to carry out that ideal negation, that deferred assassination which is what my language is.
>
> (p.43)

In other words, mortality is the condition under which language can proceed to that idealizing destruction of a singular reality in the flesh, thus making it ideal and, by the same token, the object of a possible address. Without the prior annihilation of immediate existence by means of which the latter is separated from itself, made other than itself in its singular and unique existence, it could not possibly become an Other for me to address.[21] But for me to speak, I too must be a universal subject, that is, I must also be distanced from myself. 'The power to speak is alone linked to my absence from being', Blanchot explains (p.43). As soon as I say 'I', 'it is as though I were chanting my own dirge' (p.43). It is not as a full, dominating, and self-certain presence that I achieve the ideal destruction through which the Other becomes not only the Other of a possible address but an Other in the first place. 'No fullness, no certainty can ever speak; something essential is lacking in anyone who expresses himself', Blanchot notes (p.43). Death thus appears to be intrinsically linked to the possibility of language. Without negation of the singular being in the name, no Other would arise, nor would I be in a position to be a possible speaker. Moreover, negation not only separates the other being from the uniqueness of its existence, or myself from myself, but also opens the space between me and an Other, thus providing the essential condition for all possible communication and understanding.

My speech is a warning that at this very moment death is loose in the world, that it has suddenly appeared between me, as I speak, and the being I address: it is there between us as the distance that separates us, but this distance is also what prevents us from being separated, because it contains the condition for all understanding.

And in conclusion, Blanchot can therefore say that 'without death, everything would sink into absurdity' (p.43).

Several consequences follow: if the one who speaks must negate his existence, and negate the existence of what he speaks about, 'if true language is to begin', 'language can only begin with the void' (p.43). Language, at its most fundamental, prior to any linguistic act, be it even that of naming, is the voice of mortality. 'When I first begin to speak, I do not speak in order to say something; rather a nothing demands to speak, nothing speaks, nothing finds its being in speech and the being of speech is nothing' (p.43). At its most primordial, language is death as the opening of signification; death itself become meaningful. It is the emptiness of death separated and detached from itself, the void turned to ideality, real death metamorphosed into universality. What speaks at the beginning before I say anything is nothing but signification, meaning pure and simple, language itself. We must now ask the question regarding the status of negativity in language. Undoubtedly, Blanchot is much indebted to Hegel's concepts of negation and negativity. But his emphasis on death as the condition for the ideality of language, for the constitution of the Other, and more generally for communication, shows negation to enjoy a status unlike that which it occupies in Hegel. Take, for example, the negation incurred in a linguistic relation with a human being who is at first a singular and unique existence. By annihilating it in the immediacy of its being, by making it 'other than his being' (p.43), negation in language does not transform immediacy into an Other that would simply be the Other of self, but allows the Other to emerge as the possibility of address. Such an Other is an absolutely dissymetrical Other whose address is unpredictable, and which is the place that must have been opened in advance for an Other who is the Other of a self to present itself. Unlike its Hegelian conception, negation in Blanchot allows a place for the unforeseeable.

Given that language begins with negation, and that its meaning does not derive from what exists, but rather 'from its own retreat before existence', different approaches to language become possible. The first, which corresponds to the ideal of literature, is the temptation 'to proceed no further than this retreat, to try to attain negation in itself and to make everything from nothing' (p.44). The second approach is the one taken by ordinary language, for which negation of beings only serves to resuscitate beings, now more alive than ever, in the shape of their ideas and meanings. Whereas this last approach makes language a reliable source of certitude, 'literary language is made of uneasiness; it is also made of contradictions. Its position is not very stable', Blanchot notes (p.44). The analysis of the contradictions in question will help to explain why the ideal of literature cannot but divide into two conflicting forms. Literary language seeks to attain the absence of the thing, that is, its meaning, 'absolutely in itself and for itself, to grasp in its entirety the infinite movement of comprehension' (p.44). Words here are nothing but the transparency of the absence of things and of 'the savage freedom of the negative essence'. But since words are also 'a non-existence made *word*, that is, a completely determined and objective reality' (p.44) in which the negativity in question finds itself imprisoned, this conflict, Blanchot maintains, forces literature into a struggle with ordinary language's deceptive assumption that the negating power of language can be stabilized by the limited presence of the word. As a result, literature takes the shape of a liberation, in defiance of the word, of the wild freedom of negation, and of putting the whole of language to the task of doing justice

> to the uneasy demands of one single thing that has been deprived of being and that, after having wavered between each word, tries to lay hold of them all again in order to negate them all at once, so that they will designate the void as they sink down into it – this void which they can neither fill nor represent.
>
> (p.45)

But with this the conflictual tasks of literary language are not yet exhausted. Indeed, since the negation constitutive of language, and with it of the life of the spirit and of the light of day, 'cannot be created out of anything but the reality of what it is negating' (p.46), the question arises for literary language of what it is that in the beginning was lost. Literature thus becomes haunted by the thought of what had to be put to death for language to come to life. It turns into a search for what preceded it. But this inquiry into the moment anterior to the 'wonderful power' (p.46) of speech puts literature into contradiction with itself. 'How can I recover it', Blanchot asks;

'how can I turn around and look at what exists *before*, if all my power consists of making it into what exists after?' (p.46). Indeed, the double bind in which literature finds itself caught is that the search for what had to be excluded from language for language to arise in the first place is inevitably linguistic. Literature can devote itself only to this search because it has already proceeded to the annihilation of the something in question. 'The torment of language is what it lacks because of the necessity that it be the lack of precisely this (*ce qu'il manque par la nécessité où il est d'en être le manque*). It cannot even name it' (p.46), Blanchot concludes.

Literature begins where literature becomes a question. This question, which is now addressed to language itself, shows itself to be a question that for structural reasons arises with necessity. By virtue of being 'the terrible force that draws beings into the world and illuminates them' (p.45), language must seek the 'something' that had to be excluded. But the very reasons which prompt this quest also make any satisfactory answer to this question impossible. Indeed, a definite answer to this question would amount to nothing less than a collapse of language.

In its (impossible) quest for what precedes language, literature discovers the materiality of language. This materiality – the reality, physicality, opacity of the word – no longer the obstacle that it was to a literature that sought to attain absence absolutely in and for itself, now becomes the writer's 'only chance' (p.46), Blanchot ascertains. The happy fact that language is physical – 'Yes, fortunately, language is a thing' (p.30) – becomes the chance of acceding to the senseless, the anonymous and the obscure that precedes it. But such a literature is not the world itself, a 'negation asserting itself', but rather conceives of itself as 'the presence of things before the world exists' (p.47). As Blanchot notes, literary language's attempt 'to become the revelation of what revelation destroys . . . is a tragic endeavour' (p.47). Indeed, in this inevitable quest for the moment anterior to language, literature experiences its inability to escape universality. Undoubtedly, literary language may succeed in destroying the meaning of the word as the word becomes itself an obscure thing, but this meaninglessness is itself meaningful in that it represents what had to disappear for language to become meaningful:

> When literature refuses to name anything, when it turns a name into something obscure and meaningless, witness to the primordial obscurity, what has disappeared in this case – the meaning of the

name – is really destroyed, but signification in general has
appeared in its place, the meaning of the meaninglessness
embedded in the word as expression of the obscurity of existence,
so that although the precise meaning of the term has faded, what
asserts itself now is the very possibility of signifying, the empty
power of bestowing meaning – a strange impersonal light.

(p.48)

In its quest for what language excludes, literature discovers signification in general, but not as a transcendental in the strict sense of
language's capacity to make something appear, but as an inescapable
degree zero of meaning to which even the meaningless must bend.
Literature thus experiences the condemnation of language to signify,
its inability to disappear, and stop making sense. As it seeks to
disclose the secret of the day (of meaning, universality, ideality),
literature discovers (only) the fatality of light: 'day in the form of
fatality is the being of what is prior to the day, the existence we must
turn away from in order to speak and comprehend' (p.48).

But the other ideal of literary language, that of reaching absence
absolutely in and for itself, is no less tragic. It too encounters contradiction. Seeking to achieve meaning in its fullest extent by
destroying the totality of particular things, this language cannot
avoid resurrecting in spite of itself this particularity in the being of
the words. According to Blanchot, literary language in this sense

is the movement through which whatever disappears keeps
appearing. When it names something, what it designates is abolished; but whatever is abolished is also sustained, and the thing
has found a refuge (in the being which is the word) rather than a
threat.

(p.48)

Literature, thus divided between two slopes, each divided in itself, is
'made of uneasiness', 'made of contradictions', 'not very stable or
secure' (p.44). But this contradictory condition is the chance of literature. Were it possible to resolve any of its contradictions, not only
would the variegated manifestations of the language of literature
disappear, but literary language itself would cease to exist. Only
because it is structurally deficient – having to perform negation
absolutely, yet being capable of doing so only by providing a refuge
for the things that have been abolished in the form of the word, on
the one hand, and, on the other, having to inquire into the moment
that precedes language while coming up against signification in

general – can literary language be viable at all, and show its infinite possibilities, or riches. Everything that Blanchot advances about the two internally divided slopes of literature demonstrates that limitation is the sole condition under which the respective quests can be successful. Were it not for the inner obstacles that prevent the two kinds of literature from realizing themselves in purity, literature would have no chance.

A literature that composes with the movement of negation 'by which things are separated from themselves and destroyed in order to be known, subjugated, communicated' cannot content itself with partial or fragmentary results. 'It wants to grasp the movement itself', in its totality, that is, the 'unreal whole' of the world to which all real things refer back (p.49). Non-realism is thus necessarily inscribed in the realism characteristic of the first slope. Literature, on this slope,

> looks at things from the point of view of this still *imaginary* whole which they would *really* constitute if negation could be achieved. Hence its non-realism – the shadow which is its prey. Hence its distrust of words, its need to apply the movement of negation to language itself and to exhaust it by realizing it as that totality on the basis of which each term would be nothing.
>
> (p.49)

In short, if the literature of realism strives to make things known, it must grasp the movement of negation required to achieve this task as such. But in so doing, this kind of literature applies the movement of negation to its own language, disembodying its own words, making them nothing, but thereby running the risk of losing its capacity to communicate. In other words, the realism of literature on the first slope is a viable possibility only under the condition that its intrinsic non-realism threatens its very possibility. If, by contrast, literature shows a concern for the reality of things before they acquire linguistic meaning, it must ally itself 'with the reality of language', now 'a matter without contour', in which words have become opaque and hence meaningless (p.49). But there are also limits to this latter drift. Blanchot remarks:

> Beyond the change that has solidified, petrified, and stupefied words two things reappear in its metamorphosis: the meaning of this metamorphosis, which illuminates the words, and the meaning the words contain by virtue of their apparition as things. . . . Literature has certainly triumphed over the meaning of words, but

what it has found considered apart from their meaning is meaning
that has become thing: and thus it is meaning detached from its
conditions . . . wandering like an empty power . . . the simple
inability to cease to be, but which, because of that, appear[s] to be
the proper determination of indeterminate and meaningless existence.

(pp.49–50)

In sum, then, on this second slope of literature on which meaning
was to be left at the threshold, meaning reappears as the impossibility of leaving meaning behind. Its success at making things reveal
their pre-linguistic reality by turning language itself into an opaque
thing obtains only where this reality and its opaqueness *signify the
absence of meaning*, hence where the project of this kind of literature fails and meaning returns as the meaningful absence of
meaning. In conclusion it is thus to be remarked that, for both slopes,
successful achievement depends on an exigency that, although intimately tied with each slope, limits their ultimate accomplishment.
However, without this uneasy condition, without the intrinsic impossibility that inhabits each slope, there would be no slope to begin
with, and hence no literature. What Blanchot says about the impossibility of realizing in purity each one of the two seemingly incompatible slopes, and in 'distinctly different works or goals', (p.51), serves
to emphasize further the constitutive power of the unresolvable
contradictions.

'An art which purports to follow one slope is already on the
other', Blanchot writes (p.51). In an absolute sense, this contamination of one slope by the other undercuts the possibility of 'distinctly
different works or goals' (p.51). But the lack of incompatibility that
such contamination implies entails neither the loss of their respective distinctiveness nor their annihilation, but rather serves to guarantee a certain specificity to each slope. The lapse into its opposite,
its lack of purity, allows the distinction and difference of one slope
from the other. How is this point made in 'Literature and the right to
death'? As we have seen, on the first slope is a literature of realism,
like that of Flaubert, that seeks its realization through meaningful
prose, that is, by means of a language that expresses things
according to their meaning. Yet Flaubert's realism demonstrates that
such a language, in so far as it corresponds to everyday speech, is not
sufficiently meaningful. Meaningful prose must therefore correct
this situation by seeking a language able to recapture the movement
of negation itself, without which there is no meaning. Meaningful

prose discovers this language, and its corresponding art form, in the language and art of Mallarmé. In contradistinction to ordinary prose, Mallarmé's language, which 'represents the world for us . . . teaches us to discover the total being of the world', safeguards the movement of negativity by which meaning becomes truth (p.51). On the second slope is *poetical language*, that side of Mallarmé's poetry, for example, concerned not with negation and meaning but with the materiality of language. Poetical language is interested 'in what things and beings would be if there were no world', Blanchot states. Francis Ponge, who 'has gone over to the side of objects: sometimes he is water, sometimes a pebble, sometimes a tree' (52), is exemplary of the literature of this slope. But, as Blanchot points out, and though none of the works characteristic of the second slope can be called works of prose, their attempt to describe things as they would describe themselves cannot but have recourse to meaningful prose if they are to give expression to the muteness of things, or the senseless. While it is true that those prose descriptions of poetical language do not belong to the world in the same way as Flaubert's realism, but rather 'to the underside of the world', they remain 'perfectly meaningful prose' (p.53), harbouring a language of negativity and meaning in poetical language itself.

Each slope veers away from itself to the other. But as the discussion of poetical language in 'Literature and the right to death' demonstrates, being always already on the opposite slope is the sole condition under which literature can hope to be truthful. One cannot choose one's spot in literature 'because literature has already insidiously caused you to pass from one slope to the other and changed you into something you were not before. This is its treachery', Blanchot writes, but 'this is also its cunning version of the truth' ('Là est sa traîtrise, là aussi sa vérité retorse') (p.53). Blanchot's discussion of how both meaningful prose and poetical language supplement, correct or fulfill each other heightens the possibilizing or enabling function of literature's treachery by demonstrating that the other is always other in a specific way. Indeed, the Mallarmé who creeps into Flaubert is not the same as the one who has recourse to Flaubert. No cancellation of one slope by the other occurs here. If the two slopes stand against one another, they are not, for that matter, reversible. No neutralization takes place here. Rather, the insidious passage of one slope into the other is always a passage to a distinct Other that helps accomplish the truth of the first slope. This truth is, no doubt, a twisted truth, but a truth nonetheless. Although the two slopes, like affirmation and negation in Kafka's writings, are 'constantly threatened by reciprocity', the fact that the other slope is present in the first in a particular shape eliminates the danger of their mutual annihilation.[22] I recall here that the division of literature into two slopes derives only from a certain point of view. 'If one looks at it in a certain way, literature has two slopes', Blanchot writes (p.48). Further, he notes that they are only 'apparently incompatible' (p.51). Indeed, the division in question does not establish that literature is duplicitous, that is, made up of parts standing in binary opposition. The slopes are not symmetrically opposed. Rather, the attempt to recapture the movement of negation itself on the first slope endows it with a privilege unlike any that poetical language might claim for itself. And, as seen, the second slope arises with necessity from the destruction of particular things on the first slope, a destruction that allows these things to be known and communicated, and does not escape the light of day brought forth by the first.

Because the treacherous conversion of one slope into the other which insidiously undercuts all wishful identity on its part also enables the first slope to achieve a certain distinctness, there is also no end to the conversion in question. As little as the two slopes cancel each other out in reciprocity, does the recourse that each slope must make to its other in order to be what it is know a fulfilment. Having wondered at the exact point at which Lautréamont's transparent prose turns poetically opaque and meaningless, or at which point in Sade's clearest prose one hears 'an impersonal, inhuman sound' (p.54), that is, the muteness of things before the world was created, Blanchot asks: 'Where is the end? Where is that death which is the hope of language? But language is *the life that endures death and maintains itself in it*' (p.54). The passage from one slope to the other never ceases. It does not die. Indeed, death, to the extent that it might be the hope of language, is not simply an end, but the negative to be held out for language to achieve truth. I now return to the question of the contradictions, equivocalities and paradoxes that constitute literary language on all its levels and in all its manifestations. Is there a matrix for all of literature's ambiguities? More precisely, where does this ambiguity originate and what is its ultimate and most economical structure? It has been observed that 'a fundamental ambiguity seems to inhabit all of Blanchot's thinking'.[23] Hence, my question is whether this ambiguity can be described in such a way that the manifold paradoxes, contradictions, equivocalities can be derived from it. Yet, what would a 'fundamental ambiguity' have to be for it to have a grounding or explicatory value? What 'fundamental ambiguity' could, beyond indistinctness, uncertainty and obscurity, have a constituting function? The last pages of 'Literature and the right to death' perhaps harbour an answer to these questions.

'If we want to restore literature to the movement which allows all its ambiguities to be grasped, that movement is here: literature, like ordinary speech, *begins* with the *end*, which is the only thing that allows us to understand', Blanchot remarks (pp. 54–5). In the last resort, then, all the ambiguities that make up literature and its language stem from this fundamental ambiguity that it must begin with the end, in other words, with death, with death's intrinsic ambiguity.

> If we are to speak, we must see death, we must see it behind us. When we speak we are leaning on a tomb, and the void of that tomb is what makes language true, but at the same time [this] void is reality and death becomes being. There is being – that is to say, a logical and expressible truth – and there is a world, because we can destroy things and suspend existence. This is why we can say that there is being because there is nothingness: death is man's possibility, his chance, it is through death that the future of a finished world is still there for us (*c'est par elle que nous reste l'avenir d'un monde achevé*); death is man's greatest hope, his only hope of being man.
>
> (p.55)

The argument of this passage, which also illuminates the title of Blanchot's piece, is familiar by now. Without the real possibility of death, no idealizing detachment of beings from themselves, and hence no universally shareable meaning, is possible.[24] Man's humanity depends on his eventual death, to which man as man must thus claim to have a right. If he could no longer die, nor could he be human. But as this passage also underscores, although death is a necessary condition, a right, it is not a sufficient reason for ideality, universality and communality to occur. Death entails no guarantee whatsoever that being, man or literature will be. No cause or mechanical relation exists between death and what it can render possible. Death is merely the possibility, chance or hope for being, man, the world, literature to come into being. Death is ambiguous in more than one sense, but, first and foremost, in the following: its negation can be final, without any effect, on the one hand; on the other, it is a possibility for something to occur, come, arrive – for the world to be a world, to have a future, for a future of the finished world. This fundamental ambiguity is communicated to everything for which the end becomes the chance for a beginning. This ambiguity that structures death, death's structural ambiguity, needs further illumination.

In Blanchot's discussion of Kafka's belief that literature might be a way out of the ambiguity of the human condition in which he shows that such a quest merely transforms death as the impossibility of dying into the mockery of immortality, he raises the question of the power of literature. Why, he asks, could 'a man like Kafka decide that if he had to fall short of his destiny, being a writer was the only way to fall short of it truthfully?' (p.59). This question, posed against all the contradictions, equivocalities and paradoxes of literature that have been staged up to this point, seems unanswerable. But the reason for its being unanswerable is not contingent: as will become clear later, it is unanswerable by right if answering means 'to clear it up' (p.59). 'Perhaps this is an unintelligible enigma', Blanchot holds, 'but if it is, the source of the mystery is literature's right to affix a negative or positive sign indiscriminately to each of its moments and each of its results' (p.59). This 'strange right', he claims, is 'linked to the question of ambiguity in general' (p.59). This right, in which the power of literature is rooted, is thus not one more characteristic of literature added to its contradictory, equivocal, paradoxical nature. For not only does the contradictory nature of literature follow from this right, but it will also help us to understand ambiguity in general, and in particular, the reason, or rather the minimal ambiguity, on which all of literature's ambiguity hinges.

'Why is there ambiguity in the world?', Blanchot asks. 'Ambiguity is its own answer. We can't answer it except by rediscovering it in the ambiguity of our answer, and an ambiguous answer is a question about ambiguity. One of the ways it seduces us is by making us want to clear it up', he tells us (p.59). The question regarding ambiguity is thus structurally unanswerable. It is a question whose answer invariably turns into a question again. 'Literature is language turning into ambiguity (*qui se fait ambiguïté*)' (p.59). Earlier in *La Part du feu*, he had written: 'Literary art is ambiguous. This means that none of its exigencies can exclude the opposite exigency. On the contrary, the more they are in opposition the more they call upon one another'.[25] Whereas ordinary language seeks to remove ambiguity and to limit equivocality by putting a term to understanding, in literary language ambiguity is set free and held out. In contrast to ordinary language, ambiguity in literary language is 'in some sense abandoned to its excesses by the opportunities it finds and exhausted by the extent of the abuses it can commit' (p.59). But literature is not only a place where this ambiguity is met; in a final ambiguity, literature renders it inoffensive.

It is as though there were a hidden trap here to force ambiguity to reveal its own traps, and as though in surrendering unreservedly to ambiguity literature were attempting to keep it – out of sight of the world and of the thought of the world – in a place where it fulfils itself without endangering anything. Here ambiguity struggles with itself (*l'ambiguïté est là aux prises avec elle-même*).

(p.59)

But precisely because in literary language ambiguity becomes ambiguous itself – as the event in which ambiguity is faced in and for itself, literature also immediately becomes a neutralizing event – the struggle, in literature, of ambiguity with itself perhaps reveals something essential about ambiguity itself. In literary language,

> each moment of language can become ambiguous and say something different from what it is saying, but . . . the general meaning of language is unclear: we do not know if it is expressing or representing, if it is a thing or means the thing.

(p.59)

The struggle of ambiguity with itself concerns not only the possibility of determining the singular moments of language, but literary language itself and ultimately the ambiguity itself that is its most essential characteristic. The possibility constitutive of literature of affixing indiscriminately opposite, contradictory, equivocal values to any moment of language, to literature as a whole, and to ambiguity itself shows literature to be the event of a proliferation of ambiguity. It is an ambiguous event itself in that it remains undecidable whether this proliferation is of the order of a generalization or a *mise en abîme* of ambiguity. Literature *is* this ambiguity.

If Blanchot could claim that ambiguity is its own answer, it is because ambiguity is fundamentally a question. It is a question to such an extent that it even returns in the answers that it solicits. But if 'ambiguity . . . is the essential movement of poetic activity', then literature is also *all* question, a silent question identical with the structure of literature itself. Ambiguous through and through, including its determination as being ambiguous, literature's ambiguity is indicative of what Blanchot terms 'an ultimate ambiguity', to which all of its contradictions, divisions and oppositions, refer back (p.60). 'The reversals from *pro* to *contra* . . . have different causes' and differ in 'kind, and meaning' (p.60). They are not modifications of a homogeneous realm of contradictions, but are heterogeneous in nature. Yet, in their very disparity, they 'refer back to an ultimate ambiguity whose strange effect is to attract literature to an unstable point where it can indiscriminately change both its meaning and its sign' (p.60). It is because literature refers to this ultimate ambiguity that is the reason for the ambiguity that affects it own characterization that literature can be the place where and in which contradictions, divisions and opposites of incompatible nature and status can meet. One ultimate ambiguity is then to be construed as the reason for all the divergent reversals that we have seen and which, rather than homogenizing them, explains why they can cohere in literature in spite of their disparity. What is this final ambiguity responsible for literature's essential instability which manifests itself in the dilemma particular to every work of choosing between the 'daylight of affirmation or the backlight of negation' (p.60)? What is this last ambiguity that 'deep within' the literary work and in silence, for neither 'the content of the words nor their form is involved here', 'is always in the process of changing the work from ground up' (p.60)? It is, says Blanchot, the ambiguity of *'that life which supports death and maintains itself in it* – death, the amazing power of the negative, or freedom, through whose work existence is detached from itself and made significant' (p.61). The question then is: what *is* death for it to play this – however invisible – pivotal role? In what sense can it be the ultimate ambiguity with which consequently everything begins and to which its ambiguity is communicated with the result that what *begins* has also already reached its end?

Death is this last point of instability in the life that maintains itself in it – that is, the life of daylight, language, universally communicable meaning, and so forth – hence of the possibility of the indifferent reversals of negative and positive values, because, at the very moment that it makes meaning possible, death 'continues to assert itself (*s'affirme encore*) as a continually differing possibility (*comme une possibilité toujours autre*)' (p.61). Within the meaning that it renders possible, death remains as the affirmation of its negation, and as the possibility of an always other possibility. Death is the power of an always other or alternate possibility (*alternative*) and hence the 'cause' of ambiguity, because even though it allows ideality, universality and meaning to come about, it continues to perpetuate 'an irreducible *double meaning*, a choice whose terms are covered over with the ambiguity that makes them identical to one another as it makes them opposite' (p.61). Indeed, death is the inevitable power of the additional possibility of a foundering of meaning, a lack of meaning, and losing the chance of its occurrence.

Ideality and universality are always in jeopardy. There is always the possibility that they may not occur. This also means that all relation to an Other, and all possible address could possibly be missing. Needless to say, the possibility of such infelicity is not the simple symmetric opposite of meaning. All the reversals discussed up to this point have their matrix in this dissymetrically always other possibility that death may be what too lightly, perhaps, one terms 'real death'. If, for Blanchot, death is the ultimate ambiguity, it is because, as an always other possibility, it is the minimal ambiguity presupposed by any other ambiguity. 'The nothingness of death' (p.62) to which death as the chance of meaning continues to refer as a possibility, that is, the possibility that death 'becomes the disappearance of every way out' (p.62), but of every issue as well, this is what makes all meaning ultimately ambiguous.

Blanchot ends 'Literature and the right to death' as follows:

> This original double meaning, which lies deep inside every word like a condemnation that is still unknown and a happiness (*bonheur*) that is still invisible, is the source of literature, because literature is the form this double meaning has chosen in which to show itself behind the meaning and the value of words, and the question it asks is the question asked by literature.
>
> (p.62)

Literature, it now appears to us, becomes a question – the question asked by literature – when it becomes the form in which the original ambiguity manifests itself. Literature silently poses the question posed by the original double meaning. To conclude, I should like to discuss one more time the irreducible double meaning deep within literature and its language. I recall that for Blanchot death is the power of detachment from which meaning arises. But once everything – the whole, totality, the world – begins in detachment, the power of the other possibility is already at work. Detachment is not only the origin of ideality, universality and meaning. It is not only the condition under which a relation to an Other can arise. Detachment is also a laceration, a tearing, or ripping apart. 'Death ends in being: this is man's laceration (*déchirure*), the source of his unhappy fate, since by man death comes to being and by man meaning rests on nothingness' (p.62), Blanchot writes. Detachment, consequently, is always already the power of alternatives. Without this possibility of the always other possibility, death could not inaugurate the idealizing process of language in detachment. Without this possibility no Other could possibly emerge, and no address take

66 *Rodolphe Gasché*

place. Death is thus first and foremost this minimal ambiguity of an always other possibility. It is the prodigious power of the negative only because it is first of all the opening for the occurrence of an other possibility. As seen, this possibility is that of the arrival of an unpredictable (non-Hegelian) Other. It is a structural trait inscribed everywhere. As we have seen, this trait is the mark in everything that it also may not have come forth, of the possibility that rather than something nothingness could have prevailed. But this trait's minimal ambiguity does not stop here. Indeed, this mark is also positively the mark of something that has become meaningful through the detachment of death. It also points to the possibility that meaning can spring forth from negation and destruction. It affirms that there is a chance for meaning to occur, that an Other can present itself in an address, and that it/he/she is a possible addressee for us. The 'always other possibility' is thus ambiguous as well – nothingness/the chance of everything. This compels me to define death, beyond the negative and positive valorizations that it can affix to just anything, as affirmation – of the possibility of nothingness, of the chance for being to be. But death as such a *yes* manifests itself in that it asks. Its beginning in affirmation ends in a question. Death as the affirmation of an always other possibility begins in that it asks. It is in literature that death asks this question, the silent question of the possibility of literature.

NOTES

1 Maurice Blanchot, 'Literature and the right to death,' in *The Gaze of Orpheus*, trans. Lydia Davis (Barrytown, N.Y.: Station Hill Press, 1981). All quotations in the text refer to this edition.
2 Roger Laporte, *Etudes* (Paris: POL, 1990), p. 23.
3 Maurice Blanchot, *La Part du feu* (Paris: Gallimard, 1949), p. 123. All further references are to this edition. All translations are mine.
4 Ibid., p. 11.
5 Ibid., p. 108.
6 The concepts borrowed from Hegel do not simply project their dialectical power upon Blanchot's developments; they suffer also a significant mutation within Blanchot's text, thus exhibiting possibilities that Hegel might not have accounted for. Let me also refer here to Andrzej Warminski's *Readings in Interpretation: Hölderlin, Hegel, Heidegger* (Minneapolis: University of Minnesota Press, 1987), who argues that what takes place in Blanchot's readings of Hegel in the 1940s is a 'rewriting of Hegel's . . . (concepts, in particular, the concepts of the negative and death) in another place, to the side' (p. 185).
7 Maurice Blanchot, *The Space of Literature*, trans. A. Smock (Lincoln and London: University of Nebraska Press, 1982), p. 109.

8 To substantiate this point, a careful and patient parallel reading of Blanchot's essay and Hegel's *Phenomenology* would of course be required. Such a comparison would have to determine scrupulously the exact points of Blanchot's departure from Hegel. Here a few hints must suffice, first and foremost that there is never anything marvellous about a dialectical inversion. It occurs with necessity, in all logical rigour.

9 G. W. F. Hegel, *Phenomenology of Spirit*, trans. A. V. Miller (Oxford: Oxford University Press, 1977), pp. 240–1.

10 Blanchot, *La Part du feu*, p. 292.

11 In his analysis of the different ways in which consciousness deceives itself and others, Hegel distinguishes different modes in which things happen to it independently of its own making, but which it claims nonetheless for itself. In case it is 'an event of historical importance (*Weltbegebenheit*) which does not really concern him, he makes it likewise his own; and an interest for which he has done nothing is, in his own eyes, a party interest which he has favoured or opposed, and even combated or supported', Hegel writes (p. 249).

12 Blanchot, *La Part du feu*, p. 133. See also p. 87.

13 Ibid., p. 59.

14 Ibid., p. 87.

15 Ibid., p. 78.

16 Ibid.

17 Ibid., p. 70.

18 The writer is a stoic if he endures his condition, one that, however, allows him the acquisition not of personal, but of universal freedom. He is a sceptic, or nihilist, as Blanchot also calls him, if 'he negates everything at once, and he is obliged to negate everything since he only deals with everything'. Finally, he is an unhappy consciousness 'since he is a writer only by virtue of his fragmented consciousness divided into irreconcilable moments' (p. 38).

19 To suspect that Blanchot's discussion of revolutionary terror represents a hidden reference to his own association with right-wing movements in pre-war France and is a late attempt to come critically to grips with it completely misreads the status of the fourth temptation. Blanchot takes up the theme of terror for the same reason that he has discussed the dialectic between talent and work, work and individual, respectively the three temptations of stoicism, scepticism and unhappy consciousness, namely because he borrows his themes from Hegel's *Phenomenology*, at times even following the latter's order of exposition. If, indeed, this theme enjoys a special privilege over all the other themes, it is not because it would stand in for a personal past of guilt, but because deriving from the conflicts previously discussed, it becomes the place par excellence for exemplifying all the paradoxes that make up literature and literary activity. Moreover, the theme of revolutionary terror in question concerns terror in the name of freedom, and not the terror of the far right. To take this discussion to be an implicit acknowledgement by Blanchot of his own political past is not only to give in to arbitrary association; it also spells out a whole 'philosophy' of the literary text. Whatever the critical methods are, including the seemingly progressive ones of structuralism, by means of which associations of this kind are

made, the literary text is reduced to the expression of, in this case, a shameful experience. A literary criticism thus limited to hunting down in the literary text the signs of scandalous political involvement is indeed nothing but a pretext for a return to an autobiographical and anecdotal understanding of literature. Apart from foreclosing all reflection on how the 'universally' valid medium of literature relates to empirical (and in particular to private, secret, hidden) factuality, such an approach trivializes history, by reducing its constituting agents or forces, its course and disasters, to the simple effects of individual actions. A common-sense, or rather vulgar conception of work, writer and history presides over such an approach. This is, of course, not to disqualify all socio-political contextualization of the text, or even to deny encrypted within it a reference to a secret. Such analyses, however, require that the text be first recognized as text.

20 In 1941, Jean Paulhan, in *Les Fleurs de Tarbes ou La Terreur dans les Lettres*, compared the violently anti-rhetorical and subjectivist literary criticism that begins with Sainte-Beuve and that finds in Henri Bergson its metaphysical legitimation – a criticism bent on coinciding with the spirit of the creator, and oblivious of the fact that literature requires rhetorical skills, in other words, that it is made of words – to the Terror during the French Revolution, whose first victims, as Paulhan argues, were also those distinguished by their talents (Paris: Gallimard, 1990), pp. 61ff.). The designation of literature as the 'Reign of the Terror' refers, of course, to that work by Jean Paulhan.

21 It has been remarked with barely withheld indignation that in 'Literature and the right to death', Blanchot's main example to illustrate the destructive power of language is that of a woman: 'For me to be able to say, "This woman" I must somehow take her flesh and blood reality away from her, cause her to be absent, annihilate her' (p.42). The choice of the example is not fortuitous, of course. In question are indeed the linguistic and ontological conditions under which a thing in general, an animal (the cat) and a human being can become an Other to begin with. To elaborate on how something can become an Other is also to inquire into the conditions of possibility of relation, communication, exchange. It would seem that this can be done most poignantly by taking 'woman' as the example.

22 Blanchot, *La Part du feu*, p. 90.

23 Françoise Collin, *Maurice Blanchot et la question de l'écriture* (Paris: Gallimard, 1971), p. 92.

24 Henry Meschonnic, in an essay entitled 'Maurice Blanchot ou l'écriture hors langage' (*Les Cahiers du chemin*, 20 (1974)), has taken Blanchot to task for linking language as a medium of ideality and universality to destruction, negation and death. Meschonnic, who opposes a scientific or semiotico-semantic interpretation of language to what he deems to be a 'mythology of language' (p.90), whose dualism reveals its metaphysical postulates (p.95), primarily objects to Blanchot's privileging of the word as characteristic of language as a whole. No doubt, in 'Literature and the right to death', Blanchot approaches language (and its idealizing function) primarily from the name. But the name is, for Blanchot, clearly, and first of all, a word. Where language becomes conceived in

its materiality, the 'name ceases to be the ephemeral passing of nonexistence and becomes a concrete ball, a solid mass of existence' (Blanchot, 'Literature and the right to death', p. 46). Here the name is shown to regress to the word. It is the words that for Blanchot make up language, and the word is not thought from the name. 'The meaning for meaning of words' which can either be that of materiality or negativity springs from 'an ambiguous indeterminacy that wavers between yes and no', and which, as the end of the essay demonstrates, is that of death (p. 61). Moreover, in his analysis of the word, he draws on a variety of implications that come with the traditional concept of the word itself, and that thoroughly displace its metaphysical status, as well as its potential for giving rise to what Meschonnic terms a 'mysticism of lost unity and of the end to come' (p. 100). As an example of such emphasis on potentially dislocating traits of the word, I quote the following from Blanchot's essay: 'Take the trouble to listen to a single word: in that word, nothingness is struggling and toiling away, it digs tirelessly, doing its utmost to find a way out, nullifying what encloses it – it is infinite disquiet, formless and nameless (*sans nom*) vigilance' (p.45).

25 Blanchot, *La Part du feu*, p. 197.

4   Crossing the threshold

On 'Literature and the right to death'

Christopher Fynsk

Literature begins, Blanchot says, when it becomes a question, when the language of a work becomes literature in a question about language itself.[1] This question concerns the source of literature's ambiguity: its 'origin' in an irreducible 'double meaning' that is not a movement between irreconcilable meanings, but between meaning and a 'meaning of meaning' that is itself irreducibly ambiguous, material and ideal, neither material nor ideal: a 'point of instability', a 'power of metamorphosis', an 'imminence of change' (pp. 61–2/330–1) that gives itself in language beyond either the meaning language takes on, or its 'reality'.

The question, as Blanchot stages it in 'Literature and the right to death', opens in both a temptation and an obsession, a 'torment'. Only the latter will provide my focus here, since my aim is to bring forth the way the ambiguity of literature constitutes an offering of the *il y a*, and to read the relation (the *pas* of relation) marked by this offering as the site of what Blanchot will later thematize as the encounter with *autrui*. But to approach this second dimension of the essay and the infinite movement on to which it opens, I shall start with a few notes on the first, and what Blanchot describes as the temptation of the negative.

'Any writer who is not led by the very fact of writing to think: "I am the revolution, freedom alone makes me write", in reality is not writing' (p.40/311). Blanchot makes this statement categorically in the first moment of his movement through what we might call 'the two versions of the imaginary'. The declaration introduces Sade, whom Blanchot identifies as 'the writer par excellence', and this by virtue of his identification with the French Revolution and the Terror – his engagement with the passion of death as a negativity that gives itself up to the *jouissance* of an 'absolute sovereignty' (p.41/311). Blanchot will lean to Mallarmé (and others: Flaubert, for example,

or the surrealists) in subsequent references to literature's drive to
realize the negation inherent in language. Along this first slope of
literature's double movement (p.51/318), we find the prosaic search
for a transparent meaning, and beyond this the tropological movements by which literature seeks the flower that is 'absent from all
bouquets', or the ground of essence itself in the movement of
thought (though when this movement reaches 'Igitur' we are clearly
on the 'second slope', where we have in fact also already been with
Flaubert). But in seeking to illustrate the irreducibly *imaginary*
dimension of this negation (the 'imaginary' ground of its very
opening), and its 'irrational', even 'aberrant' character as the passion
of that 'life that bears death and maintains itself in it',[2] Blanchot
turns to Sade.

The reference is undoubtedly dictated in part by the subversion of
the Hegelian dialectic to which Blanchot dedicates himself in the
first half of the essay; to release a kind of excess in the negative,
Blanchot writes Sade into a very particular moment offered by Hegel
himself (one that communicates with moments signalled by Bataille
in 'Hegel, la mort et le sacrifice'[3]). The Terror, he suggests, represents for literature that specular, speculative moment where literature 'contemplates itself', 'recognizes itself', and 'justifies itself'
(p.41/311) in the realization of absolute freedom. In the Terror, literature passes into the world. It becomes 'real', we might say, it
embraces existence, but only inasmuch as existence has become
fabulous in giving itself over to the absolute character of the word
wherein all finite determinations dissolve.[4] What is terrible about the
Terror is its abstraction, the fact that its incarnation of absolute
freedom, its synthesis of the universal and the singular, the ideal and
the real, remains 'ideal (literary)' (p.40/310). The 'life that bears
death and maintains itself in it' represents the sacrifice of 'life', if
life names existence as it is given in the always singular experience
of human finitude. To put it more succinctly, it is the sacrifice of
'our' dying.

Once again, Blanchot's subversive aim is to write Sade into the
dialectic at a moment indicated by Hegel himself, to draw forth the
'imaginary' character of the negation from which literature proceeds
when it works to offer a presentation of the meaning of being in its
totality, or the world as such; 'the meaning and absence' of the
whole of what is (p.36/308). The finite, 'imaginary' character of the
transcendence offered by language (and the possibility of its uncon-
trollable passage into the *jouissance* of 'absolute sovereignty': 'life
elevated to the point of passion, passion become cruelty and folly'

(p. 41/311)) haunts the negativity of meaning no less than the becoming-image of the word, as we shall see, haunts its material presence. Ultimately, Blanchot suggests (this is the conclusion of his essay and its challenge), the one veers into the other and is even indistinguishable from it; the ambiguity of literature lies in the communication of the image and the imaginary (the word, in its 'reality' and 'significance', doubly *limiting* this communication). Nevertheless, the foregrounding of the Sadean temptation is striking. 'I am the revolution' – could this phrase *also* characterize Kafka and Ponge? (Kafka perhaps, but Ponge?) Or has Blanchot allowed himself to be carried into the movement he is describing when he claims that every writer knows such delirium? And could he be capturing something that not only haunts his own more literary writing, but also constitutes a temptation he has known in seeking to pass from literature to reality? Could he be thinking here of his own past political passions? This would be to point to something more than a 'national aestheticism', something far more profound (where identification or 'mimesis' is concerned) and more unsettling.

This last question is not without interest for Blanchot scholarship, but it certainly points beyond his person. Blanchot notes that in literature's specular and speculative identification with that historical moment where '"life bears death and maintains itself in death itself" in order to obtain from it the possibility and the truth of speech' (p.41/311), the question of literature itself opens. Without transition, Blanchot writes: 'That is the question . . .' (p.41/311). The question, we may presume, has to do with the abstract character of the negation to which literature commits itself, possibly even the delirious character of this engagement when it is undertaken without reserve, but equally with something that haunts its murderous power: something that haunts its movement of negation and becomes an obsession.

Blanchot returns to Hegel here, a young Hegel, 'the friend and neighbour of Hölderlin', who recognizes in the 'right to death' (p.39/309) afforded by the negation borne by language a 'strange right' (p.42/312) (they are 'friend and neighbour' more by this recognition than by their physical proximity at the *Stift*). Adam's act of naming, Hegel wrote in a text prior to the *Phenomenology*, is an act of annihilation – an act, Blanchot adds, to which every instance of naming or designation alludes. 'The meaning of speech requires . . . that before any word is spoken there be a sort of immense hecatomb: a prior deluge, plunging into a total sea all of creation' (pp.42/312–13). All of being must be given over to death for speech to be possible. Language itself brings this death, and we speak only *from* it. Blanchot's words are worth following closely here:

> Of course, my language does not kill anyone. And yet: when I say 'this woman', real death is announced and already present in my language; my language means that this person, who is there right now, can be detached from herself, removed from her existence and her presence and plunged suddenly into a nothingness of existence and presence. My language essentially signifies the possibility of this destruction; it is, at every moment, a resolute allusion to such an event. My language does not kill anyone. But, if this woman were not really capable of dying, if she were not threatened by death at every moment of her life, bound and united to it by an essential bond, I would not be able to accomplish that ideal negation, that deferred assassination that is my language.
>
> (pp.42–3/313)

Most will be familiar now with the argument that says that for a word to be a sign, it must signify beyond any concrete context in which it might appear. Signification presupposes the possible absence of a referent and the absence of the speaker who might initially claim this language as their own. But Blanchot also appears to be saying something more that should be noted here, something in the order of an ontological claim. It is not only that language signifies in the possible absence of its speaker and its referent; it is that a 'real death' has occurred. The woman negated when I say 'this woman' must have been '*really capable of dying*', bound *essentially* to death. Language is thus constantly referring back to its origin in the essential bond between the existent being and the possibility of the death that offers this being to language. How do we think this offering or opening – in what manner does the living being give itself to language? How does death mark itself? I shall not try as yet to answer this question, but I would note that this mark is what Blanchot names (in much of his earlier writing) 'the image'.

Before any speech, there is the offering of a dying and the offering of my own dying. ('I' speak from my power to distance myself from myself, to be other than my being – in other words, from my death.) Might this help to explain why Blanchot figures the effort to return to what exists *before* language as the effort to recover a corpse? (As we shall see, Blanchot will argue in 'Two versions of the imaginary' that the becoming-image of the thing is best figured by the cadaver.) If what is 'before' language is not life, but life bound to death, life offering itself to language in the image (and in this, already language, at least as 'the image of a sign', to borrow Benjamin's phrase[5]), is the before not already an 'after' (life)?

The question of the 'before' torments language. Were literature to cede to the temptation to gather to itself its very separation from existence, to attain and offer negation in itself and make the nothing (as the ground of meaning) everything, it would already have 'a strange and awkward task'. But literature cannot forget the initial murder.

> It recalls the first name that would have been the murder of which Hegel speaks. The 'existent' was called out of its existence by the word and it became being. The *Lazare, veni foras* made the obscure cadaverous reality leave its original depths and gave it, in exchange, only the life of the spirit. Language knows that its realm is the day and not the intimacy of the unrevealed; it knows that for the day to begin . . . something must be excluded. Negation realizes itself only from the basis of the reality it negates; language draws its value and its pride from being the accomplishment of this negation; but what was lost at the outset? The torment of language is what it lacks by the necessity that it be the lack of it. It cannot even name it.
>
> (pp.45–6/315–16)

Since the first 'slope' of language's movement is the slope of negation and the assumption and accomplishment of the murder from which meaning proceeds, one would expect the 'before' to be figured under the names of life. And indeed much of Blanchot's language in this passage points in that direction (everything surrounding the evocations, 'this woman', 'a flower', 'the cat'). But the living reality evoked by these words is unavoidably *idea* – entirely a product of language; and how can one avoid thinking the before without reference to some Eden? Blanchot's move is to substitute a figure of death where we expect life, and a figure of the 'after' for the before. Literature, seeking what it has lost, does not want the living Lazarus, but the dead Lazarus. The resurrected Lazarus is short-changed in the tropological movement of negation – he gets only the life of spirit, not the death of material existence. The (un) revealed Lazarus would be Lazarus in this death. In a 'commensurate' exchange, he would be brought forth *as* death; or, beyond metaphor (as we read in *Thomas the Obscure*), he would *be* death (an absolute aporia), the death that is the non-dialectical *other* of living existence.

The language of literature is the search for this moment that precedes it. Literature generally names it existence; it wants the cat as it exists, the pebble in its *siding with things*, not man, but this one here, and in this one here what man rejects to say it, the foundation of speech and what speech excludes in order to speak, the abyss, the Lazarus of the tomb and not the Lazarus brought into the day, the one who already smells bad, who is Evil, the lost Lazarus and not the Lazarus saved and resuscitated.

(p.46/316)

'The foundation of speech' – could this be, once again, the 'real death' of the existent 'really capable of dying' and bound to death by an 'essential bond'? And what abyss lies in this 'real'? For Blanchot's evocation of the corpse of Lazarus suggests, I believe, that literature's torment drives it actually beyond the threshold that is the opening of language and towards what, for spirit, appears initially as a tomb ('appears' in the sense that spirit knows here a lure – as Blanchot consistently suggests, spirit sees its outside first as something tempting). For the cadaver presents a materiality that refuses itself to language and gives only its refusal. The cadaver, in effect, is 'exemplary' in this way; a strange 'non-thing', it is of the earth, as Heidegger might say, but in the extreme form of the ab-ject, a residue that has always fallen from signification as inassimilable (in *cadaver* we should hear the Latin *cadere*). What 'object' is more other, more *unheimlich*, more charged in its obtrusive but fleeting presence, and what leaves a more indelible image when we chance upon it? A material (non-) presence that is not quite of nature, no longer of the world and given in the absence of life, the corpse presents the inassimilable other of spirit and meaning that has in fact always been there.

That has also always been there in words. Literature's chance for returning to what language has left behind lies in the materiality of language. Its way back lies in the abandonment of meaning and a flight into the physical character of the word: 'rhythm, weight, mass, shape, and then the paper on which one writes, the trail of the ink, the book' (pp.46/316–17). It finds there not only the thingly character of the word, but its primitive force:

The word acts not as an ideal force but as an obscure power, as an incantation that coerces things, makes them *really* present outside themselves. It is an element, a part barely detached from its subterranean surroundings: no longer a name, but a moment of the

universal anonymity, a brute affirmation, the stupor of a confrontation in the depths of obscurity.

(pp.46–7/317)

It is a thing and it draws forth the thing in its 'hidden intimacy'
(p.41/312), leaving behind ideality and the consciousness of the
writer in its negative force. It communicates the presence of things
before consciousness:

> It is not beyond the world, but neither is it the world: it is the
> presence of things before the *world* comes to be, their persever-
> ance after the world has disappeared, the stubbornness of what
> subsists when everything is effaced and the dazedness of what
> appears when there is nothing. This is why it cannot be confused
> with the consciousness that illuminates and decides; it is *my*
> consciousness *without me*, the radiant passivity of mineral
> substances, lucidity in the depths of torpor. It is not the night, it is
> what haunts the night; not the night but the consciousness of the
> night that lies awake ceaselessly in order to catch itself and for this
> reason dissipates itself without respite. It is not the day, but the
> side of the day that the day rejected to become light. And it is not
> death either, for in it there shows existence without being, the
> existence that remains beneath existence like an inexorable affir-
> mation, without beginning and without end, death as the impossi-
> bility of dying.

(p.47/317)

I cite at length for the beauty of this passage (this night that dissipates itself in a vain effort at self-reflection), but also because the
movement of Blanchot's argument as he follows literature's way
back must be followed with the greatest care. Sinking into its physicality, Blanchot suggests, literature communicates an uncommuni-
cating presence that is not quite self-presence and never quite posits
itself, but nevertheless stirs and persists ('moment', 'affirmation',
'presence', 'perseverance', 'stubbornness', 'appearance', 'passivity',
'lucidity'). The 'nature' of words, 'what is given to me and gives me
more than I can grasp' (p.46/316), thus communicates something of
what Blanchot, following Levinas, terms the *il y a*: 'The anonymous
and impersonal current of being that precedes all being: being as the
fatality of being' (p.51/320). Given that Blanchot thinks the *il y a* as
an abyssal opening, we could in fact have more grounds for comparison with Heidegger's *es gibt* than one might at first assume (inasmuch as Hegel appears to be the determinant philosophical

reference). One might in fact stage the confrontation between Heidegger and Blanchot around precisely these words of 'thought' that normally serve as translations for one another but also *resist* with the diversity of the idiom. For Blanchot as for Heidegger, *il y a/ es gibt* names the opening of essence; but the *pas* of this opening in Blanchot (to which I shall return) also paralyses the setting underway and turns the way itself into an endless detour. The *il y a* is a name for what might be called the 'underside' of the hermeneutic circle, the abyssal opening from which Heidegger consistently turns away even as he remarks its presence. But rather than pursue Blanchot's relation to Heidegger directly, let me continue to follow the movement of Blanchot's meditation, for it is the 'signifying' structure of the communication we have seen that most interests me here (and precisely in its bearing on Heidegger's reflections on language).

The paragraph following the one from which I have cited at length appears to take back what is given in the first: the effort to return to what is before revelation (which by all 'appearances' has been a success) is now labelled 'tragic'. Literature may well have succeeded in abandoning a signified meaning, but it cannot avoid signifying this abandonment: its language continues to show its own intention and expose its pretence:

> It says: 'I no longer represent, I am; I do not signify, I present.' But this will to be a thing, this refusal to mean that is immersed in words turned to salt, in short, this destiny that literature becomes as it becomes the language of no one, the written of no writer, the light of a consciousness deprived of self, this insane effort to bury itself in itself, to hide itself behind the fact that it appears – all this is what literature now manifests, what literature now shows. Should it become as mute as stone, as passive as the cadaver enclosed behind this stone, the decision to lose the capacity to speak would continue to be read on the stone and would be enough to awaken this false corpse.

> (pp.47/317–18)

The 'death' it thought it could find (and by all appearances it found: nothing of the preceding paragraph was qualified as illusory) turns out to be 'false'. But then we recognize in retrospect that it wasn't exactly the 'death' of the cadaver or the silence of the stone in which it is enclosed that was supposedly found. If literature set out to find the 'real' beyond language in the form of a materiality that gives itself only in refusal, it actually found something else: the obscure reflection without reflection of the *il y a*, that affirmation that is a failure of negation to negate itself, the fatality of the day. The turn in Blanchot's argument from the first to the second paragraph remarks the traits of reflection (without reflection) in the preceding paragraph, but only then to recover them in the succeeding paragraph in a more affirmative manner. It is as though the ineradicable reflection of language's intention and self-offering remarks the prior reflection in such a way as to offer its 'truth'. For when Blanchot summarizes the movement that has just occurred in the preceding paragraphs, it changes sign once again. Literature knows that it cannot go beyond itself: 'it is the movement by which what disappears appears' (a statement that recalls the first slope but is also already ambiguous since what 'disappears' is also what refuses itself). He then goes on, summarizing the second movement:

> When it refuses to name, when it makes of the name an obscure, insignificant thing, witness to the primordial obscurity, what has disappeared here – the meaning of the name – has indeed been destroyed, but in its place signification in general has come forth, the meaning of the insignificance encrusted in the word as an expression of the obscurity of existence. So that, if the precise meaning of the terms has been extinguished, the very possibility of signifying now affirms itself, the empty power to give a meaning, a strange impersonal light.
>
> (p.48/318)

The inability to avoid signifying its intention (its *vouloir dire*) has become the presentation of signification in general, the very possibility of signifying. Words that *would* become things, that offer themselves *as* things, remain *words* that offer themselves in this way; but the persistence of the word as word ('qu'il y a – ici – langage') becomes the indication or expression of the *il y a* itself. All of the ambiguity of this movement is expressed in the phrase, 'in its place has arisen . . . the meaning of the insignificance encrusted in the word as an expression of the obscurity of existence'. 'The meaning of the insignificance' may be read, after the preceding paragraph, as referring to the marking of the fatal destiny of the word in its effort to be a thing (p.47/317), the ineradicable designation that this insignificant 'thing' is a word offering itself as insignificant. But 'meaning' here also takes on another meaning: for it is the obscurity of existence appearing *as* insignificance – the appearance of insignificance *as such*. The self-reflection or self-offering of language becomes the showing of the *il y a*. The tragic undermining of literature's endeavour has become a *discovery* of the fatality of the day (tragedy itself changing meaning with a new sense of 'fatality'):

> Negating the day, literature reconstructs the day as fatality; affirming the night, it finds night as the impossibility of the night. That is its discovery. . . . If we call the day to account, if we reach the point of pushing it away in order to find what there is before the day, beneath the day, we then discover that it is already present, and that what there is before the day is still the day, but as a powerlessness to disappear and not as the power to make appear, an obscure necessity and not the light of freedom.
>
> (p.48/318)

The inability to avoid signifying, become the 'empty power to give a meaning', is the expression of the 'powerlessness to disappear' of the being of what is before the day, the existence from which one must turn away to speak and to understand.

Has Blanchot worked a kind of dialectical sleight of hand here – have we read something more on the order of a slippage than an argumentation? It may well be a slippage, but Blanchot would suggest, I believe, that this is the 'slippage' that makes dialectic possible (and impossible). Blanchot will return to it once again after a summary of his two slopes in what seems an effort to catch more precisely the movement we have just followed. Summarizing the second slope, Blanchot affirms that literature's effort to refuse to say is not in fact tragically undermined. The metamorphosis in itself has not failed, he says:

> It is quite true that the words are transformed. They no longer *signify* shadow, earth, they no longer represent the absence of shadow and earth that is meaning, that is the shadow's light, the transparency of the earth; opacity is their response; the rustle of closing wings is their speech; material weight presents itself in them with the stifling density of a syllabic accumulation that has lost all meaning. The metamorphosis has taken place.
>
> (p.49/319)

But in this metamorphosis, he continues, and beyond the solidification of words, there reappears (like a 'revenant', a kind of spectral return) 'the meaning of this metamorphosis which illuminates them and the meaning they draw from their appearance as things or even, if this should happen, as vague, indeterminate, ungraspable existence where nothing appears, the heart of depth without appearance'. The meaning of the metamorphosis refers us back once again to language's inability not to present itself as language offering its abandonment of meaning, an inability not to show itself *as* language offering itself as thing. But the appearance of the meaning language draws from its appearance *as* a thing, or, 'if it should happen', as non-appearance, is also the appearance of meaning itself, or more precisely, 'meaning in general', the 'empty power of signification'. The possibility of the 'as such' of meaning is given as the word gives itself as a word giving itself as a thing. Once again, these are *words* appearing *as things appear*, offering this *as* by which a thing may appear as a thing, or even by which insignificance may appear *as* insignificance, but doing so by their own self-giving, which is a giving as. This is a presentation of the possibility of the as such via a self-presentation that is irreducibly a marking of dissimulation. The word gives (itself) as, thereby giving 'meaning' as

> detached from its conditions, separated from its moments, wandering like an empty power with which nothing can be done, a power without power, a simple powerlessness to cease to be, but which, because of this, appears as the proper determination of indeterminate and senseless existence.
>
> (p.50/320)

The word showing itself offering itself as (existence in its refusal to signified meaning) – giving itself giving as – is the condition of signifying or offering to understanding (or better, thought) what escapes signification. 'Qu'il y a langage' – a remarking of the fact of language, but in its irreducible figurality: this is what literature produces as a 'question' (or perhaps a stunned discovery: something related to Kafka's joy when he writes, 'He was looking out the window' (p.26/298)) as it says the fact of Being – as it says 'is' – in its fundamental dissimulation. Literature, on one of its slopes at least, is language remarking an irreducible figurality, its own, but as a saying of the dissimulation that belongs, as Blanchot asserts, to Being itself; 'mimesis', we might say, 'figuring' (itself) like a wandering corpse.

The image, once again, is from 'Two versions of the imaginary'. Borrowing this title and summarizing the movement we have followed thus far, we might say that the two slopes of literature's ambiguity are constituted by the movement between the 'imaginary' point of view literature adopts in seeking to give expression to the world that is the meaning of things in their totality ('I am the revolution') and the becoming-image of the word ('I no longer represent, I am'). As Blanchot suggests in his concluding footnote to

'The essential solitude',[6] the language of literature is language that has become entirely image. Not a language full of images, but a language that has become the image of language, figuring by this non-reflection the dissimulation of Being itself which is the condition of appearance in general and which appears when the thing is absorbed by its image. The damaged tool offers such an appearance, Blanchot remarks (recalling Heidegger):

> The category of art is linked to this possibility that objects have of 'appearing', that is to say, of abandoning themselves to pure and simple resemblance behind which there is nothing – except being. Only what has surrendered itself to the image appears, and everything that appears is, in this sense, imaginary.[7]

The corpse, again, is most 'exemplary' here, though it figures this time (on another 'slope') not only a materiality that offers its refusal to signification via the absence of life, but an 'ideality' that has grown thick with 'the elemental strangeness and formless heaviness of being that is present in absence'[8] – it figures, in other words, the very possibility of appearing, vacillating between ideality and materiality and marking their point of confusion (which is also the 'confusion' of the idealism of classical art, as Blanchot notes with a certain perverse irony). As a cadaver falls from the hold of our affective interests and the world of names and identities, Blanchot writes, it will come to resemble itself and in this 'self'-reflection that reflects no one and nothing (it is not 'simply' a corpse, nor is it a human being, for the being that appears is 'impersonal', a monumental double of the one we have known: 'the apparition of the original – until then unknown – sentence of last Judgment inscribed in the depths of being and triumphantly expressing itself with the help of distance'[9]) it will offer resemblance itself, resemblance absorbing the thing:

> The cadaver is its own image. It no longer has any relations with this world, in which it still appears, except those of an image, an obscure possibility, a shadow present at all times behind the living form and that now, far from separating itself from this form, transforms it entirely into shadow. The cadaver is the reflection becoming master of the reflected life, absorbing it, identifying itself substantially with it in making it pass from its use and truth value to something incredible – unusual and neutral. And if the cadaver is so resemblant, this is because it is, at a certain moment, resemblance par excellence, entirely resemblance, and

also nothing more. It is the like, like to an absolute degree, overwhelming and marvellous. But what does it resemble? Nothing.[10]

Perhaps it would suffice to stop here with the observation that with his thought of the image, Blanchot has effectively generalized the *Verstellung* that Heidegger recognizes as belonging essentially to truth and that art offers in its own withdrawal and thingly quality. Heidegger's 'that' – what the work of art *says* as it offers the event of truth in a movement of simultaneous approach and withdrawal – has been rethought as the 'that' of language (which in fact it was for Heidegger inasmuch as the essence of art is said to reside in language). But here the 'that' marks an irreducible figurality that undermines any stability in the pose. The re-presentation of language is the remarking of the 'imaginary' dimension of truth – the remarking of the dissimulation of Being.

Could we go further? Is this not a limit for thought? It is a limit, but a limit of a very particular kind. For we might observe in each of Blanchot's descriptions of the becoming-image of the word that it marks a 'meaning of meaning' (or perhaps better, a meaning *without* meaning) that is neither material nor ideal, but something prior to each of these categories that embraces both while *inclining* towards an 'elementary depth' in an infinite movement towards what Blanchot names the 'neutral'.[11] The image is a threshold – a limit, as Blanchot will emphasize in asserting that it has a protective function,[12] but a limit that marks an infinite abyssal relation and that is therefore already a crossing towards what Blanchot calls in *The Space of Literature* the 'other' night. For the consciousness that undertakes this crossing (though initiative will reveal itself always to have been the fatality of desire), it will be a movement towards the other of consciousness – towards itself as other:

> The *other* night is always the other, and he who hears it becomes the other, he who approaches it departs from himself, is no longer the one who approaches, but the one who turns aside, goes hither and yon. He who, having entered the first night, seeks intrepidly to go toward its profoundest intimacy, toward the essential, hears at a certain moment the *other* night – hears himself, hears the eternally reverberating echo of his own progress, a progress toward silence, but the echo sends it back to him as the whispering immensity, toward the void, and the void is now a presence that comes to his encounter.[13]

The noise at the threshold is the echo of approach, but an echo that reverberates with an otherness that *itself* becomes approach. What consciousness hears is its own absence, itself becoming other in opening to the other – something that can be 'known' only as a kind of madness. Or as a kind of exposure. Here is the same movement across the threshold I have just followed as it is described in 'Literature and the right to death':

> In this effort, literature does not confine itself to rediscovering in the interior what it wanted to abandon on the threshold. For what it finds, as the interior, is the outside which, once an exit, has now changed into the impossibility of leaving – and what it finds as the obscurity of existence is the being of the day which has changed from an explicatory light, creative of meaning, into the harassment of what one cannot prevent oneself from understanding and the stifling haunting of a reason without principle and without beginning, which one cannot account for. Literature is that experience by which consciousness discovers its being in its powerlessness to lose consciousness, in the movement in which, disappearing, tearing itself from the punctuality of a self, it reconstitutes itself, past unconsciousness, in an impersonal spontaneity, the desperate eagerness of a haggard knowledge, that knows nothing, that no one knows, and that ignorance finds always behind itself as its own shadow changed into a gaze.
>
> (p.50/320)

This is consciousness become the gaze of fascination, a blind seeing that is *contact* with the outside and the impossibility of not seeing what obtrudes with the collapse of the separation that is constitutive of consciousness. Consciousness become a passivity or an opening that proceeds from an effraction or a touch: thus it is the *passion* of the image when the thing becomes image in withdrawing from the world and the passion of writing when the word veers towards the image and opens on to the outside – the passion of the outside.

To write is to arrange language under fascination and, through language, in language, remain in contact with the absolute milieu, where the thing becomes an image again, where the image, once an allusion to a figure, becomes an allusion to what is without figure, and where, once a form sketched on absence, it becomes the formless presence of that absence, the opaque and empty opening on what is when there is no more world, when there is no world yet.[14]

It is a seeing that is at once a suspended self-reflection ('a lost neutral glimmer that does not go out, that does not illuminate, the circle, closed upon itself, of the gaze'[15] and a *being seen* – once again, an exposure. In 'solitude', Blanchot writes, 'I am not alone, but in this present I am already returning to myself under the form of Someone (*Quelqu'un*).'[16] And then further on the same page:

> Where I am alone, the day is no longer anything but the loss of an abode, intimacy with the outside that is placeless and without repose. The coming, here, makes it so that he who comes belongs to dispersion, to the fissure where the exterior is a stifling intrusion, the nakedness, the cold of that in which one remains discovered, where space is the vertigo of spacing.[17]

My consciousness *without me*, appearing *as other* in the form of an impersonal anonymity that is less a presence than the presence of an absence, the intrusion of the outside, *relation* with an irreducible alterity. Fascination is hetero-affection, 'self'-affection that is an infinite becoming-other in a fundamental passivity. The coming of *on*, *il* or *quelqu'un* is an infinite opening to the outside, not a 'human' presence, but the presence of the other to a self that is no longer the 'same', no longer a 'self'. Where Blanchot names the other – 'Eurydice', for example – this name is a figure for a nameless other dissimulated by the night, the 'other' night or 'dissimulation itself', an infinite, abyssal movement.

Thus the image is not a limit, if by this we mean a point where reflection – or thought – must stop. Rather, it is a site of engagement and passage where reflection halts, but in becoming the approach to/of the outside. It is a threshold, in this sense, but a threshold already marked by a crossing, a passage, that Derrida has identified and engaged in exemplary fashion by tracking the *pas* (both adverb of negation and noun: 'step') that echoes throughout Blanchot's text.[18] I shall not try to subject this extraordinarily rich demonstration to summary, precisely because it works to demonstrate *pas*, describing the movement in question in both a thematic manner and in a trajectory (like the *viens* which it attempts to think while making it sound). But I should like to note the point of juncture with the current discussion by observing that in Derrida's reading, *pas* names and 'is' what happens in the becoming-image of the word. *Pas* is what is marked (or marks itself) in the powerlessness of the word to efface its own re-presentation of its effacement of meaning, in this remarking of the very possibility of meaning that inhabits it as a wandering, empty power whose 'ghostly' presence Blanchot figures as a movement, 'a walking staircase, a corridor that unfolds ahead', as he describes it in 'Literature and the right to death' (p.54/323).[19] Together with *sans*, as Blanchot uses this term almost formulaically to mark the same effacement of meaning and a passive opening to the other, it is the 're-trait' – at once remarking and withdrawal – of a movement of distancing that infinitely suspends the 'as' given in language's re-presentation of its possibility, rendering this 'giving as' abyssal.[20] If the 'as' I have isolated marks the very possibility of metaphor or figurality in general, the *pas* that marks it is the re-trait of metaphor, and, as set to work in the text, the marking of what exceeds the order of the signifiable – or the signifier – in a movement beyond meaning and beyond Being. The step (not) beyond that occurs in and with the opening to the *il y a* in the becoming-image of the word is the *opening* (and closing) of a thought of Being. Here is Derrida's inscription of *pas* in this becoming-image that we have followed in 'Literature and the right to death':

> To remain near oneself in one's effacement [the movement from *je* to *il* we have seen], to sign it still, to remain in one's absence as remainder, there is the impossible, death as the impossibility of dying on the basis of which death without death announces itself. The remainder without remainder of this effacement that no longer effaces *itself*, here is what *there is* perhaps (by chance) but that *is* (not) *pas*: here is *pas* under the name of forgetting as he uses it, as one can no longer think it, think it that is, starting from (*à partir de*) a thought-of-Being. If 'Being is another name for forgetting', it names a forgetting of forgetting (that it violently encrypts) and not a synonym of forgetting, exchanging itself with it as its equivalent, giving it to be thought. Or naming it, it unnames it, makes it disappear in its name. This *thought* which is no longer of Being or of the presence of the present, this thought of forgetting tells us perhaps what was to be heard under this name (*thought*), which named, as you remember, without declaring her name, she (*elle: la pensée*) to whom *Death Sentence* said 'eternally: "Come", and eternally, she is there'; or the unique word to which, in *He who*, 'Come' is said so that it (*elle: la parole*) should cry its name. 'When I say "this woman. . . ." That's you, that's your name.'[21]

Derrida (or more precisely, one of the interlocutors in this dialogue – the 'counterpart' to the one marked as feminine: 'Derrida', as Blanchot might put it, only to the extent that he is not 'himself') goes on to say here that this forgetting that gives forgetting to be thought (*pas d'oubli*), this forgetting that gives (thought), is *il y a*. To which he adds: 'this *il y a* enjoins *viens*'.

The becoming-image of the word is the opening to a call, Derrida suggests, that must have already occurred for the *pas* to have been engaged in the first place. *Viens* is the 'invitation' that provokes the *pas* of approach, but that this step provokes in its turn in such a way as to allow it to sound for a first time as the word of the other. *Viens* is the word of approach, the word that is written in approach (on the body) as the word of/to the other that comes to our encounter (never 'our' encounter). This other, once again, is not another human being. What approaches is the other night, an infinite alterity whose coming is the opening of what is named in *Thomas the Obscure* 'the supreme relation which is sufficient unto itself'.[22] *There is* (*il y a*) joins in approach, en-joins itself in a giving prior to the law that is the birth of the law. The call is wholly anonymous, wholly other.

Blanchot will emphasize later that this joining of relation occurs only in engagement with the Other as *autrui*. As one of the voices from his own dialogue in *The Infinite Conversation* asserts, 'All alterity presupposes man as *autrui* and not the inverse.' This voice then continues:

> Only it follows from this that, for me, the Other man who is 'autrui' also risks being always Other than man, close to what cannot be close to me: close to death, close to the night, and certainly as repulsive as anything that comes to me from these regions without horizon.
> – We well know that when a man dies close to us, however indifferent his existence might be to us, in that instant and forever he is for us the Other.
> – But remember: the Other speaks to me; the decisive interruption of relation speaks precisely as infinite relation in the speech of the Other. You are not claiming that when you speak to *autrui*, you are speaking to him as though to a kind of dead person, calling to him from the other side of the partition?
> – When I speak to the Other, the speech that relates me to this other 'accomplishes' and 'measures' that inordinate distance (a distance beyond measure) that is the infinite movement of dying, where dying puts impossibility into play. And in speaking to him, I myself speak rather than die, which means also that I speak in the place where there is a place for dying.[23]

The address comes from the other (human being) as the address of the other. *Viens* marks an infinite relation to which the other (human beings) give themselves up in giving themselves to language. This is 'real death' as Blanchot emphasizes in 'Literature and the right to death' – a 'real' dying into language that Blanchot defies us in *The Writing of the Disaster* to distinguish from a murder.[24] But this death is infinite. The others, in their dying, 'know' the *il y a*, the absence of being ('such an absence that everything has forever and for always been lost in it, to the point that the knowledge affirms and dissipates itself there that nothing is what there is, and first of all nothing beyond').[25] This is what they 'give' in their dying: 'the absence of being through the mortifying gaze of Orpheus'.[26] This is why Derrida can assert that behind the 'thought' to which *Death Sentence* addresses itself (or behind the 'word' addressed in *Celui*) there is the 'thought' of the *il y a*. The presence of the others in their infinite dying, in the 'infinite' of their dying (and which 'I' approach only in forgetting), is the presence of an infinite absence.

Literature happens, we noted at the outset, when its language becomes a question addressed to language itself. We may add now, perhaps, that literature becomes a question *in response*, in fascinated and repeated response, to the speaking that occurs as language remarks 'that there is language'. That there is language is the *opening* of the question (in response) – the question of Being or difference, we might say now (recognizing how abyssal this question is for Blanchot), but also, and only, as it comes to us from a 'real dying' Blanchot persistently assigns to the self (prior to the self) *and* to another. Not the dying of 'this woman', but of 'her' whom this designation returned to the night. A distinction, I would have to add immediately, that is crucial but ultimately untenable, as Derrida suggests, I believe, when he takes up the question of citation and repetition in Blanchot's narratives, arguing that writing introduces what he calls an irreducible contamination in the address of the other.[27] The deconstructive move in literary criticism would be to stress the contamination to which Derrida refers. Such a move is in no way a falsification; indeed, it has been a necessary one both in the context of the politics of criticism and in relation to the matter at hand. But this emphasis on the 'contamination' of writing and its citationality has served to purify the recitation of contamination by what I am tempted to call a *reference*, i.e. a relation to the other that opens in the singular event of address.

When we figure this speaking in relation to 'Literature and the right to death', and give it a word (*viens*), we undoubtedly precipitate a movement that will only be made thematically by Blanchot in subsequent texts. But is not the condition of writing *viens* something like the haunting 'real' presence of an other? And can it be called a new 'departure' when Blanchot draws out the thematics of *autrui* in *The Infinite Conversation*, for example (disregarding for the moment what he offers in his fiction, where the question of *autrui* is almost always present)? Has he not drawn out something of the relation already marked in his text?

It is undeniable that a step is made when Blanchot takes up overtly the problematic of *autrui* in *The Infinite Conversation*. And though I am hesitant to use the same language in comparing narratives, I am tempted to say (and will have to demonstrate elsewhere) that a step has been made between texts such as *Thomas the Obscure* and *Death Sentence* with regard to the question that has furtively appeared here. But the insistence of what I am prompted to call the question of *reference* in Blanchot's thought on literary language marks out the site of the problematic of *autrui*. Literature becomes a question, Blanchot seems to suggest, because a 'touch' of some kind has occurred. Literature's origin is the 'signifying' of that touch: the writing of an infinite relation that opens there, the writing, for example, of *viens*. Here is one version of its structure (one that I find particularly useful for approaching *Death Sentence*):

> In the room: When he turns back toward the time when he signalled to her, he senses clearly that he is signalling to her in turning back. And if she comes and if he grasps her, in an instant of freedom of which he has nothing to say and that for some time he has marvellously forgotten, he owes to the power of forgetting (and to the necessity of speech) that grants him this instant the initiative to which her presence responds.[28]

Here we have *pas*, 'forgetting' and '*viens*' unfolding in the space of writing. It goes without saying that we must not reduce the touch to an empirical event. The event *would only have happened* in writing. But it would only have happened had it already happened in a past that is no less 'real' for being immemorial. There has been a touch. A text such as *Death Sentence*, I want to suggest, remarks it as the 'real' condition of the infinite relation in which it is given and lost. The step Blanchot makes (has always made) draws it out as the touch of *autrui*.

NOTES

1 Maurice Blanchot, 'Literature and the right to death', in *The Gaze of Orpheus and Other Literary Essays*, trans. Lydia Davis, ed. and with an

Afterword by P. Adams Sitney (Barrytown, N.Y.: Station Hill Press, 1981), p. 21. All quotations in the text refer to this edition. The additional page numbers immediately following these numbers refer to the French edition published in *La Part du feu* (Paris: Gallimard, 1949). I have occasionally modified the English translations.

2 *'The life that endures death and maintains itself in it'* (Ibid., p. 54/224) – both 'the life that brings death' (as in a murder) and 'the life that bears death' (the death it can never murder or be done with, not even in suicide).

3 A translation of this essay is published in *On Bataille*, Yale French Studies 78, ed. Allan Stoekl, trans. Jonathan Strauss (New Haven: Yale University Press, 1990), pp. 9–28.

4 'At this moment, freedom pretends to realize itself in the *immediate* form of *everything* is possible, everything can be done. A fabulous moment – and no one who has known it can completely recover from it, for he has known history as his own history and his own freedom as universal freedom. Fabulous moments indeed: in them, fable speaks, in them, the speech of fable becomes action.' Blanchot, 'Literature and the right to death', p. 38/309.

5 See 'On language as such and on the language of man', in *Reflections*, ed. Peter Demetz, trans. Edmund Jephcott (New York: Schocken, 1978), p. 326.

6 Maurice Blanchot, 'The essential solitude', in *The Gaze of Orpheus*, p. 77.

7 Ibid., p. 84.

8 Ibid., p. 83.

9 Ibid.

10 Ibid.

11 See, for example, the opening paragraphs of 'Two versions of the imaginary', in *The Space of Literature*, trans. and with an Introduction by Ann Smock (Lincoln and London: University of Nebraska Press, 1982).

12 The point is suggested in 'Literature and the right to death', p. 60/328; for a reference to the image as a limit, see 'Two versions of the imaginary', in *The Gaze of Orpheus*, p. 79.

13 *The Space of Literature*, p. 16.

14 *The Gaze of Orpheus*, p. 77.

15 Ibid., p. 75.

16 Ibid., p. 74.

17 Ibid.

18 See 'Pas (*préambule*)', *Gramma*, 3/4 (1975), pp. 111–215. A slightly modified version of this essay appears in *Parages* (Paris: Galilée, 1986), pp. 19–116. In this text I shall cite the original version. All translations mine.

19 These phrases mark what Derrida identifies as the labyrinthine topology – or tropology? – of *pas*: the vertiginous *spacing* of *pas*.

20 'Il y va de l'autre', Derrida writes, 'qui ne peut s'approcher *comme autre*, dans son phénomène d'autre, qu'en s'en éloignant, et apparaître en son lointain d'altérité infini qu'à se rapprocher' (approximately and reductively, starting with the first words: 'It is a matter of the other: which can only approach *as other*, in its phenomenon as other, by

distancing itself, and *appear* in its distance of infinite alterity by drawing nearer' ('Pas', p. 130)). The engagement of/with/in that movement of *Entfernung, é-loignement*, is *pas*.

21 Ibid., 'Pas', pp. 196–7.
22 See Maurice Blanchot, *Thomas the Obscure*, trans. Robert Lamberton (New York: David Lewis, 1988), p. 105.
23 Maurice Blanchot, *The Infinite Conversation*, trans. and Foreword by Susan Hanson (Minneapolis and London: University of Minnesota Press, 1993), p. 72.
24 Maurice Blanchot, *The Writing of the Disaster*, trans. Ann Smock (Lincoln and London: University of Nebraska Press, 1982), pp. 65–71.
25 Ibid., p. 72 (translation modified).
26 Blanchot, *The Infinite Conversation*, p. 38.
27 'Between (her) who "is there" *for* (not only *in order to* but also *by the fact of*) responding to "Viens" and (her) who *already* will have given all her force and called "Viens", there is no incompatibility, no contradiction, but also no synthesis or reconciliation, no dialectic. Hence the boundless affliction. And the impossibility of deciding between an eternal return of the affirmation in which the recited . . . is intact, good only once, the unique force of a "Viens" that never reproduces itself (saving "Viens") and, on the other hand, but at the same time, a repetition of what has already been reissued in quotation marks, writing and citation in the everyday sense. Contamination by the everyday sense is not an accident but it belongs to the structure of affirmation; it is always risked inasmuch as it demands the narrative. Writing is also this irreducible contamination, the narrative the boundless affliction of which he can say, "I rejoice immeasurably"' (Derrida, 'Pas', p. 117).
28 This passage from *L'Attente L'Oubli* is cited ibid., p. 128.

5 The work and the absence of the work

Paul Davies

There has always been something odd about the question 'What is the work of art?' For some this oddness, simply asserted, attests to the strength of the category of the work, underlining its avant-garde potential. For others it merely marks its capacity to mystify and so to conceal the means by which artistic practices are regulated and defined, a point which presumably must needs apply to the adjective 'artistic' as well. For some the work resists and for others it serves a dominant culture. For some it is essentially a value term, synonymous with 'good work', and for others, whatever it is, it is essentially not that. Maurice Blanchot, content neither with celebrating nor with disparaging the work, also insists on the awkwardness attached to the question concerning it, a question he suggests that the work itself perhaps *silences*.

In *The Space of Literature* Blanchot makes much of the distinctions between the book and the work and between writing and reading, sometimes seeming to map the latter distinction on to the former. The writer writes a book, while the reader reads *the* work; a book is never the work and the writer never a reader. But although it is in its being read that the book can be said to become a work, a correct formulation of that becoming should already have introduced the work. 'Reading simply "makes" the book, the work, become a work.'[1] That the making here is not a matter of production and that reading cannot accordingly be seen as a productive activity is borne out by the first occurrence of the word 'work' in this sentence suggesting that it is not a straightforward matter of first a book and then a work but rather that despite the writer's exile from the work the first word does not fall to reading. Reading does not solicit the work. Any solicitation 'can only come from the work itself'.[2] The work, the result of the transition and that for the sake of which there is a transition, already pre-empts any straightforward presentation of the transition. From the first there is the work to the extent that, from the first, the writer belongs to what does not belong to the writer. This indifference to the writer on the part of the work is taken by the writer to be evidence that the work is as yet unfinished. It is heard as an obligation to continue writing. But it is a call to an impossible task, an attempt to finish the interminable and to give an original personal voice to what is essentially anonymous. The work, Blanchot says, 'closes in around [the writer's] absence as the impersonal, anonymous affirmation that it is – and nothing more'. A presentiment of this situation – the not yet of the work as the being of the work rather than the accident of its remaining unfinished – is given to the writer 'in the impression of a strange worklessness (*désœuvrement*)'.[3] In making 'the book, the work, become a work' reading affirms the being of the work and so confirms the writer's predicament. From the first the work unworks itself. Everything here from the writer's unrealizable project, his always being bound to a forthcoming work, to the reader's affirmation prior to all interpretation, and the transition itself, is somehow *of the work*. And amongst all of Blanchot's most difficult constructions these three words will for a while be the hardest to read.

During the course of *The Space of Literature*, Blanchot refers to the solitude of the work, the demand of the work and the concern of the work. In each case, although the genitive allows of a double reading, it is the alteration wrought in and on the words 'solitude', 'demand' and 'concern' by their being taken to belong to the work that is of primary importance. The text begins with the claim that an experience of what is meant by 'solitude' teaches us something about art, but the solitude at issue is neither a subjective nor even a human condition but rather the essential solitude. This solitude is not a means of defining the work. On the contrary, it signifies the inevitable failure of any attempt to provide criteria for ascribing an identity or essence to the work. If in the phrase 'the solitude of the work' the meaning of the word 'solitude' is affected by being predicated of the work, then in speaking of this altered solitude as the essential solitude the same can be said of the word 'essence'. To say something of the work, as philosophy or criticism does, is to seek to bring the work positively closer, the thematize it, to say what it is. For Blanchot these positive ascriptions are undermined by an examination of what is at stake in this 'of the work'. For him the work's only positivity is its distance, its receding from thematization. The work opens up a space, and although the work must always be absent from that space, the space itself can only be thought as being 'of the work'. And if reading lets all of this be, then that letting be as well is already 'of the work'.

Reading, we read, 'makes of the book what the sea and the wind make of objects fashioned by men: a smoother stone, a fragment fallen from the sky without a past, without a future, the sight of which silences questions'.[4] One of the questions presumably silenced in the reading that lets the work be a work is the philosophical question: what is a work and what is the work? Strictly speaking, nothing in Blanchot's account here is unprecedented – the work considered, for a moment, as a quasi-natural accomplishment, the strange resistance of the work to a philosophical interrogation – and yet the manner in which that account might impinge upon the philosophical scene remains obscure. At least I should like to say that it remains obscure and then to go on to consider Blanchot's treatment of the work in the context of that philosophy for which the notion of the work of art is both a prerequisite and a problem, but something intrudes. Another context, namely the context of Blanchot's own project and therefore arguably one for which Blanchot's treatment of the work is almost wholly responsible, seems to render the question of the philosophical context redundant. For is not everything that could be said of Blanchot and the work in relation to philosophy and the work already clearly marked out in the appeal to the work's irreducibility to a philosophy of the work? Is it not sufficient simply to repeat this point? And is this not what Blanchot does when he comes to situate *The Space of Literature* and its treatment of the work in the context of the development of his own writing, thereby both assuming and addressing the consequences of the work's irreducibility?

FROM CATEGORY TO WORD: BLANCHOT'S PROJECT

A footnote to that section of *The Infinite Conversation* entitled 'Forgetting, unreason' harks back to the earlier text: 'I return here to *The Space of Literature* where the category of worklessness, the absence of the work, begins to emerge.'[5] This is deceptively simple; there are however a few things worth remarking at the outset: the confident juxtaposition of terms – worklessness, the absence of the work – with little regard for the differences between them, at least the different ways in which *The Space of Literature* and *The Infinite Conversation* would have introduced them; their juxtaposition as a 'category', and so their philosophical genealogy and purpose retrospectively assured. Moreover, as the context is a discussion of

Foucault, it is maybe a matter of Blanchot's considering the wider
implications of his earlier analyses, touching on questions of application, of influence and of contemporaneity.

To follow Blanchot and to return to the pages of *The Space of
Literature* from a reading of *Le Pas au-delà* and *The Writing of the
Disaster* is first to be reminded of just how crucial a role the notion of
the work plays there and, second, to feel inclined to wonder whether
anything in the discussion of the work as perpetually and necessarily
bound up with its absence, with worklessness, prepares the reader for
the subsequent, implicit and gradual withdrawal of the word itself
from Blanchot's vocabulary. There is some justification for saying
that the matter is one of vocabulary in that Blanchot seems increasingly interested in the writing and marshalling of a particular series of
words and phrases: 'outside', 'fragment', 'neuter', 'the absence of
the book', *désastre*, 'return', etc. None of these would function as a
concept, yet each would engage a certain conceptualization. Each
would sustain, albeit precariously and perhaps as its enabling and dis-
enabling condition, a conceptualizing of communication, say, or of
experience, of the book. In Blanchot's writings, in the years after *The
Space of Literature*, these and other concepts, now identified as the
constituents of a philosophical discourse, are characterized by and
held accountable to a worklessness which itself somehow warrants
this *other* writing, the extraordinary writing of these extraordinary
words and phrases. It is as if, following the investigation into the
characteristics of the work in *The Space of Literature*, the work, the
word 'work', is consumed by the word 'worklessness'. A text in
which one reads *œuvre* primarily within *désœuvrement,* as though the
word were now a fragment and its occurrences fragmentary, is going
to differ from a text in which it retains a positive role serving as both
the point of departure for and the object of the study.

It is the writings that make up *The Infinite Conversation* which
seem to mark the transition, the step away from an investigation into
the work. Utilizing a narrative drawn from his readings of Hegel and
Hölderlin or, more accurately, a narrative which functions as a sort
of Hölderlinian variation on the Hegelian theme of the death of art,
Blanchot argues that we have moved from the notion of the masterpiece (*chef d'œuvre*) to that of the work and, by way of the sort of
analysis we find in *The Space of Literature*, from the notion of the
work itself to the thought and the affirmation of the work's absence.
At several moments in *The Infinite Conversation* Blanchot alludes to
his earlier critical writings, summarizing them and allowing them, in
part, to determine and to introduce a new issue or question. The

thought of *désœuvrement* derives from a particular engagement with the work; the task *now* is to write, think and live with this thought. It is interesting that these summaries could never have been given in this form in and by those writings themselves and that they seem to be given now for the sake of a writing that would be as far removed as possible from a summarizing tone or desire. It seems as though in order to arrive at a non-summarizable and non-summarizing writing Blanchot must summarize a series of investigations into the work which themselves always scrupulously precluded such a gesture.

But perhaps it is not so much a withdrawing of the word *œuvre* as it is its replacement and reattribution. How else are we to understand the manner in which Blanchot, in these lines from *Le Pas au-delà*, seems to redescribe solely in terms of writing and its irreducibility to presence what was once so forcefully described in terms of the work: 'The past was written, the future will be read. This could be expressed in this form: what was written in the past will be read in the future, without any relation of presence being able to establish itself *between* writing and reading'?[6] Consider too the retention of the idea of demand or exigency in a formula such as 'the demand of writing' or 'the demand of the fragmentary' (*l'exigence du fragmentaire*). And if Blanchot continues to associate the work of art with the relation to death, he seems to do so by concealing the word. In one of the very few passages in *The Writing of the Disaster* in which we come across it, Blanchot insists on linking it cryptically to a name, to a tradition, writing it – but in an unelucidated manner – in the shadow of a proper name; it is as much a matter of mentioning it as of using it:

> Schleiermacher: By producing a work, I renounce the idea of my producing and formulating myself; I fulfill myself in something exterior and inscribe myself in the anonymous continuity of humanity – whence the relation between the work of art and the encounter with death: in both cases, we approach a perilous threshold, a crucial point where we are abruptly turned back.[7]

Later in the same text, Blanchot writes:

> It is through reverence that the work, always already in ruins, is frozen: through reverence which prolongs, maintains, consecrates it (through the idolatry proper to titles), it congeals, or is added to the catalogue of the good works of culture.[8]

One is closest to what in the work resists cultural appropriation when one does not call it by a name,[9] and perhaps now not even by the name 'work'.

Since the earliest literary essays it seems fair to say that Blanchot has attempted 'to grasp the *general* importance of the *singular* works of art that culture rejects even as it receives them'.[10] But it is not until the more programmatic statements of the 1960s that one finds the attempt being described in quite these terms. If these statements do mark a transition, then, contemporaneous with Blanchot's break from an explicitly fictional writing, they seem to prepare the way for the later 'fragmentary', no longer simply fictional or non-fictional writings. And in those writings the word 'work', on the handful of occasions on which it is used, is read in the context of neither an investigation into its 'characteristics' nor a statement as to the outcome of the success or failure of such an investigation, but rather as a word which can only be used warily, hermetically, as though one must always be aware that wherever it belongs (philosophy, the past), it does not belong here.[11]

In the 'note' at the beginning of *The Infinite Conversation*, Blanchot envisages a writing devoted to an absence of identity, bound to itself solely in and as the *exigence* of writing: a writing which

> little by little brings forth possibilities that are entirely other: an anonymous, distracted, deferred, and dispersed way of being in relation, by which everything is brought into question – and first of all the idea of God, of the Self, of the Subject, then of Truth and the One, then finally the idea of the Book and the Work.[12]

Here the narrative into which an account of Blanchot's previous critical writing can be inserted not only invites us to consider the development of Blanchot's writing as a whole but also explicitly sets that development up in relation to philosophy, in relation to the various logics of relation which have served the ideas and the categories of God, the Self, the Subject, Truth, the One, and the Book and the Work. Perhaps it is to be a matter of moving from 'categories' to precisely 'words', *le parole fragment*, words conveying the inexchangeable. 'Désœuvrement' as the presentiment of the anonymity and the interminability of the work is both the name of what removes the work from all determinable relations to a writer, an interpretation, truth, etc., and the name of that which still insists that the work *relate*. It is a matter of emphasis: the work or the thought of this other relation. If Blanchot no longer speaks so much of the work (and of the 'of the work'), is it not because of his developing interest in this engagement, his choosing to write less about works and more about the tasks of a writing responsive to the thought of 'désœuvre-ment'?[13]

Blanchot's writing would move from an analysis of the category of the work to a summarizing of that analysis in terms of the category of worklessness, the absence of the work. This latter category – the last category? – will, in turn, inaugurate a different writing; generically unstable, its fragmentary advance will hinge on the writing and reading of *words*, words deemed too fragile, too strange, sometimes too familiar, too impoverished to be taken as categories, as technical or theoretical terms. But if the category 'work' can never really be one of Blanchot's words, does it and the reading of *The Space of Literature* to which it seems indebted fit so easily into this presentation of Blanchot's development? Is its role to be confined to the sustaining of such a presentation?

In *The Writing of the Disaster* Blanchot again alludes to *The Space of Literature*, but here it is very definitely not for the sake of summary. Blanchot recalls the descriptions of the unsettling vigilance that is the condition of insomnia, a condition that unsettles the presence and the self-consciousness of a subject and so marks the slippage from the first to the third person, the becoming anonymous of the one who sought to sleep. It is also the condition of the writer, that daytime insomniac, whose quest for his or her own voice is destined to the same slippage, the same turning into anonymity. Blanchot writes:

> Why this recollection? Why is it that despite what they say about the uninterrupted wake which persists behind the dream, and about the inspirational night of insomnia, still these words seem to need to be taken up again, repeated, in order to escape the meaning which animates them, and to be turned away from themselves, away from the discourse which employs them? But taken up anew they reintroduce an assurance to which one thought one had ceased to subscribe. They have an air of truth; they say something – they aspire to coherence. They say: you thought all this long ago; you are thus authorised to think it again. They restore this reasonable continuity which forms systems; they employ the past as a guarantee, letting it become active, it cites, incites. Thus they prevent the invisible ruin which the perpetual wake, outside consciousness-unconsciousness, gives back to the neuter.[14]

The passage concludes with what is perhaps the first and certainly the most enduring of Blanchot's words. But it does so in such a way that one is forced to sense its inevitable hardening, its becoming a term or terminus. For as a word it seems dependent on a narrative that cannot help but monumentalize, and a word in such a narrative, albeit one from category to word, just is a category. Later in The *Writing of the Disaster* Blanchot will seem to concede the word *neutre* to an authorizing reassurance. He will move on, but without any sense that this moving on entails an obvious or even possible summary. He will move on when it is a question, once again, of a work, of a particular writer's work, Kafka's. The point is not to rule against the *neutre*, whose own introductions in *The Infinite Conversation* and in the passage cited here unsettle any easy contextualization; such a ruling against would simply sustain the recollection Blanchot is simultaneously performing and showing cannot be performed, endorsing and showing cannot be endorsed.

The confidence with which one can speak of Blanchot's development, of his movement towards an ever more reticent and less confident writing, is not only self-refuting, employing the sort of narrative that would lead us to the above passage as both a check to and an achievement of that narrative. If Blanchot here reflects on the way in which simply to have continued writing and thinking gives an authority to one's continuing, to the stories one can tell oneself (and others themselves) about it, are we not, more than anything, back with the writer's predicament at the very start of *The Space of Literature*, with the presentiment that going on as if the work could be finished leaves one strangely workless? To set worklessness to work either in an account of Blanchot's development or in the engineering of an encounter between Blanchot and philosophy is to forget something of what was meant by worklessness and the impossible obligation to which it would introduce us.

It is not wrong to assert that Blanchot's treatment of the work shows it to be irreducible to a philosophy of the work, but it is confusing, especially when that treatment is itself said to consist in little more than the claim that the work is so irreducible. This would be one of the temptations facing the sort of account we have been considering.

PHILOSOPHY AND THE WORK

'Investigations on the subject of art such as those the aesthetician pursues bear no relation to the concern of the work of which we speak. Aesthetics talks about art, makes of it an object of reflection and of knowledge. Aesthetics explains art by reducing it, but in all events art for the aesthetician is a present reality around which he constructs plausible thoug'ıts at no risk'.¹⁵ How can it plausibly be a matter of Blanchot and aesthetics? Everything is clear. Neither engagement nor compromise: aesthetics bears 'no relation to the concern of the work of which we speak'. But what if to the claim that 'art for the aesthetician is a present reality around which he constructs plausible thoughts . . .' we add the words 'despite everything': despite everything that *from the first* troubles the reality of the work and so troubles that upon which the 'present reality of art' depends?

In the *Critique of Judgement*, under the heading 'Art in general', Kant insists upon a threefold distinction. Art is first distinguished from nature, then from science, and finally as 'free art' from craft (or 'mercenary art').¹⁶ The order is crucial. To follow these moves is to come slowly but surely to the notion of the work of art as that exemplary and expressive product whose essential features are to be judged in terms of a resistance to paraphrase or summary and a response, a feeling, proper to such a resistance. In the clarification of the first move, the distinguishing of art from nature, Kant provides the following well-known formulation: '(a)rt is distinguished from nature as doing is from acting or operating in general; and the product or result of art is distinguished from that of nature, the first being a work, the second an effect'.¹⁷ If one might sometimes speak of effects as works, as when one admires the 'regularly constructed honeycombs made by bees', to do so is always to speak analogically. The labour of the bee, unlike the freely chosen activity of the artist, is wholly dictated by the bee's nature. A little later, having gone on to distinguish art from science and craft and having provided an initial statement about fine or beautiful art, Kant seems to draw another analogy: 'Nature we say is beautiful if it also looks like art; and art can be called beautiful art only if we are conscious that it is art while yet it looks like nature'.¹⁸ I say that Kant *seems* to draw an analogy because not only does he not mention that this comparison is made solely by virtue of an analogical relation, but also he gives us reason to suppose that here the comparison is necessary. When it is a question of the beautiful, we have to think of works of art as if they were effects of nature and of effects of nature as if they were works of art, where the 'as if' is part of the content of the thought. In the first clearly signalled analogy the honeycomb is thought as a work because it can be described in such a way as to emphasize certain features that it can be said to have in common with the products of human labour. But in distinguishing art from science and craft, Kant makes it clear that this is not sufficient for a thing to be called a work. The honeycomb is like a work of art in the sense that it is like any artefact. The process that produces it is as much like the process that produces a scientific result or a piece of craft, that is, a process (a human activity) for which a rule can be given, as it is like the fundamentally mysterious process that leads to the work of art.

The second passage concerns the now clarified notion of the work, a notion obviously implicit in the first passage, but not one that could be grasped solely in terms of what distinguishes it from nature. And yet, so clarified, it is once again, but far more profoundly because exceptionally, to be brought into proximity with the effect of nature. Here it is precisely because the work is not like an artefact, not like a technical or scientific achievement, indeed not like any human *product* at all, that it is as if it were (i.e. not simply analogous to) an effect of nature. But surely the point is simply that when I regard an effect of nature as beautiful I delight in it as if it were made solely for that delight. Likewise, when I judge a work of art to be beautiful or judge a thing to be a beautiful work of art my attention is drawn to nothing in the work which would betray the fact that it is the result of a rule-governed activity; this being the paradox of the work that the rule which enabled the artist to produce it can be neither inferred nor taught, neither communicated nor imagined, is thus no human rule at all but rather given by nature. It is true that in the first passage an effect of nature is like a work of art because it is like the result of a human process, while in the second a work of art is like an effect of nature because it is not like the result of a human process, but any inconsistency can be put down to the fact that between the two passages we find the first clarification and first real introduction of the notion of the work of art. Note, however, a curious and far from superficial consequence of this introduction in this context. If in experiencing the work of art I am experiencing it as if it were an effect of nature, and if to experience an effect of nature as beautiful is to experience it as if it were a work of art, then we can say that in experiencing the work of art it is as if it were only as if it were a work. The formulation is awkward, but it addresses the symptomatic awkwardness that attends both the introduction of the notion of the work and the residual inconsistency in the analogies with nature. It suggests as well that the aesthetic discourse around the work and for which the notion of the work is necessary has to find a way to keep that notion at a distance. The claim that to treat the beautiful in nature is to treat it as if it were a work of art implies that the whole account of natural beauty is somehow already dependent upon the yet to be introduced notion of the thing we call the work of art. Yet, with its introduction, this thing is scarcely conceivable as a thing. Its strangeness as a thing and as a product leads us to discuss it solely in terms of the quasi-natural process which produces it (genius) and the aesthetic response for which it calls. But what of the work *itself*? The question is deflected by the command to consider it as if it were an effect of nature. It is as if the command is issued for the whole purpose of this deflection. But the command can only be understood on the basis of a prior allusion to the work and to an implicit affirmation of the work as somehow always already there. We can, with Kant, speak of 'art in general', but it seems that any attempt to speak of the work in general or of the work itself is to be frustrated.

Whatever its inclination or affiliation – be it analytic, continental or otherwise – philosophy has for a long time conceded that the notion of the work is a rather strange one. It has been frequently willing to acknowledge the notion's historicity, the work's complicity with a romanticism itself responding to some of the aspects which make the notion so difficult yet so provocative in its Kantian determination. More than anything else it is romanticism that turns the theoretical instability of the work into the artistic quest for the work. Romantic writing on the work will henceforth also be a writing on the absence of the work. Any philosophical engagement with the question of art is obliged, it seems, both to use the notion of the work and to confess that it has very little idea about that to which it refers. If the book I am reading, the piece of music I am playing or listening to, the film I am watching, the painting or sculpture I am looking at are in some way inseparable from the work to which I refer when I refer to one of them, it also seems that in each case there are properties pertaining to the work which do not pertain to them. Is it a matter best addressed in terms of universals and particular instances, or in terms of types and tokens? Neither of these proposals has proved effective. The work, neither universal nor type, seems too close to the things we call works for these binary logics to operate. The things we persist in calling works never conform simply to instances or types. But it is also the case that the work never seems wholly present when these things are present, never quite to occur when these things are occurring.

In asking about the sort of thing the work is, the ontology of art, it seems, is forced to remain incomplete. There are perhaps two main ways of responding to this predicament.

(1) One could respond by arguing that the more important issue for the philosophy of art is not what the work is but how or when a

thing comes to be regarded as a work. There is something instantly credible and rather tempting here. Yet nothing can prevent the ontological question from returning: what *is* the work of art when it is a work of art? What *is* the work of art now that this thing is said to have become a work of art? In any attempt to introduce the formula 'a work of art is a thing + *y*' where the thing is an artefact or an event and where y denotes an experience, a value, a process, an interpretation, etc., the suspicion arises again that the notion of the work has already determined the thing to which we wish to add the essential and defining term. There seems to be something in principle unsatisfactory, for example, in my asking how or why these lines on a canvas come to be accepted as comprising a work of art. An answer of the order that they are made or drawn by Paul Klee, that a particular institution or set of institutions has deemed the canvas worthy of exhibition, or that they produce a certain response in the mind or body of the qualified viewer merely underlines the fact that when I describe these marks and lines I am already describing a work of art. Again, if in a rather different fashion, at the very moment a theory wishes to introduce the notion of the work and to insist on this moment as the moment of its introduction, it could be argued that the theory has from the first been drawing upon that notion, as though that notion were the non-theorizable condition for the very possibility of the theory. The thing the theorist would need to be able to refer to as being *not yet* the work – i.e. not yet evaluated, not yet interpreted, the thing before the addition of *y* – instantly coalesces with the work, the work itself.

It is at this point that Blanchot's account of the relation between the book and the work might be usefully recalled. For is there not in his claim that '(r)eading simply "makes" the book, the work, become a work' the same ambivalent precedence accorded the work, a precedence that confers an ambiguity on the very introduction of the work *as* the work? In implying a step from a book to a work, Blanchot seems to share the move the 'where or when is art' theorists seek to theorize. In letting the work interrupt that move, he seems to be mimicking and pointing out the impossibility of such a theory. But is the ambiguity sufficient for his purposes? To get a clearer sense of what is at stake in such a question, we need to consider Blanchot's reaction or contribution to a second possible response to the faltering of the ontological inquiry.

(2) One could respond by letting the question as to the being of the work rebound on to the question of the being of the thing, in other words by contending that the tension provoked by the work in the

ontology of art should be seen as having consequences for ontology itself, even a fundamental ontology. If one takes this response in its Heideggerian form, it will entail moving not from the thing to the work but precisely from the work to the thing. To ask how a thing becomes a work is not only to presuppose what a thing is *as* a thing but also to subordinate the work to that ontology. Thus it is a question of how a thing as traditionally conceived can become a work. Consequently the instability of the work in this context can be read against that traditional conception of the thing. Note, however, that the instability of the work does not derive from its contextualization and it does not simply vanish on the work's being retrieved from its subordination to a traditional ontology. There is a tension at the heart of the work which – again on Heidegger's terms – enables it to be thought as an origin, as an original occurrence in which a thing can be shown as the thing it is and from which the work can be thought as the work it is.

For some it will be obvious that this is where we should have begun, with Heidegger's dismantling of an aesthetic tradition and, more specifically, with his disparaging of any account of the work which seeks either to reconcile it with or to limit it to a subjectivism, the language of 'expression' and 'experience'. After all, is this not the easiest way of diagnosing the seemingly intractable ambiguity of the work in Kant's text, in romanticism, and in the various 'where or when is art' theories? Blanchot's own comments about aesthetics and its inability, in its apparent concern for the work, to think the concern *of the work* would tie in nicely here. In linking the work, from the first, with the words 'being' and 'beginning' is Blanchot not making it clear that it is Heidegger's introduction, clarification and problematization of the work that serve as the backdrop for his own investigations? For example, when Blanchot considers the topic of genius, although what he says is not exactly what Heidegger says or would say, the effect is surely the same, the same emphatic (re)turn to the work itself. In *Le Livre à venir*, Blanchot argues that there is something odd about employing the idea of a quasi-natural expression in order to explain the artist's obsessive commitment to his or her work. There must be something wrong with the ease with which one links the drive to create with the artist's having something to say. Blanchot writes:

> Can we be content with the belief that the passion . . . which called Cézanne, brush in hand, to his death and for which he could not spare a day to bury his mother, has no other source than the need to

express himself?'[19]

The passion to express, if it can be so called, concerns neither Cézanne the man nor Cézanne the genius. It concerns the painting, the work, alone. It is surprising, however, that this way of retrieving the painting from expression characterizes not only the thinking that would bring Blanchot into proximity with Heidegger but also to a great extent Blanchot's treatment of Heidegger.

In the Foreword to *Erläuterungen zu Hölderlins Dichtung*, Heidegger likens the work of his commentary (*Erläuterung*), the act of commenting on a poem, to snow falling on to a bell, the bell ringing out as the snow melts. The image of this snowfall, of the bell and its ringing (*läuten*), comes from some lines of Hölderlin's cited by Heidegger. The commentary thus seeks to describe itself in terms given by the very poet the commentary would serve. This service which would allow the poet's words to be heard, to ring out, occurs as a sort of self-occluding on the part of the commentary. It is as though the commentary were not a way of speaking but a way of keeping silent. Blanchot remarks on this gesture in the 1963 Preface to the second edition of his *Lautréamont et Sade*, but feels the need to go further. If, drawing on this account of commentary, criticism becomes 'the open space in which the poem is communicated',[20] if it thereby stages a disappearance for the sake of the poem's appearance, then rather than giving an identity or function to criticism or commentary, rather than serving to introduce or to preface a commentary or critical reading, this movement of disappearing has to be thought of as already belonging to the work itself. If Heidegger thought that words belonging to the poem could somehow give to commentary what can then be seen as belonging to it, that is, its capacity to disappear and to let the work be, then Blanchot suggests an inversion. What is most compelling here is the drama of appearing and disappearing that such an appropriation is said to demonstrate. The disappearing of commentary is not the achievement of a particularly sensitive and self-aware commentary but *of the work*, moreover of the work considered as itself a disappearing or self-effacing.

So much would need to be said at this juncture. Blanchot's inversion raises the whole question of Heidegger's attempt to adduce from the essence of the poem an essence for thinking, for commentary, be it by analogy, reflection or reading. Since *La Part du feu* Blanchot has been interested in Heidegger's renegotiation of the question of the work and in his attempts to bring philosophy into a different relation with poetry. *The Space of Literature* and the 1963 Preface allow us to pose a question to this different relation. To what extent does Heidegger's encounter with Hölderlin presuppose a certain conception of the work, and to what extent is Hölderlin held apart from some of the implications of that conception? In 'The origin of the work of art', Heidegger presents us with several famous examples of works, notably: the Van Gogh painting, the Greek temple, the Meyer poem. The essay ends with, again, some lines of Hölderlin's, from 'The journey', lines allowed to stand in partial answer, or in place of an answer, to the question whether we are yet at an origin. Is this poem another example? Clearly not. Is it, then, a work? When Heidegger cites it, is he citing a work and giving an example of what it might be now, after the account of the work as an origin, to cite a work? Or is it a matter of a temporary relaxing of the question of the work? For Blanchot, the work silences the question concerning it even in the form that would, when answered, think the work as an origin.

The main text of *The Space of Literature* closes with the word 'beginning'. It closes with the word being announced by the poem, the work, in a solitude, now understood, by way of a reading of Hölderlin, to be a solitude incapable of originating anything. On our reading, it thus makes explicit what must remain implicit in Heidegger's citing of Hölderlin at the close of his essay. If the work announces 'beginning', it does so because it is always not quite or not yet this beginning. It is as if the work silences the question 'what is the work?' by always transposing it into the logically derivative 'where or when is the work?' And so of Heidegger one could ask: what is the work when it is an origin?

The last appendix to *The Space of Literature* also ends the book with a reading of Hölderlin, of Hölderlin's itinerary as a turning and returning which prohibits even the most generous or self-denigrating of philosophical commentaries and the most intricate of developmental narratives.

On the one hand, we could, confronted with these difficult insinuations, envisage Blanchot as somehow succeeding Heidegger: from the traditional understanding of the work to Heidegger's thought of the work as origin to Blanchot's thought of the work as other than origin, perhaps as disastrous pre-origin. In his review of *The Space of Literature*, entitled 'Le Regard du poète', Levinas seems to view Blanchot's project as inherently negative, one whose value for philosophy, and especially for Levinas's philosophy, derives from the narrative it can be seen as engendering. In a sense we do this as

well when we move too quickly to the matter of Blanchot's development, to a presentation of his writings, and especially those writings
prior to *The Infinite Conversation*, as somehow completed, their
results understood and acted upon. When, in *The Writing of the
Disaster*, Blanchot 'remembers' *The Space of Literature*, it is
perhaps more a matter of his *itinerary* than his development, and it is
to the thought of such an itinerary that the analyses of the work and
of the 'of the work' in *The Space of Literature* always invite us and
always return us. On the other hand, given Blanchot's problema-
tizing of the means by which Heidegger would claim to think the
work against the tradition, we could underline the manner in which
Blanchot's insistence on the work's irreducibility to aesthetics, to a
philosophy of art, requires a reconsideration of how this irreducibility is marked in and by that philosophy itself. It is there that
we can see what it is to attempt to think away from the very *thing*
you believe yourself to be thinking towards. And this too would be a
project, one whose diagnosable indifference to the work will always
have been indebted to the undiagnosable indifference *of the work*.
What are the implications of beginning to think of it as such?

NOTES

1 Maurice Blanchot, *The Space of Literature*, trans. Ann Smock (Lincoln
  and London: University of Nebraska Press, 1982), p. 94. The sentence
  continues: 'beyond the man who produced it, the experience that is
  expressed in it and even beyond all the artistic resources which tradition
  has made available'.
2 Ibid., p. 196.
3 Ibid., p. 23. It is as the content of this impression, the writer's impression, that we first come across the word *désœuvrement* in *The Space of
  Literature*.
4 Ibid., p. 193.
5 Maurice Blanchot, *The Infinite Conversation*, trans. Susan Hanson
  (Minneapolis and London: University of Minnesota Press, 1993), p.
  453.
6 Maurice Blanchot, *The Step Not Beyond*, trans. Lycette Nelson (Albany:
  State University of New York Press, 1982), p. 34.
7 Maurice Blanchot, *The Writing of the Disaster*, trans. Ann Smock
  (Lincoln and London: University of Nebraska Press, 1986), p. 7.
8 Ibid., p. 80.
9 One is reminded of the clichés, 'I refuse to look at that', 'I can't bear it',
  which Blanchot says point to the absolute intolerance of the work of art
  far more forcefully than does the suspect self-satisfaction of the one
  who feels at ease with music, with painting, all the things of art and
  culture. 'It is quite true', Blanchot writes, 'one cannot live with a
  painting in plain sight' (*The Space of Literature*, p. 192).

10 Blanchot, *The Infinite Conversation*, p. 201.
11 There is, to my knowledge, only one occasion on which Blanchot writes the word 'work' so as to let it resonate without a reference to its contexts, its philosophical determinations, but also without any clue as to how it might engage those determinations or alter those contexts (cf. *The Step Not Beyond*, p. 88)
12 Blanchot, *The Infinite Conversation*, p. xii.
13 Note that Blanchot will return to *œuvre* and *désœuvrement* in *The Unavowable Community*, where it is a matter of responding to a particular and polemical application of his own terminology by Nancy and a matter of a particular work, Marguerite Duras's *The Malady of Death*.
14 Blanchot, *The Writing of the Disaster*, p. 59.
15 Blanchot, *The Space of Literature*, p. 234.
16 Immanuel Kant, *Critique of Judgement*, trans. W. S. Pluhar, (Indianapolis: Hackett, 1987), p. 170
17 Ibid.
18 Ibid., p. 174.
19 Maurice Blanchot, *Le Livre à venir* (Paris: Gallimard, 1959), p. 46.
20 Maurice Blanchot, *Lautréamont et Sade*, (Paris: Editions de Minuit, 1963), p. 12.

6   *Il y a* – Holding Levinas's hand to Blanchot's fire[1]

Simon Critchley

Death is not the *noema* of a *noesis*. It is not the object or meaningful fulfilment of an intentional act. Death, or rather, dying, is by definition ungraspable; it is that which exceeds intentionality and the noetico-noematic correlative structures of phenomenology. There can thus be no phenomenology of dying, because it is a state of affairs about which one could neither have an adequate intention nor find intuitive fulfilment. The ultimate meaning of human finitude is that we cannot find meaningful fulfilment for the finite. In this sense, dying is meaningless and, consequently, the work of mourning is infinite (which is to say that mourning is not a Work).

Since direct contact with death would demand the death of the person who entered into contact, the only relation that the living can maintain with death is through a representation, an image, a picture of death, whether visual or verbal. And yet, we immediately confront a paradox: namely that the representation of death is not the representation of a presence, an object of perception or intuition – we cannot draw a likeness of death, a portrait, a still life, or whatever. Thus, representations of death are *misrepresentations*, or rather they are representations of an absence.[2] The paradox at the heart of the representation of death is perhaps best conveyed by the figure of prosopopoeia, that is, the rhetorical trope by which an absent or imaginary person is presented as speaking or acting. Etymologically, prosopopoeia means to make a face (*prosopon* + *poien*); in this sense we might think of a death mask or *memento mori*, a form which indicates the failure of presence, a face which withdraws behind the form which presents it.[3] In a manner analogous to what Nietzsche writes about the function of *Schein* in *The Birth of Tragedy*, such a prosopopoeic image both allows us to glimpse the interminability of dying in the Apollonian mask of the tragic hero and redeems us from the nauseating contact with the truth of tragedy, the abyss of the

Dionysian, the wisdom of Sile us: 'What is best of all is . . . not to be born, not to *be*, to be *nothing*. But the second best for you is – to die soon.'[4] I believe that many of the haunting images – or death masks – in Blanchot's *récits* (I am thinking of the various death scenes in *Thomas the Obscure*, *Death Sentence* and *The Last Man*, but also of the figures of Eurydice or the Sirens) have a prosopopoeic function: they are a face for that which has no face, and they show the necessary inadequacy of our relation to death. To anticipate myself a little, my question to Levinas will be: *must the face of the Other always be a death mask?*

However, as I show elsewhere with reference to Blanchot's reading of Kafka's *Diaries*, the writer's (and philosopher's) relation with death is necessarily self-deceptive: it is a relation with what is believed to be a possibility, containing the possibility of meaningful fulfilment, but which is revealed to be an impossibility.[5] The infinite time of dying evades the writer's grasp and s/he mistakes *le mourir* for *la mort*, dying for death. Death is disclosed upon the horizon of possibility and thus remains within the bounds of phenomenology or what Levinas would call 'the economy of the Same'. To conceive of death as possibility is to conceive of it as *my* possibility; that is, the relation with death is always a relation with *my* death. As Heidegger famously points out in *Sein und Zeit*, my relation to the death of others cannot substitute for my relation with my own death; death is in each case *mine*.[6] In this sense, death is a self-relation or even self-reflection that permits the totality of *Dasein* to be grasped. Death is like a mirror in which I allegedly achieve narcissistic self-communion; it is the event in relation to which I am constituted as a Subject. Being-towards-death permits the achievement of authentic selfhood, which, I have argued elsewhere,[7] repeats the traditional structure of autarchy or autonomy, allowing the self to assume its fate and the community to assume its destiny. One might say that the community briefly but decisively envisaged in Paragraph 74 of *Sein und Zeit* is a community of death, where commonality is found in a sharing of finitude, where individual fates are taken up into a common destiny, where death is the Work of the community.

The radicality of the thought of dying in Blanchot is that death becomes impossible and ungraspable. It is meta-phenomenological. In Levinas's terms, dying belongs to the order of the enigma rather than the phenomenon (which, of course, passes over the complex question whether there can be a phenomenology of the enigmatic or the inapparent). Dying transgresses the boundary of the self's jurisdiction. This is why suicide is impossible for Blanchot: I cannot *want* to die; death is not an object of the will. Thus, the thought of the impossibility of death introduces the possibility of an encounter with some aspect of experience or some state of affairs that is not reducible to the self and which does not relate or return to self; that is to say, something other. The ungraspable facticity of dying establishes an opening on to a meta-phenomenological alterity, irreducible to the power of the Subject, the will or *Dasein* (as I see it, this is the central argument of *Time and the Other*). Dying is the impossibility of possibility and thus undermines the residual heroism, virility and potency of Being-towards-death. In the infinite time of dying, all possibility becomes impossible, and I am left passive and impotent. Dying is the sensible passivity of senescence, the wrinkling of the skin – crispation: the helplessly ageing face looking back at you in the mirror.

In this way, perhaps (and that is a significant 'perhaps'), the guiding intention of Levinas's work is achieved: namely that if death is not a self-relation, if it does not result in self-communion and the achievement of a meaning to finitude, then this means that a certain plurality has insinuated itself at the heart of the self. The facticity of dying structures the self as Being-for-the-other, as substitution, which also means that death is not revealed in a relation to *my* death but rather in the alterity of death or the death of the Other. As Levinas writes in a late text, it is 'As if the invisible death which the face of the other faces were *my* affair, as if this death regarded me'.[8]

This relation between dying and plurality allows us to raise the question of what vision of community could be derived from this anti-Heideggerian account of dying, from this fundamental axiom of heteronomy. If, as Levinas suggests, the social ideal has been conceived from Plato to Heidegger in terms of fusion, a collectivity that says 'we' and feels the solidarity of the Other at its side, what Nancy calls 'immanentism', then a Levinasian vision of community would be 'a collectivity that is not a communion',[9] *une communauté désœuvrée*, a community unworked through the irreducibility of plurality that opens in the relation to death. This is a point made by Alphonso Lingis:

> Community forms when one exposes oneself to the naked one, the destitute one, the outcast, the dying one. One enters into community not by affirming oneself and one's forces but by exposing oneself to expenditure at a loss, to sacrifice.[10]

To conceive of death as possibility is to project on to a future as the fundamental dimension of freedom and, with Heidegger, to establish the future as the basic phenomenon of time. Yet, such a future is always *my* future and *my* possibility, a future ultimately grasped from within the solitary fate of the Subject or the shared destiny of the community. I would claim that such a future is *never future enough for the time of dying*, which is a temporality of infinite delay, patience, senescence or *différance*. Dying thus opens a relation with the future which is always ungraspable, impossible and enigmatic; that is to say, it opens the possibility of a future without me, an infinite future, *a future which is not my future.*[11]

What is a future that is not my future? It is another future or the future of an Other, that is, the future that is always ahead of me and my projective freedom, that is always to come and from where the basic phenomenon of time arises, what Levinas calls dia-chrony. But what or who is the Other? Does the word 'Other' translate the impersonal *autre* or the personal *autrui*? For Blanchot, writing establishes a relation with alterity that would appear to be strictly impersonal: a relation with the exteriority of *le neutre*. It would seem that the latter must be rigorously distinguished from the personal alterity sought by Levinas, the alterity of *autrui*, which is ultimately the alterity of the child, that is, of the son, and the alterity of illeity, of a (personal) God.[12] It would seem that although the experience of alterity in Blanchot and Levinas opens with the impossibility of death, that is, with their critique of Heidegger's Being-towards-death, one might conclude that there is only a formal or structural similarity between the alterity of the relation to the neuter and the alterity of *autrui* and that it is here that one can draw the line between Levinas and Blanchot. However, in opposition to this, I should like to muddy the distinction between Blanchot and Levinas by tracking an alternative destiny for the *il y a* in Levinas's work and indicating the direction that could be taken by a Blanchot-inspired re-reading of Levinas.

* * *

I show elsewhere that the experience of literature for Blanchot has its source in 'the primal scene' of what he variously calls 'the other night', 'the energy of exteriority prior to law' or 'the impossibility of death', and that this experience can be understood with reference to Levinas's notion of the *il y a*.[13] However, although Levinas's thinking begins with the *il y a*, which is his deformation of the Heideggerian understanding of Being (an appropriation and ruination of the *Seinsfrage*), his entire subsequent work would seem, on a first reading, to be premised upon the necessity to surmount the *il y a* in order to move on to the hypostasis of the Subject and ultimately the ethical relation to the Other, a relation whose alterity is underwritten by the trace of illeity. In order to establish that ethics is first philosophy (i.e. that philosophy is *first*), Levinas must overcome the neutrality of the *il y a*, the ambiguous instance of literature.

Now, to read Levinas in this way would be to adopt what Paul Davies has called 'a linear narrative',[14] which would begin with one ('bad') experience of neutrality in the *il y a* and end up with another ('good') experience of neutrality in illeity, after having passed through the mediating moments of the Subject and *autrui* (roughly, Sections II and III of *Totality and Infinity*). To read Levinas in this way would be to follow a line from the *il y a* to the Subject, to *autrui*, to illeity. However, the question that must be asked is: can or, indeed, *should* one read Levinas in a linear fashion, as if the claim to ethics as first philosophy were a linear ascent to a new metaphysical summit, as if *Totality and Infinity* were an anti-Hegelian rewriting of the *Phenomenology of Spirit* (which might yet be true at the level of Levinas's intentions)? Is the neutrality of the *il y a* ever decisively surmounted in Levinas's work? And if this is so, why does the *il y a* keep on returning like the proverbial repressed, relentlessly disturbing the linearity of the exposition? Is the moment of the *il y a* – that is to say, the instance of the literary, of rhetoric and ambiguity – in any way reducible or controllable in Levinas's work? Or might one track an alternative destiny of the *il y a*, where it is not decisively surmounted but where it returns to interrupt that work at certain critical moments? Might this not plot a different itinerary for reading Levinas, where the name of Blanchot would function as a clue or key for the entire problematic of literature, writing, neutrality and ambiguity in the articulation of ethics as first philosophy? Is literature ever decisively overcome in the establishment of ethics as first philosophy?

Let me give a couple of instances of this tracking of the *il y a* before provisionally sketching what I see as the important consequences of such a reading.[15]

The problem with the *il y a* is that it stubbornly refuses to disappear and that Levinas keeps on reintroducing it at crucial moments in the analysis. It functions like a standing reserve of non-sense from which Levinas will repeatedly draw the possibility of ethical significance, like an incessant buzzing in the ears that returns once the day falls silent and one tries to sleep. To pick a few examples, almost at random: (1) in the 'Phenomenology of eros', the night of the *il y a* appears alongside the night of the erotic, where 'the face fades and the relation to the other becomes a neutral, ambiguous, animal play'.[16] In eros, we move beyond the face and risk entering the twilight zone of the *il y a*, where the relation to the Other becomes profane and language becomes lascivious and wanton, like the speeches of the witches in Macbeth. But, as is well known, the moment of eros, of sexual difference, cannot be reduced or by-passed in Levinas's work, where it functions as what Levinas calls in *Time and the Other* an 'alterity content'[17] that ensures the possibility of fecundity, plurality within Being and consequently the break with Parmenides. (2) More curious is the way in which Levinas will emphasize the possible ambivalence between the impersonal alterity of the *il y a* and the personal alterity of the ethical relation, claiming in 'God and philosophy' that the transcendence of the neighbour is transcendent almost to the point of possible confusion with the *il y a*.[18] (3) Or, again, in the concluding lines of 'Transcendence and intelligibility', at the end of a very conservative and measured restatement of his main lines of argumentation, Levinas notes that the account of subjectivity affected by the unpresentable alterity of the infinite could be said to announce itself in insomnia, that is to say, in the troubled vigilance of the psyche in the *il y a*.[19] It would appear that Levinas wants to emphasize the sheer radicality of the alterity revealed in the ethical relation by stressing the possible confusion that the Subject might have in distinguishing between the alterity of the *il y a* and that of illeity, a confusion emphasized by the homophony and linked etymology of the two terms.

In *Existence and Existents*, Levinas recounts the Russian folk-tale of Little John the Simpleton, who throws his father's lunch to his shadow in order to try and slip away from it, only to discover that his shadow still clings to him, like an inalienable companion.[20] Is not the place of the *il y a* in Levinas's work like Little John's shadow, stretching mockingly beneath the feet of the philosopher who proclaims ethics as first philosophy? Is not the *il y a* like a shadow or ghost that haunts Levinas's work, a *revenant* that returns it again and again to the moment of nonsense, neutrality and ambiguity, as Banquo's ghost returns Macbeth to the scene of his crime, or like the ghostly return of scepticism after its refutation by reason? Thus, if the *il y a* is the first step on Levinas's itinerary of thought, a neutrality that must be surmounted in the advent of the Subject and *autrui*, then might one not wonder why he keeps stumbling on the first step of a ladder that he sometimes claims to have thrown away? Or, more curiously – and more interestingly – *must* Levinas's thought keep stumbling on this first step in order to preserve the possibility of ethical sense? Might one not wonder whether the ambiguity of the relation between the *il y a* and illeity is essential to the articulation of the ethical in a manner that is analogous to the model of scepticism and its refutation, where the ghost of scepticism returns to haunt reason after each refutation? Isn't this what Levinas means in 'God and philosophy' (but other examples could be cited) when he insists that the alternating rhythm of the Saying and the Said must be substituted for the unity of discourse in the articulation of the relation to the Other?[21]

Which brings me to a hypothesis in the form of a question: might not the *fascination* (a word favoured by Blanchot) that Levinas's writing continues to exert, the way that it captivates us without our ever feeling that we have captured it, be found in the way it keeps open the question of ambiguity, the ambiguity that defines the experience of language and literature itself for Blanchot, the ambiguity of the Saying and the Said, of scepticism and reason, of the *il y a* and illeity, that is also to say – perhaps – of evil and goodness?

(Let us note in passing that there is a certain thematization, perhaps even a staging, of ambiguity in Levinas's later texts. For example, he speaks in *Otherwise than Being* of the beyond of being 'returning and not returning to ontology . . . becoming and not becoming the meaning of being'.[22] Or again, in the discussion of testimony in Chapter 5 of the same text,

> Transcendence, the beyond essence which is also being-in-the-world, needs ambiguity, a blinking of meaning which is not only a chance certainty, but a frontier both ineffaceable and finer than the outline (*le tracé*) of an ideal line.[23]

Transcendence *needs* ambiguity in order for transcendence to 'be' transcendence. But is not this thematization of ambiguity by Levinas an attempt to *control* ambiguity? My query concerns the possibility of such control: might not ambiguity be out of control in Levinas's text?)

What is the place of evil in Levinas's work? If I am right in my suggestion that the *il y a* is never simply left behind or surmounted and that Levinas's work always retains a memory of the *il y a* which could possibly provoke confusion on the part of the Subject between the alterity of the *il y a* and the alterity of illeity, then one consequence of such confusion is the felt ambiguity between the transcendence of evil and that of goodness. On a Levinasian account, what is there to choose experientially between the transcendence of evil and the transcendence of goodness?[24] This is not such a strange question as it sounds, particularly if one recalls the way in which ethical subjectivity is described in *Otherwise than Being* . . . in terms of trauma, possession, madness and even psychosis, predicates that are not so distant from the horror of the *il y a*. How and in virtue of what – what criterion, as Wittgenstein would say, or what evidence, as Husserl would say – is one to decide between possession by the good and possession by evil in the way Levinas describes it?

(Of course, the paradox is that there can be no criterion or evidence for Levinas, for this would presume the thematizability or phenomenologizability of transcendence. But this still begs the question of how Levinas convinces his readers: is it through demonstration or persuasion, argumentation or edification, philosophy or rhetoric? Of course, Levinas is critical of rhetoric in conventionally Platonic terms, which commits him, like Plato, to an anti-rhetorical rhetoric, a writing against writing.)

Let me pursue this question of evil by taking a literary example of possession mentioned in passing by Levinas in his discussion of the *il y a*, when he speaks of 'the smiling horror of Maupassant's tales'.[25] In Maupassant, as in Poe, it is as though death were never dead enough and there is always the terrifying possibility of the dead coming back to life to haunt us. In particular, I am thinking of the impossibility of murdering the eponymous Horla in Maupassant's famous tale. The Horla is a being that will not die and cannot be killed, and, as such, it exceeds the limit of the human. The Horla is a form of overman, 'after man, the Horla'.[26] What takes place in the tale – to suspend the temptation to psychoanalyse – is a case of possession by the Other, an invisible Other with which I am in relation but which continually absolves itself (incidentally, the Horla is always described using the neutral, third-person pronoun – the *il*) from the relation, producing a trauma within the self and an irreducible responsibility. What interests me here is that in Maupassant the possession is clearly intended as a description of possession by evil, but does not this structure of possession by an alterity that can neither be comprehended nor refused closely resemble the structure of ethical subjectivity found in substitution? That is to say, does not the trauma occasioned in the Subject possessed by evil more adequately describe the ethical Subject than possession by the good? Is it not in the excessive experience of evil and horror – the insurmountable memory of the *il y a* – that the ethical Subject first assumes its shape? Does this not begin to explain why the royal road to ethical metaphysics must begin by making Levinas a master of the literature of horror? But if this is the case, why is radical Otherness goodness? Why is alterity ethical? Why is it not rather evil or an-ethical or neutral?[27]

Let us suppose – as I indeed believe – that Levinas offers a convincing account of the primacy of radical alterity, whether it is the alterity of *autrui* in *Totality and Infinity* or the alterity within the Subject described in *Otherwise than Being* . . . Now, how can one conclude from the 'evidence' (given that there can be no evidence) for radical alterity that such alterity is goodness? In virtue of what further 'evidence' can one predicate goodness of alterity? Is this not, as I suspect, *to smuggle a metaphysical presupposition into a quasi-phenomenological description*? Such a claim is, interestingly, analo-gous to possible criticisms of the *causa sui* demonstration for the existence of God.[28] Let's suppose that I am convinced that in order to avoid the vertigo of infinite regress (although one might wonder why such regress must be avoided; why is infinite regress bad?) there must be an uncaused cause, but in virtue of what is one then permitted to go on and claim that this uncaused cause is God (who is, moreover, infinitely good)? Where is the argument for the move from an uncaused cause to God *as* the uncaused cause? What neces-sitates the substantialization of an uncaused cause into a being that one can then predicate with various other metaphysical or divine attributes? Returning the analogy to Levinas, I can see why there has to be a radical alterity in the relation to the Other and at the heart of the Subject in order to avoid the philosophies of totality, but, to play devil's advocate, I do not see why such alterity then receives the predicate 'goodness'. Why does radical Otherness have to be deter-mined as good or evil in an absolute metaphysical sense? Could one – and this is the question motivating this critique – accept Levinas's quasi-phenomenological descriptions of radical alterity whilst suspending or bracketing out their ethico-metaphysical conse-quences? If one followed this through, then what sort of picture of Levinas would emerge?

The picture that emerges, and which I offer in closing as one possible reading of Levinas, as one way of arguing with him, is broadly consistent with that given by Blanchot in his three conversa-tions on *Totality and Infinity* in *The Infinite Conversation*.[29] In the latter work, Blanchot gives his first extended critical attention to a theme central to his *récits*, the question of *autrui* and the nature of the relation to *autrui*. What fascinates Blanchot in his discussion of Levinas is the notion of an absolute relation – *le rapport sans rapport* – that monstrous contradiction (which refuses to recognize the principle of non-contradiction) at the theoretical core of *Totality and Infinity*, where the terms of the relation simultaneously absolve themselves from the relation. For Blanchot, the absolute relation offers a *non-dialectical account of intersubjectivity*,[30] that is, a picture of the relation between humans which is not – *contra* Kojève's Hegel – founded in the struggle for recognition where the self is dependent upon the other for its constitution as a Subject. For Levinas, the interhuman relation is an event of radical asymmetry which resists the symmetry and reciprocity of Hegelian and post-Hegelian models of intersubjectivity (in Sartre and Lacan, for example) through what Levinas calls, in a favourite formulation, 'the curvature of intersubjective space'.[31]

For Blanchot, Levinas restores the strangeness and terror of the interhuman relation as the central concern of philosophy and shows how transcendence can be understood in terms of a social relation. But, and here we move on to Blanchot's discreet critique of Levinas, the absolute relation can *only* be understood socially, and Blanchot carefully holds back from two Levinasian affirmations: first, that the relation to alterity can be understood *ethically* in some novel meta-physical sense, and second, that the relation has *theological* implica-tions (i.e. the trace of illeity). So, in embracing Levinas's account of the relation to *autrui* (in a way which is not itself without problems), Blanchot places brackets around the terms 'ethics' and 'God' and hence holds back from the metaphysical affirmation of the Good beyond Being. Blanchot holds to the ambiguity or tension in the rela-tion to *autrui* that cannot be reduced either through the affirmation of the positivity of the Good or the negativity of Evil. The relation to the Other is neither positive nor negative in any absolute metaphys-ical sense; it is rather neutral, an experience of neutrality which – importantly – is *not* impersonal and which opens in and as that ambiguous form of language that Blanchot calls literature (if I had the space and competence, it is here that I could begin a reading of Blanchot's *récits* in terms of the absolute relation to the *autrui*).

Where does this leave us? For me, Levinas's essential teaching is the primacy of the human relation as that which can neither be refused nor comprehended and his account of a subjectivity *disposed* towards responsibility, or better, responsivity (*Responsivität* rather than *Verantwortung*, to follow Bernhard Waldenfels's distinction).[32] Prior to any metaphysical affirmation of the transcendence of the Good or of the God that arises in this relation, and to which I have to confess myself quite deaf (I have tried hard to listen for many years), what continues to grip me in Levinas is the attention to the Other, to the Other's claim on me and how that claim changes and challenges my self-conception.[33] Now, how is this claim made? Returning to my starting point with the question of death, I should like to emphasize something broached early in Levinas's work, in *Time and the Other*,[34] but not satisfactorily pursued to my mind, where the first experience of an alterity that cannot be reduced to the self occurs in the relation to death, to the ungraspable facticity of dying. Staying with this thought, I should want to claim, with Blanchot, that what opens up in the relation to the alterity of death, of my dying and the Other's dying, is not the transcendence of the Good beyond Being or the trace of God, but the neutral alterity of the *il y a*, the primal scene of emptiness, absence and disaster, what I am tempted to call, rather awkwardly, atheist transcendence.[35]

We are mortals, you and I. There is only my dying and your dying and nothing beyond. You will die and there is nothing beyond. I shall slowly disappear until my heart stops its soft padding against the lining of my chest. Until then, the drive to speak continues, incessantly. Until then, we carry on. After that there is nothing.

NOTES

1 This chapter is the development of a long discussion of Blanchot's critical writings, whose focus in his important early essay 'Literature and the right to death', and where I employ Levinas's notion of the *il y a* as a clue to understanding what Blanchot means by literature or writing (see '*Il y a* – a dying stronger than death', *Oxford Literary Review*, 15 (1993), pp. 81–131). My suggestion is that the *il y a* is the origin of the artwork. However, the substantive thesis that is introduced in my earlier discussion and developed here concerns the question of death and presupposes the (negative) agreement of Levinas and Blanchot in their critique of Heidegger's conception of death as *Dasein*'s ownmost possibility, as the possibility of impossibility. I try to draw the philosophical consequences of Blanchot's terminological distinction between *la mort* and *le mourir*, death and dying, where the former is synonymous with *possibility* and consequently with the project of grasping the meaning of human finitude, whereas the latter can be identified with *impossibility* and entails the ungraspable facticity of death, where I can no longer lay hold of a meaning for human finitude. My suggestion is simply that the notion of dying yields an approach to human finitude at once more profound, more troubling, less heroic and less virile than that found in *Sein und Zeit*, a suggestion that I make good through a discussion of dying in the work of Samuel Beckett, which will appear in my *Very Little . . . Almost Nothing* (London and New York: Routledge, forthcoming). I owe my title to Gerald Bruns, whose extremely thoughtful remarks greatly aided the revision of this paper for publication. I also

owe a debt to Donna Brody, former research student at the University of
Essex, who first brought the radicality of the *il y a* to my attention and
whose work has been invaluable in thinking through these issues.

2 In this regard, see Elisabeth Bronfen's and Sarah Webster Goodwin's
interesting introduction to *Death and Representation* (Baltimore: John
Hopkins University Press, 1993), pp. 3–25, esp. pp. 7, 20.

3 This idea is borrowed from J. Hillis Miller's *Versions of Pygmalion*
(Cambridge, Mass.: Harvard University Press, 1990); see especially the
excellent discussion of Blanchot, 'Death mask: Blanchot's *L'arrêt de
mort*', pp. 179–210.

4 Fredrich Nietzsche, *The Birth of Tragedy*, trans. W. Kaufmann (New
York: Vintage, 1967), p. 42.

5 See Critchley, 'A dying stronger than death', pp. 120–8. Please note that
the reference to Kafka here is to his *Diaries* (cited p. 121) and not to his
fiction, which, of course, often says exactly the opposite. Indeed, it
would be interesting to pursue the theme of the impossibility of death in
relation to Kafka's short tale 'Die Sorge des Hausvaters' and the spectral, deathless figure of Odradek (in *Erzählungen* (New York: Schocken,
1967), pp. 170–2).

6 *Sein und Zeit*, 15th edn (Tübingen: Niemeyer, 1984), p. 240. *Being and
Time*, trans. J. Macquarrie and E. Robinson (Oxford: Blackwell, 1962),
p. 284. For Levinas's most sustained critique of Heidegger on death, see
the recently published lecture series 'La Mort et le temps', in *Emmanuel
Levinas: cahier de l'Herne* (Paris: L'Herne, 1991), pp. 21–75. My opposition between death as possibility and impossibility as a way of organizing the difference between Heidegger, on the one hand, and Levinas
and Blanchot, on the other, only tells half the story and, as Derrida has
shown us, matters are rarely univocal in relation to Heidegger, particularly on the question of death and the entire thematic of authenticity and
inauthenticity. For more nuanced accounts of Heidegger on death, see
Christopher Fynsk, *Thought and Historicity* (Ithaca: Cornell University
Press, 1986); and Françoise Dastur, *La Mort: essai sur la finitude* (Paris:
Hatier, 1994).

7 See 'Prolegomena to any post-deconstructive subjectivity', in
Deconstructive Subjectivities, ed. S. Critchley and P. Dews (Albany:
State University of New York Press, 1996), pp. 19–20.

8 'Paix et proximité', in *Les Cahiers de la nuit surveillée* 3 (Lagrasse:
Verdier, 1984), p. 344.

9 See Emmanuel Levinas, *Time and the Other*, trans. R. Cohen
(Pittsburgh: Duquesne University Press, 1987), p. 84.

10 Alphonso Lingis, *The Community of Those who have Nothing in
Common* (Bloomington: Indiana University Press, 1994), p. 12. A question left unresolved here concerns the relation of death to femininity in
Levinas, particularly in *Time and the Other* (pp. 85–8), that is, between
the *mystery* of death and the *mystery* of the feminine, and whether, in the
light of Elizabeth Bronfen's work, this repeats a persistent masculinist
trope (see *Over Her Dead Body: Death, Femininity and the Aesthetic*
(Manchester: Manchester University Press, 1992)). This also entails the
related point concerning the extent to which the Levinasian account of
plurality is dependent upon his notion of fecundity and hence upon his

account of the child, that is to say, the son, and therefore entails a male lineage of community that fails to acknowledge mother–daughter relations (see below, n. 14).

11 I borrow this formulation from Paul Davies. In this regard, see the following passage from 'Meaning and sense': 'To renounce being the contemporary of the triumph of one's work is to envisage this triumph in a *time without me*, to aim at this world below without me, to aim at a time beyond the horizon of my time, in an eschatology without hope for oneself, or in a liberation from my time.

To be *for* a time that would be without me, *for* a time after my time, over and beyond the celebrated "being for death", is not an ordinary thought which is extrapolating from my own duration; it is the passage to the time of the other' (Emmanuel Levinas, *Collected Philosophical Papers*, trans. A. Lingis (Dordrecht: Kluwer, 1987), p. 92).

12 In 'Questions to Emmanuel Levinas: on the divinity of love', in *The Irigaray Reader*, ed. M. Whitford (Oxford: Blackwell, 1991), pp. 178–89, Irigaray rightly questions Levinas as to whether the alterity of the child as the future for the father that is not the father's future does not still remain within the sphere of the *pour soi*, where the child is *for* the father, a project beyond his powers of projection, but still *his* project (see esp. p. 181).

13 Critchley, 'A dying stronger than death', pp. 102–20.

14 See 'A linear narrative? Blanchot with Heidegger in the work of Levinas', in *Philosophers' Poets* (London: Routledge, 1990), pp. 37–69.

15 A point of clarification here: in lectures given on Levinas at Essex University in November 1994, Rudi Visker spoke of an 'ethicization of the *il y a*' in Levinas's work. The claim is that the overcoming or surmounting of the *il y a* in the move to the hypostasis of the Subject that characterized Levinas's earlier analyses is abandoned in the later work, where the *il y a* is accorded an ethical significance previously denied to it. Now, there is some truth to this claim, and it would be a question of giving (which I cannot give here) a detailed periodization of the *il y a* across Levinas's work, noting differences of nuance in different texts written at different periods. It is certainly true to say, as Levinas says himself in *Ethique et infini*, that in his later work, although he scarcely speaks of the *il y a* as a theme, 'the shadow of the *il y a* and non-sense still appeared to me necessary as the very ordeal of dis-interestedness' ((Paris: Fayard, 1982), p. 42). The *il y a* is the shadow or spectre of nonsense that haunts ethical sense, but – and this is crucial – ethical sense cannot, in the final instance, be confused or conflated with an-ethical nonsense. The *il y a* is a threat, but it is a threat that must and can be repelled. This would seem to be confirmed by the 1978 Preface to *De l'existence à l'existent*, where, after writing that the *il y a* is the 'principal feature' of the book, he goes on to describe the *il y a* in terms of 'inhuman neutrality' and 'a neutrality to be surmounted' (2nd edn (Paris: Vrin, 1986), pp. 10–11; missing from the English translation by A. Lingis, *Existence and Existents* (The Hague: Nijhoff, 1978)). Thus, Levinas's basic philosophical *intention* does not alter, but whether his *text* is saying something at odds with this intention is another matter.

16 Emmanuel Levinas, *Totality and Infinity*, trans. A. Lingis (Pittsburgh:

Duquesne University Press, 1969), p. 263.

17 Levinas, *Time and the Other*, p. 36.

18 See *Collected Philosophical Papers*, pp. 165–6: 'And this implies that God is not simply the "first other", the "other par excellence", or the "absolutely other", other than the other (*autrui*), other otherwise, other with an alterity prior to the alterity of the other (*autrui*), prior to the ethical bond with the other (*autrui*) and different from every neighbour, transcendent to the point of absence, to the point of a possible confusion with the stirring of the *il y a*.'

19 *Transcendence et intelligibilité* (Geneva: Labor et Fides, 1984), p. 29; trans. S. Critchley and T. Wright in *Emmanuel Levinas: Basic Philosophical Writings* (Bloomington: Indiana University Press, 1996), p. 159: 'But perhaps this theology already announces itself in the very wakefulness of insomnia, in the vigil and troubled vigilance of the psyche before the moment when the finitude of being, wounded by the infinite, is prompted to gather itself into the hegemonic and atheist Ego of knowledge.'

20 See Levinas, *Existence and Existents*, p. 28.

21 Levinas, 'God and philosophy', in *Collected Philosophical Papers*, p. 173.

22 Emmanuel Levinas, *Otherwise than Being or Beyond Essence*, trans. A. Lingis (The Hague: Martinus Nijhoff, 1981), p. 19.

23 Ibid., p. 152.

24 Levinas goes some way to discussing this question in 'Transcendence and evil' in *Collected Philosophical Papers*, pp. 175–86, where, although Levinas recognizes the 'non-integratability' (p. 180) or excess of evil, the horror of evil is understood by Levinas as the horror of evil in the other man and, hence, as the breakthrough of the Good (p. 185) and the 'approach of the infinite God' (p. 186).

25 Levinas, *Existence and Existents*, p. 60.

26 Guy de Maupassant, *Contes et nouvelles*, ed. L. Forestier (Paris: Gallimard, 1979), pp. 913–38, esp. p. 938; *Selected Short Stories*, trans. R. Colet (Harmondsworth: Penguin 1971), pp. 313–44, esp. p. 344.

27 Several years ago, I corresponded with Michel Haar after some discussions we had at the Collegium Phaenomenologicum in Perugia, where I had tried to explain my fascination with Levinas. He wrote, and I recall from a memory long troubled by his words, 'Je ne vois pas qu'il y a éthique dès qu'il y a altérité' ('I don't see why there is ethics since there is alterity'). For Haar's powerful critique of Levinas, see 'L'Obsession de l'autre: l'éthique comme traumatisme', *Emmanuel Levinas: cahier de l'Herne*, pp. 444–53.

28 I owe this analogy to a conversation with Jay Bernstein.

29 Maurice Blanchot, *The Infinite Conversation*, trans. and Foreword by Susan Hanson (Minneapolis and London: University of Minnesota Press, 1993), pp. 49–74. In this context I shall have to pass over the interesting and difficult question of whether Blanchot's relation to Levinas alters in *The Writing of the Disaster*, trans. Ann Smock (Lincoln and London: University of Nebraska Press, 1986), which might justifiably be approached as a deeply sympathetic but subtly reconstructive reading of Levinas's *Otherwise than Being*.

30 Blanchot, *The Infinite Conversation*, pp. 70–1.
31 Levinas, *Totality and Infinity*, p. 291.
32 See Bernhard Waldenfels, *Ordnung in Zwielicht* (Frankfurt-am-Main: Suhrkamp, 1987).
33 After the thoughts contained here were already loosely formulated, I made the happy discovery that many of my claims are strikingly similar to those proposed by John D. Caputo in his attempt to think obligation without reference to any substantive ethics. See his *Against Ethics* (Bloomington: Indiana University Press, 1993).
34 See Levinas, Lecture III in *Time and the Other*, pp. 67–79.
35 Blanchot's reservations on the subject of whether the neuter can be described as transcendent should be noted here. In *The Infinite Conversation*, he writes, 'One of the essential traits of the neutral, in fact, is that it does not allow itself to be grasped either in terms of immanence or in terms of transcendence, drawing us into an entirely different sort of relation' (p. 463).

7   Conversation

Ann Smock

THE MEETING PLACE

In *L'Attente L'Oubli* (*Waiting, Forgetting*),[1] it seems that a man, looking out of a hotel room window, saw a woman on her balcony and signalled to her. Moreover, he called. He called, and she came, and they met in his room, where they stayed, speaking together all night long. For example, in the course of their long conversation – in the course of *L'Attente L'Oubli* – she asks him repeatedly to describe the room they are in.

She asks him to describe their meeting place as though, strangely, it weren't right there, and they right in it both together: as though they were meeting in a place which isn't found there. Or, where they don't find themselves. In fact, they seem to be looking for the way that leads to where they are. 'It's as if they still had to look for the road to arrive where they already are' (p. 122).

Now, *L'Attente L'Oubli* doesn't ever exactly begin. Rather, it stops on page one, its starting point. Its first sentence states that 'here, on this sentence', he was obliged to quit. It appears that he had been writing everything she said, but she made him stop here, because she didn't recognize her words. She couldn't gauge where she was or who was speaking; she'd 'lost the centre and everything was turning before her eyes' (p.8).

So, *L'Attente L'Oubli* doesn't exactly start at its starting point – it stops, instead (at its start it arrives instead at its finish) – but of course it doesn't exactly stop there either: about one hundred and fifty pages follow the sentence which states on page one that it is the last. In place of the start a stop; in place of this stop a start. It is in this manner that start and finish cannot be disentangled and that in this tangle neither is to be found. There is neither start nor stop to *L'Attente L'Oubli* but in place of each the intervention of the other, and this inseparability – this indifference of the two – gives the interval, the difference; it gives the separation, the divide, the entire stretch between the start and finish. Which is to say: *L'Attente L'Oubli*. *L'Attente L'Oubli* is the conjunction of its start and stop interfering, intervening or interceding; *L'Attente L'Oubli* interrupts the 'same' thing, the convergence or the meeting 'itself'; it displaces the place it 'is', the meeting place. *L'Attente L'Oubli*: the place not found there, not found but lost ('she had lost the centre . . .').

The place not found but lost there – or again: the place *en route* there. The place approaching it. Suddenly, with the advent of *L'Attente L'Oubli*, *L'Attente L'Oubli* is over, to be sure – forgotten upon arrival – but how could this abrupt cut-off have occurred yet? There never was anything at all to interrupt, consign to the past or forget till afterwards, till now, that is, now that there's *L'Attente L'Oubli* stretching out – tending, turning towards, awaiting its interruption, which is to say, 'itself', the convergence of its stop and start which it 'is' – is rather, diverging from and thereby returning towards. And departing the better to approach, and seeking the better to lose. Turning, turning.

To wait is to experience this type of swerve, this sort of veering off of and from the conditions under which, for example, one might ever *find oneself*, or, indeed, under which anything at all might do so: might manage to be where and what it is at that point. To wait is notably to experience the diversion of language from the reflexive structures, the auto-referential patterns that would have been reassuring, just above, when we were attempting to articulate the effect that *L'Attente L'Oubli* has on *L'Attente L'Oubli*: it would have been handy to be able to say, *L'Attente L'Oubli interrupts itself*, but what is interrupted is precisely the possibility of such a construction, and among the results is the appearance, on and off in the following, of unanchored, floating pronouns: *L'Attente L'Oubli interrupts it*, for example. Or, *the place approaches it*. Another possible example: *language says it*. Language diverted in this manner – turned away from itself – turned away by its turn back, and returned by its departure, converses, we want to suggest.

But we were intending, at the start of the paragraph we have just left behind, to describe the swerve in question in terms of waiting which, in Blanchot's thinking, defers waiting and introduces a wait instead. If one ever waits, it's simply because one cannot do so, not yet. One just has to wait, instead. Whoever waits thus *in lieu* of waiting endures a mysterious difference – endures waiting which isn't waiting, but which isn't anything else, either. It is not itself, but there is no other waiting, no 'waiting itself' from which it would differ. Neither of the alternative terms you might automatically employ to designate it – or, incidentally, to designate interlocutors in a conversation: *the one, the other* – suits it. It is neither: neutral.

Waiting differs, but not with respect to anything, which is to say it is a difference – or, you could also say, a sameness – that can't be measured. Whenever Blanchot speaks of the measureless – including in passages that emphasize immoderation, transgression, madness, ravishment – the dis-, the re-placement of which we try to speak here, is relevant: the motionless careening, that is, of what has no position and knows no placement whatsoever save this removal; indifferent difference, incomparable sameness; loss, but not of anything, not of anything there ever has been.

So impatient! One cannot wait, not even for a second, one quits right off. Without even waiting, one starts right in, starts right in waiting without waiting for the start. Thus for whoever waits, nothing is permitted save what is ruled out, and *that* is unavoidable; there is *only* waiting which there is absolutely not. To wait, therefore: to approach a limit one doesn't encounter; to enter the place not found there. To wait is to be held in that place, at that boundary, on that edge – and *l'entretien*, conversation, does the holding.

On the subject of what there is and what there isn't, when one waits – on the subject of waiting – Blanchot writes that 'the one is the other' (p. 53). Abundant wealth of waiting, waiting without end; utter dearth of waiting, waiting with no beginning: the one is the other. Their relation must be that of the start and finish in *L'Attente L'Oubli* (waiting must be this *relation*). That is, it would seem that there is neither infinite waiting nor none whatsoever, but in place of each the other, the intervention of the other, and this inseparableness of wealth and dearth must give the in-between, the vacant interval – in short, the wait: one thing, as it were, or 'the one'. But the one is the other. Wealth and dearth, in other words, are one thing – waiting (*l'attente*) – but *it* isn't the same.

Blanchot asks this question about conversation at the beginning of *The Infinite Conversation*: 'Why two to say one thing?' The answer: 'Because whoever says it is the other'.[2] So it seems that whatever is said in conversation is said by no one; it requires two, that it ('one thing') might be said at all – said, that is, by neither. By no one. We have suggested that the indifference of end and beginning – or of infinite waiting and extreme impatience – introduces the interval, the difference, the empty in-between where one and the other do not find themselves and are not found. Here there is no one. Not even the other one. No one at all, only the other. Perhaps it is this in-between that says 'one thing'.

In fact, there is plenty in *L'Attente L'Oubli* to suggest that this interval (*l'entre-deux*) is the in-between of conversation (*l'entretien*), and that the interlocutors are *held* there (*tenus*) in the interval: *tenus entre, entretenus ensemble*. There is plenty in *L'Attente L'Oubli* to suggest that the two who meet and spend a whole night speaking together are held both together in between themselves, or maintained (*entretenus*) there where neither is – in a convergence which intervenes to interrupt it (consigning it to the past and delaying it indefinitely). For the man and the woman who speak together in this story feel that they are together because of having parted instead, and they suggest moreover that their being together prevents them from meeting. 'Are we together? – Only if we could be apart. – We are apart, I'm afraid. – But together because of that. Together, apart' (p. 42).

So conversation isn't, perhaps, anything at all that he says or she says or that they say, and even its characteristic movement – its back-and-forth, to-and-fro – isn't, perhaps, a function of their being two distinct persons taking turns talking, but rather a function of their being neither one nor two. Conversation may be something like the pulse of their relation: together–apart; separate–joined; divided–united. Perhaps conversation could be described as the throb of that ambiguity (discontinuous–uninterrupted; without cease–without start; surging up–subsiding). And the interval where the two of them, the woman and the man (or rather just the one – or rather neither two nor one) are *maintained* far from themselves and, as it were, *conversed* (*entretenus, entretenus*) – perhaps this interval must be felt as a beat. 'Know what rhythm holds men', Blanchot writes, quoting Archilochus.[3] In any case, when the man called to the woman in *L'Attente L'Oubli* and she came to him, the call and the answer appear to have intervened each in place of the other to form a relation which seems similar to that of start and stop in our earlier discussion, or of patience and impatience (the one is the other): 'He had called her, she had come, coming in the call, calling in her advent' (p. 71). The call arrives, the arrival calls; the call calls for the first time only later, in the answer, which came already earlier, in the call. Call and answer, address and response seem fused at a single point, which, however, precedes and follows . . . it. It: that is to say, the single point, which it has left behind and which lies still further on; the midpoint or meeting place from which it turns away, and back again towards which it thereby turns, saying, saying it.

'She had lost the centre and everything was turning before her eyes . . .'

THE CENTRAL POINT

Every so often in *L'Attente L'Oubli*, while the man and woman speak together, she says to him, 'I'd like to speak to you. Make it so I can speak to you'. He is willing, but what should he do? 'Hear me', she says. 'Make me hear that you hear me.'[4]

When you hear another asking you to hear her so that she can speak – when you hear her asking you to hear what she can't say until you've made her know you've heard it – how can you possibly reply? Nothing follows from such a prayer. So, you must lead. Thus, in *L'Attente L'Oubli*, like Orpheus leading Eurydice, the man leads the woman: 'He had to precede her and always go on ahead, without ever being sure she followed' (p. 53). All the while, however, it is he who follows, for he comes after and in response to her – in response to speech he hasn't heard yet but which he must repeat, as if retracing the steps of a stranger through a trackless expanse. 'Words one must repeat before having heard them', we read; 'rumor of which there is no trace and which he follows; rumor wandering nowhere, abiding everywhere' (p. 13).

When the woman speaks, she doesn't say anything, she just says; and when she asks him to make it so that she can speak, she doesn't really ask for anything, she just asks (p. 80). And when he asks her what they are waiting for, she is surprised: she doesn't understand how waiting could be waiting for anything (p. 21). Indeed, the answer she awaits from him is given in her demand or prayer, for she asks to speak and she is speaking – except that there is nothing for her words to answer, no demand for them to satisfy, because her speech consists in postponing speech, putting off the demand, the prayer. 'She speaks deferring speech' (p. 111). Speaking, she asks to speak and only speaks because she can't get started, and if she can't begin it's only because she cannot cease; her speech is an intervening obstacle which interrupts it. A speech impediment. 'Speaking, she is silenced (*interdite*)' (p. 15). Her words seem to comprise a point of convergence (start and finish, speech and silence, call and answer – also interdiction and transgression) which isn't found there, but diverges, as it were, or recedes.

To meet her is to approach this point, a 'central point' which Blanchot elsewhere says draws poets to it from deep inside the work they are to compose; he calls it 'the concentration of ambiguity' in *The Space of Literature*,[5] for there the work's perfection and its ruin cross, its commanding presence and its disappearance – the *here* it superbly constitutes and the *nowhere* to which it profoundly belongs. From this point there issues a muffled sound, a sort of rumour of language, which can't really be heard – 'parole sans entente' – speechlessly demanding to receive a hearing. No speaker ever employs this language or ever addresses a listener in it; it interrupts the rapport between address and response and talks – but without any start – and says, but not anything – yet there is nothing negative about it, for before it begins already it is talking and after it quits it keeps on; it hasn't started and still it persists, as if, were it ever able to start up, it could finally rest. Whoever feels he has to write, Blanchot says, feels subject to the demand that he make it so that this mute speech (this silence unable to keep still) can make him hear it. He hears a language that won't even reach him till he has found the words to repeat it in, and conferred upon it thus some moderation, got it back within bounds. He hears it calling on him, from deep inside the boundless night, drawing him into the darkness whence no poem ever arose, the way the Sirens' song attracted sailors, by being its own mysterious remove, its own not-here, not-yet, but near, soon, approaching – approaching its start or else its stop, drawing near or else sinking back.

In *L'Attente L'Oubli* the woman's talk – stillness that won't keep still, words that keep not being said – has the ambiguity of the Sirens' song, the contrariness of the 'central point' and moreover the phantom quality of Eurydice in hell, whose invisibility shows, whose disappearance appears, in whose veiled face shines the dark of night, peril Orpheus must risk but with his gaze turned away[6] just as Ulysses listens to the Sirens but lashed to the mast – and just as poets, in the account Blanchot consistently gives, have to expose themselves to the tumultuous, nocturnal excess, la *démesure*, and by *withstanding* this catastrophic immoderation, this devastating imme-diacy, bestow measure on it and on sheer boundlessness the limit of a form, in order that the mystery which poets hear might receive a hearing, thanks to their bold mediation. And yet, this boundlessness – incommunicable, demanding mediation of the poet: is it not the centre? The middle? The in-between – the interval? Mediation 'itself', perhaps. Maybe it's somehow measure 'itself', measure without measure, which threatens to overwhelm all limits and which must be modified, qualified, moderated . . . led back within bounds, at great risk corralled and made gentle, like some wild creature.

Perhaps the poet's task is to mediate the middle: *to between*, as it were, the in-between.

MEASURE, THE MEASURELESS

What does Blanchot mean by *poet*, or by *whoever has to write, whoever belongs to writing*? He just means whoever happens to encounter another human, any other at all in any other's capacity as the Other – that is, the Very High, infinitely surpassing any power that anyone can ever call upon. The approach of the Other is that of separation, infinite distance. No commonly held idea of equality or of difference has any pertinence in his regard. No shred of reciprocity mitigates the shock of his separateness. He has nothing in common with anyone, which is to say he is any other, but not under just any circumstances: the Other is any other encountered when there is nothing between the two of you, nothing at all such as shared tasks and values, common commitments, a common language to initiate by limiting (sustain by mediating, preserve by allaying) this encounter. Thus one meets the Other outside any meeting place, there where, for example, Achilles met Priam when the latter approached to beg for the body of Hector, unprotected by any human law (as stranger and suppliant, he was in the care of a god, Blanchot recalls, and was the bearer of no common language . . .). Priam was not weaker than Achilles, or than anyone: his weakness and misfortune were measureless. To encounter such an Other requires one to endure difference that differs, just differs – not from you, or from anything, without any point of reference or comparison, immeasurably. The Other: separation, but that doesn't separate anything or anyone; a boundary – even a limit – but that doesn't define or delimit anything at all.

Sheer separateness draws near and this approach says, *if only we could be different, if only we could part. Oh, let us part; oh, make it so I can approach you.* 'Make it so I can speak to you. Make me hear that you hear me . . .'

Answer me so that in your response I might find the words of this, my plea: such is the obligation, without any conceivable beginning or end, which the Other brings to bear. It is the duty to restore him to the world of limits, where rights and obligations define each other, where equality and inequality can be measured – where it is possible to recognize resemblance, distinguishing it from difference, and to gauge distance and proximity, not confounding near and far, here and elsewhere, together and apart. Thus in *L'Attente L'Oubli* the man undertakes to answer the woman in such a way as to get her back within bounds. He hears the continuous murmur of her even speech – even but not with itself or with anything, 'equal without equality', measurelessly equal. He hears her speak – it sounds like an uninterruptable echo of speech – and he undertakes to answer in such a way as to introduce measure: 'a measure of equality' (p.156). He undertakes to answer and thereby to delimit this boundless limit – perhaps to *place* this boundary, which seems unlimited to any place, but wanders no place, abiding every place. By his answer perhaps he tries to *reach* this border or this edge, and thereby to install it, within bounds.

Whence his resemblance to Orpheus. But Orpheus, in Blanchot's account, never would have undertaken to lead Eurydice back to daylight and to life – his face turned resolutely from her – if he hadn't from the start already been turning around the other way: if it weren't the disappearance of her face that he wanted to see. Nor would poets undertake to bestow on sheer immoderation the limit and propriety of form if, when they start to work, they weren't already turning the work away from its perfection and back towards its absence, the fathomless indeterminacy whence it relentlessly calls. They would never even have felt the urgent requirement to mediate if it weren't the intermediate – the in-between, measure 'itself' – that calls to them from the terrible *point central*, the deep of night whence no poet returns and no work ever arises.

Blanchot expresses this in *The Space of Literature* when he describes the work as the relation between the contrary demands that it take form in the light of day *and* that it be the devastating disintegration of form in the limitless mystery of night. These two requirements are both opposite and inseparable, he emphasizes. They never come to bear separately or even by turns, as if they were distinct from each other, for the light in which the work must appear is visibility itself: not merely the appearance of one or another thing, or of everything, but the appearance of *nothing appears*, the dawn of *all disappears*. So the work's demand – l'exigence de l'œuvre' – is that it emerge brilliantly in the light of the obscurity threatening to engulf it. Or again, the measure required is measureless, while the chaos laying claim to the work is measure 'itself'. Thus it is only by a vague sort of approximation, Blanchot says, that one can think of *l'œuvre* as a dialogue between a reader on the one hand and the writer on the other, stabilized embodiments of two distinct demands bearing on the work – or of its two poles, as he also, provisionally, puts it: possibility and impossibility; determination and the indeterminate. Such a picture only vaguely approximates the relation, the communication in question (the work, that is), for neither of its so-called poles can really reach itself and come to bear except where it cedes to the other, its contrary. They come to themselves and are themselves to the full extent of their uncompromising opposition – their unbridgeable separation – only by departing from themselves: 'quitting themselves and detaining each other together outside themselves in the restless unity of their common belonging'.[7]

Their common belonging: each one belongs to the other instead. The place where each would find itself is the place the other takes. This, then, is what they have in common: the place where, together, they do not find themselves. This is their meeting place: their violent collision interceding in between them. Parting them. The work is this intercession. This intervention. This interdiction.

SPEAK OR KILL

Language in its capacity to attenuate contradictions, modify differences, defer conflict, limit force, ward off violence, is of no avail in the face-to-face encounter with the Other as Blanchot thinks of it. To him the approach of the Other means that the two of you are utterly exposed to each other without so much as bread to share between you and certainly no common language as a middle ground. So nothing prevents you – should you wish to have recourse to *some* capacity or other in this infinitely trying situation, and finally to respond by *doing* something, at this juncture where language abandons you in all its capacities, and simply isn't there at all as a form of ability or a kind of power or even as a possibility – nothing prevents you, when you confront an Other face to face, from exerting unlimited might. 'I say this encounter is terrible, for here there is no longer either measure or limit. . . . One would have to say . . . that man facing man like this has no choice but to speak or to kill.'[8]

Speak – when speech is not a possibility – or opt instead for possibility unlimited, brute power. Speak or kill, there is no halfway in between, and the Other brings this stark alternative to bear. Yet, Blanchot adds, it is not really a matter of such a simple either/or, for to choose speech over murder is not simply to opt for one of two opposed alternatives and against the other, but rather to enter the interval between – when, however, there is no in-between. It's to approach a limit one cannot encounter, a boundary one cannot reach; it's to enter the place not found there. 'To speak is always to speak from out of this interval between speech and radical violence',

Blanchot writes, 'separating them, but maintaining each of them in a relation of vicissitude.'⁹

'Vicissitude is essential', he adds: 'il s'agit de tenir et d'entretenir.'¹⁰ Which means that it's a question, where the essential ambiguity is concerned, of holding firm (*tenir*), and of holding in-between (*entre-tenir*), and of maintaining (*entretenir*) – maintaining the ambiguity – and also of conversing, since the *entretien* or maintaining of vicissitude would also mean, in French, its conversation. Straining both English and French somewhat, one wants to say that to maintain the ambivalence (to preserve the interval) between speech and violence is 'to converse it'. And thus it seems that to speak – when the Other approaches and one *must speak* in order that he be heard – thus it seems that to speak under these circumstances, and not to kill, is to maintain (or 'converse') a relation of ambiguity between speech and violence, thereby, paradoxically, separating them. Speech is their unresolvable ambiguity, interceding in between them and warding off this devastating loss of clear boundaries, defining limits. Speech is moderation and restraint all indistinguishable from abandon and transgression, interceding to inhibit this drunken intermingling. One might as well say that the unlocatableness of the limit – between restraint and savagery – draws it. Or, that drawing it removes the boundary. This is vicissitude's *entretien*: the maintaining of ambiguity, or its conversation – this is speech.

The ambiguity that it's a matter of maintaining is the middle, the intermediate or central point. *Entretenir la vicissitude* means to hold the middle in the middle. To mediate or, if you will, *to middle* it. To keep it ambiguous – to preserve it ambiguously. To keep it pure, as it were – making sure it is adulterated. To undecide or *to between* the in-between.

To converse is the more graceful way of putting this. Or, just *to speak*.

But no one speaks this way. Only the other. Only the conversation (the *entretien*).

Often Blanchot refers to the gods when thinking of immoderation. (Of immoderation – which is to say, the preservation from it.) If the divine is linked in his writing to excess, the temptation of transgression and especially the risk of madness, this isn't because the sacred is simply the opposite of measure, law and reason, responsibilities of human proportions, but rather because it is a relation of vicissitude where law and violation, madness and reason (gods and men, the human and the divine) – madly overriding their absolute difference and the infinite distance that divides them – intervene together to safeguard it. Preventing, in this way, the intervention, the prevention, the safeguarding. Madness is this concentration of ambiguity, expressed in the disarming thought of Dionysus the mad god: not the god *of* madness or wine, but a god whose divinity overcomes him, a god like a law whose rule transgresses it and whose violation declares and preserves it. A limit, that is to say, drawn by its erasure, erased by its inscription. Waiting, as we've briefly described it in this chapter – waiting, just motionlessly waiting – could well be just such savage folly: an experience inescapably imposed by its abrupt and unappealable exclusion, not to mention vice versa. Waiting, vicissitude's *entretien*. The maintaining, in other words, of this ambiguity: *interdire, entre-dire*: to prohibit – and in particular to prohibit speech (to silence) – *and* to speak, to say, in between.

THE *RECIT* – RETURN OF THE MEETING PLACE

Among the mysterious characteristics of the *récit* – of narrative according to Blanchot – is this: there is no such thing as a *récit*, and on this account, no lack of them whatsoever. Or, conversely, there is something inevitable about the *récit*, and for this reason, no such thing. So *le récit* could be understood as a relation of vicissitude and its *entretien* or preservation: as an ambiguous rapport between impossible and inevitable – and as the safeguarding (*l'entretien*) of this rapport.

Récits generally feature but a single episode, Blanchot states, in *Le Livre à venir*: a meeting, *une rencontre*.[11] Ulysses encounters the Sirens' song, Nerval Aurélia, Breton Nadja. . . . This *rencontre* turns the person who experiences it into the one who tells of it. It's the turning of the event into the *récit* – the advent, then, of the *récit*, and thereby a turning back again the other way: the *récit* turns into the event: into the occurrence it tells about, that is. For the event the *récit* tells is the event of telling. It starts – or it will, or would – by being what it ends – if it can – by telling. Such is the meeting, then: it's the *rencontre* of the telling and of what is told – the convergence of the event the *récit* ends by telling and the same event – the end – which the telling starts by being. The meeting, *la rencontre*, is the event of their reaching one another and indeed the occasion of the *récit* which, at this meeting, finds itself. Except that that is where it disappears, or would: would disappear or lose . . . itself? Before ever having reached, or been, itself or anything? Meeting point, central point, concentration of ambiguity. . . . Another characteristic of the *récit* is that 'it seeks to meet up with itself at that point'.[12] And the *récit* would, indeed – find itself there, at the centre – except that at that spot, just as there is about to be (or rather, to be no longer) such a thing as start or stop, event or account, each one veers off and turns into the other. This is why there is event (but unaccounted for), and why there is account (but not of anything): it is because the *récit* intervenes and right at the spot it might otherwise have found – or maybe lost – 'itself', opens a measureless remove from it. It opens and it is this boundless distance, at every point the point it scrupulously skirts, and all the time rashly the precise moment it prudently avoids. The *récit* veers round, you might well say, or detours . . . it. That is why there is account and event, start and stop (wisdom and folly, care and carelessness) or rather neither one, for that is why there is only ever one, which is always the other. Which is always turning, turning into the other again, turning and returning and which simply is this swerve. At the very start of *L'Attente L'Oubli*, remember, the woman couldn't get her bearings; she had lost the centre and everything was turning before her eyes (p. 8).

Everything was turning. Turning and finding: for *trouver* (to find) – as Blanchot suggests in 'Speaking is not seeing' (a text in *The Infinite Conversation* which repeats more than one sentence from *L'Attente l'oubli*) – doesn't only or even primarily mean *trouver*, but rather *tourner* – to turn, turn round and circle, searching. 'To find is almost exactly the same word as to seek, which means to "take a turn around".'[13] Thus the centre veers off and turns – turns and finds, finds and turns – it just doesn't find itself (*L'Attente l'oubli*, p. 132). Everywhere it turns it finds, but it isn't to be found, it isn't ever there. Concerning this listing language, Blanchot recalls what Heraclitus said of sacred speech: 'I wonder', he writes, 'whether Heraclitus, when he says of sacred speech that it neither exposes nor conceals, but gives a sign, is not saying something about this.'

Now in *The Step Not Beyond*,[14] Blanchot notes a number of words which signal, give a sign, *indiquent*. *Il* is one: *it*. Also *God*, and *madness*. He calls them nameless names which do not name anything – words for which there are none, and which are words for nothing. A few words too many, it seems, and also a few words too few. By chance they are hooked, Blanchot says, on to the edge of language. *Le récit* might well be defined in the same fashion – as if it were such an extra, such a missing, such a border word. For as we've said, *a récit* is an event, it is an account, each turning uninterruptedly into the other, together ceaselessly interrupting their relation and giving either an event no story ever tells – nameless, unaccounted for (by no means hidden, though) – or else a story that recounts nothing (but which is by no means silent or secretive: it just recounts): either something unspoken or speech that says, but not anything. Or rather, neither one, exactly. For whichever one it is, is turning already, into the other. Neither event nor account, then, neither words nor what they say, signs nor what they designate, a *récit* is through and through its in-between, altogether the interval between being, and saying, it.

It is, in other words, an *entretien*, which is the form language takes when it turns altogether into the very edge of it.

Into the edge that's neither exposed nor concealed. Into the limit neither drawn nor erased, observed nor overstepped. Into the meeting place that's never either found or lost; into the middle – which signals, or points.

GIVE ME THAT

In *L'Attente L'Oubli* it seems that a man, looking out of a hotel window, saw a woman on her balcony and signalled to her. She came and they met in his room and during their long conversation, she says to him every so often, 'Give me that' (for example, pp.27, 81, 112).

But what? Give what? She doesn't say, or show, not that she keeps any secrets; but when she speaks, language just points. *That. Give me.* She says that there isn't anything so difficult in this demand or very mysterious in this pointing: everything is simple, she says. 'I am not asking you for it, I am putting it in your hand' (p. 80). Apparently *that* is not a term for it, an indication of it or of anything, but *is* something and, precisely, *that*. A term, to be sure, but not for anything; just a word, but that names nothing, an indication, but that doesn't designate or point to anything. It can't, because it is the thing it would, presumably, otherwise have designated: *that* – a nameless thing, since the word that would, presumably, name it (*that*) is the one it isn't any longer, the one withdrawn from among the names that language includes when, to the number of things there are to account for, it was added.

She doesn't ask him for anything, she doesn't indicate to him what she wishes him to give her but presents it to him; there it is, *that*, very plain, a sign, that is all, not for anything, just a pointer and yet, there being no pointer to indicate it, no sign or word for it any more, it goes all undesignated and is indeed what the woman does not say when she says. . . . When she speaks and says . . .

, there is, as it were, less than before, as if her sentence had intro-

duced its removal. What there never was before withdraws when she
speaks, as if she were marking the border whose drawing erases it.
And the prayer which presented the gift already, already turns into
the presentation asking for it. 'He called, she came, coming in the
call, calling in her advent . . .'

Language signals in this 'mysterious' way because of something
that happens at its border, Blanchot says (in *The Step Not Beyond*).
On account of words such as *it, that, God* . . . hooked, by chance, on
to its edge, language 'se fait signe'.[15] Which means turns back and
signals to itself, as the *récit* does – the *récit* which tells the event it
is, the event of telling. This is what 'se fait signe' means, but only in
so far as instead it means *becomes a sign*, which is to say, in place of
a thing its name, in place of its name, the thing. Turned thus twice
over away from itself language points, not at anything and without
any power to designate. It just points, *indique*. It is the presence to
each other of names and things, of language and its meaning – it is
this meeting place, where it finds itself, *except* that nothing names
the name and it names nothing; it is neither a name nor a thing, but is
turned away from names and away from things, like the interlocutors
in *L'Attente L'Oubli* who, ever since he turned back and gestured to
her (from his hotel room to the balcony where he glimpsed her), are
'turned away from one another in order to be present to each other in
the interval' – in the interim or delay, that is; in the wait (p. 94).
They meet in between, where their meeting is *interdite*: interrupted,
inter-spoken.

NOTES

1 Maurice Blanchot, *L'Attente L'Oubli* (Paris: Gallimard, 1962). All
references in this chapter to *L'Attente L'Oubli* will be to the Gallimard
edition, and all English translations are my own.
2 Maurice Blanchot, *The Infinite Conversation*, trans. Susan Hanson
(Minneapolis and London: University of Minnesota Press, 1993), p. ix.
3 Maurice Blanchot, *The Writing of the Disaster*, trans. Ann Smock
(Lincoln and London: University of Nebraska Press, 1986), p. 5.
4 These sentences recur in *L'Attente L'Oubli*: for example, pp. 14, 26,
110, 155.
5 Maurice Blanchot, *The Space of Literature*, trans. Ann Smock (Lincoln
and London: University of Nebraska Press, 1982), p. 44.
6 The section entitled 'Orpheus' Gaze' is the 'central point' of *The Space
of Literature*.
7 Blanchot, *The Space of Literature*, p. 200.
8 Blanchot, *The Infinite Conversation*, p. 60.
9 Ibid., p. 62.
10 Ibid., p. 30.

11 Maurice Blanchot, *Le Livre à venir*, (Paris: Gallimard, 1959). See the opening section, 'The Sirens' Song', in *The Sirens' Song, Selected Essays by Maurice Blanchot*, ed. Gabriel Josipovici, trans. Sacha Rabinovitch (Brighton: The Harvester Press, 1982).
12 'La parole vaine', in *L'Amitié* (Paris: Gallimard, 1971).
13 Blanchot, *The Infinite Conversation*, p. 25.
14 Maurice Blanchot, *The Step Not Beyond*, trans. Lycette Nelson (Albany: State University of New York Press, 1992).
15 Ibid., p. 121.

8   On unworking[1]

The image in writing according to Blanchot

Marie-Claire Ropars-Wuilleumier

Of the image too it is difficult to speak rigorously.[2]

If the writing-process according to Blanchot pertains to unworking, to 'the absence of work' and to 'interruption' in the actual idea of the work,[3] by this gesture it puts itself under the sign of the other, that is, of he who is not the one, but who always speaks in the place of the one. Such is Blanchot's critical strength, and his impact within theory: the putting into crisis of the ideas of being and of unity concerns the very essence of writing as exposed in unworking. Thought of the other and thinking through the writing-process go together. Unworking is not to be understood, then, as the disaster of the work or the impossibility of writing following the catastrophe of History. If unworking has anything to do with disaster, it is first in founding the very condition of writing on the distancing of the star (*l'astre*, as in *dés-astre*): in other words, according to *The Writing of the Disaster* itself, on 'limitless space where a sun would attest not to the day, but to the night delivered of stars, multiple night'.[4]

Night delivered of stars, night become multiple by the negative presence of light. Connected to disaster in this way, unworking does not speak the loss of the work, but the paradoxical condition of a writing where 'discourse ceases'[5] in order that 'plural speech' may come about. But if unworking must then tear itself from the work of speech in order to come outside of language, it is in language itself, and only in language, that this 'outside of any language'[6] unceasingly takes place. It can seem arbitrary, then, to connect the act of unworking to an intervention of the image. This prospect is all the more risky in that the image is not, in Blanchot, the object of a frontal approach, as is the case for notions constitutive of plural writing: unlike the 'fragmentary', the 'relation' or 'rewriting', which are analysable in themselves, the image usually intervenes in the form of its annexes, as oblique incidence, or of analogical digressions that, in *The Space of Literature* (*L'Espace littéraire*), signpost the constitutive detour of writing, supported by a myth of the turning away of the gaze: of the 'gaze of Orpheus', for example, directed by the double role of the poet who goes to fetch Eurydice only to bring her back towards night, the other night, in which the writing-process began.[7] If Orpheus turns round, and if he looks, is it not precisely to have done with sight? To go further, *The Infinite Conversation* has been read as Blanchot's renunciation of all relation to the image: as in the famous chapter 'Speaking is not seeing', understood as a disavowal of the gaze, whereas it is only the power of vision that is refused, and not the recourse to the gesture of seeing.

Insisting, on the contrary, on the image's role in putting writing into play, I shall propose a double hypothesis:

(1) The image is a marginal constant accompanying Blanchot's entire critical thought, from the gaze of Orpheus in *The Space of Literature* to the gaze of Narcissus in *The Writing of the Disaster*: this is to say that the image, without lending itself to stable definition, works at the margins of the text, where the uncertainty of the notion helps, precisely, to prevent the stabilization of the discourse in a unified utterance.

(2) The image is coextensive with the invention of unworking, but in negative form: it is not, of course, by adding the image to language that the regime of plural writing is entered, and from this point of view nothing is more foreign to the thought of Blanchot than the pursuit of some hieroglyphic starring of the text; but the plural can only act within language via the mediation of a double that casts its shadow. In this sense the image is not only a factor of analogy, prohibiting the edification of concepts; it also intervenes as an anagogical operator, leading us, by the singularity of its status, towards a thought of what is specifically unthinkable in the exercise of the writing-process.

To establish this second part of the hypothesis, I shall bring together certain features whereby the idea of image illuminates the paradox of unworking, regarding what, in unworking, is at once unfinished and incessant; but the first part of the hypothesis will bring us incessantly back to the obligation not to construct a theory of the image when, precisely, the image intervenes first in order to disavow the theoretical withdrawal (*repli*) of discourse, be it discourse of and on writing.

IMAGE AND SPLITTING

Dispensing with allegory, where meaning takes the place of the figure, and with the symbol, where the figure dissolves in the profusion of mystery, the writer's experience concerns the material and demonstrable reality of the image: this is the secret of the 'Golem', illumined by Blanchot via a Bioy Casares story ('Morel's invention') in which image-men, produced by the diabolic camera of a demiurgic scientist, lure into their retreat a fugitive who, when seduced by one of them, becomes an image in turn and dies in the wake of these immortalized shadows.[8]

I shall not, for the moment at least, consider the machine-like filmic status of these images – highly exceptional in Blanchot, who dismisses any relation between the image and audio-visual production. What matters first, in this Borgesian myth that is akin to the myth of Orpheus, is the double composition of the image-experience:

(a) the image is demonstrable, in so far as it is born of a gaze cast upon the object – in this case, exceptionally but no doubt symptomatically, a machine-gaze, preceding and informing the human gaze;

(b) far from substituting itself for the gazed upon thing or being, the image insinuates itself into the heart of the object, precipitating its ghostly becoming.

No doubt it would be appropriate to connect this experience with the experience of death, as is proposed by the second version of the imaginary, where the vision of the corpse offers a radical example of the becoming-image of the human in and through death: I shall return to this later. But this unveiling of the image in the human's mortal fall – which is also, paradoxically, the becoming-immortal of the human – should not conceal the fundamental relation that the uncovering of the image maintains with the condition of writing: the writer resides in proximity to the image, and this residence 'is his work',[9] in so far as it is the renunciation of bringing the work to light. Hence Orpheus, like Morel, enters into the logic of unworking from the moment when, looking at Eurydice, he precipitates in her the putting to death of representation by the transformation of the body into image.

Here, constituting the turning away of the work, there is a radical turning away of the mimetic principle: unworking renounces the reassuring distinction between the thing gazed upon and its aesthetic elaboration, which would succeed it; precipitating the image into the heart of the object, unworking makes the becoming-image of this thing into the very condition of a writing-process which, *by means of the gaze*, would turn away from representation and from the signification that it implies. This is the paradox set up by the image and, through the image, in the gesture of writing: because it is a process of doubling – does not image-producing imitation consist in proposing a double of the real? – the image will make visible and evident an originary splitting that will make it no longer possible to tell the double from the real, become itself its own double and as it were the shadow of itself. The image opposes representation, but by inscribing itself within representations; this is without doubt Blanchot's most fundamental contribution to a thinking about the image which, by means of the gaze, would affect all sight.

The body closed, the face sealed, the presence veiled, but as an empty futility – these are the attributes received by Eurydice twice lost in the gaze of Orpheus. She is thus given over to night, and thereby to the inspiration of Orpheus; but, as shadow, she opens at the same time the network of *resemblance* that, from text to text, designates, in Blanchot, the relation between becoming-image and exile from the self. The resemblance inscribed in being is not only the disappearance of meaning, set up as 'pure semblance' (p.359); affecting the sight of the body conveyed by dream, the splitting that makes us resemble ourselves leads us to resemble nothing, that is, to be pure resemblance, becoming itself impersonal: 'he resembles', says *L'Amitié*, of the dreamer.[10] And the extreme logic of this intransitive 'resembling' is manifest in the gaze of Narcissus, who does recognize himself in his image – an essential detail omitted by Ovid – because what Narcissus sees is an image, and because 'the similitude of an image is not likeness to anyone or anything: the image characteristically resembles nothing'.[11] Narcissus thus initiates the founding paradox of the image, simultaneously proposing imprint and exile, splitting and becoming-strange, absence to oneself in the gaze upon oneself. But already Orpheus, looking at Eurydice, experiences the expropriation and death of Eurydice: 'he himself, in this gaze, is absent'. And in referring it to the self's own image, Narcissus does no more than tighten the nut loosened by the sight of the image that, in unveiling the double in the other, unveils at the same time the attraction of the other within the double itself.

If I have insisted on the paradoxical logic of splitting that the image introduces into being and by the very semblance of being, it is because it features two basic traits of an approach to the writing-process according to Blanchot. First, in connecting the image to the ghostly, it enables an understanding of how reference to imaging can subsist even when any mention of image has disappeared from the text: if *The Infinite Conversation* seems to have done with sight and with the *récit* (narrative), it is because it is heading towards the discovery of a 'narrative voice', whose singularity, exposed by means of a critique of the notion of narrator, derives from the fact that it sends the speaking subject back into exile from the person and from speech. In this 'third person', where *I* becomes *he* without sheltering under cover of an impersonality figurable as person, we find, in Blanchot's own words,[12] the 'spectral' component that characterizes the image and that affects the bearers of speech as much as it is does narration itself. The becoming-*he* of *I* is no doubt experienced in the infinity of the conversation, where each voice holds itself *between* itself and the other voice which doubles it in echo; but this double speech can only elude the risks of dialogue, in which each would rediscover its identity, by always recalling the ghost into each of the voices, and hence recalling the double into speech itself. The narrative voice 'always tends to absent itself in its bearer':[13] body of a voice-*off* without body, divided from itself by the shadow that lures it out of itself in the very act of speaking. Thus becoming-image insinuates itself into the heart of voice, in so far as it would be specific to the image to lure, by means of resemblance, the other in place of the one.

In the term *attirance* (lure, attraction) comes a second component of this ghostly image, illuminating its role in the pursuit of the writing-process: not only does it distance from the body, by imprinting on it the mark of strangeness, but it also brings into play an attraction – Orpheus' desire or Narcissus' self-love – that precipitates its duplicity and constitutes it as the 'inaccessible proximity' evoked in *L'Amitié* regarding the image-dreamer.[14] The image is *duplicitous*, that is the paradoxical law of the image, whereby it ceases to work at unworking even as it removes itself from sight.

DUPLICITY OF THE IMAGE

The duplicity of the image operates in the order of unworking, since it is this duplicity that reveals the belonging of art and literature to dissimulation. 'Dissimulation appears' (p.28) – this would be the stake of the writing-process once essential solitude had made it enter the experience of the image. The term 'dissimulation' evades analysis, as if it brought back upon itself the power of occultation that it carries. In the afore-mentioned story of the secret of the 'Golem', dissimulation simply designates the paradoxical condition of the poet who must disown the work in order to enter the becoming of the work: 'to exercise his art he needs a means whereby he can get away from art',[15] and the image is this means. In this respect, dissimulation dissimulates nothing less than the double play of Orpheus, responding to the obligation of the detour (the proscription of the gaze upon Eurydice) by carrying over this detour on to the relation to the work: 'literature is this dissimulation'.[16] But in facing the 'profundity of unworking', the text entitled 'Approach to the space of literature' disavows any interpretation that would see in the 'disappearance' of the work the 'condition of its apotheosis'. The point to which the work leads us is also the point to which it can never lead us (p.45); and, enveloped in dissimulation, writing is nothing more than the 'approach to this point where nothing is revealed' (p.48): a doubly paradoxical point since, unconstitutable as a space, it resolves itself into the pure approach of an unveiling designated as a withdrawal from revelation.

Approach to and negation of that which is approached – dissimulation thus understood no longer authorizes the realization of literature, even in negative form: it depends upon the act of writing, in so far as this act corresponds to the contrary double movement that can be imputed to the duplicity of the image. Like Eurydice restored to the night, the image seduces, it attracts and brings about seeing, be it only seeing the presence of the image emerge in the thing: in this respect, the image fascinates; but the fascination to which essential solitude leads is due to the unveiling of the impersonal in the 'immense someone without a face (*sans figure*)' (p.27). Fascination and non-figuration go together, and that which gives itself to seeing in the 'without figure' is thus the self-absence of the figure become pure image.

On the one side attraction, on the other absence; but also on one side the gaze, which precipitates the image, and on the other the disavowal of sight in an empty image, which could in turn take possession of the gaze: 'whoever is fascinated, what he sees, he doesn't properly speaking see' (p.27); and this *not seeing*, inscribed in the heart of vision, brings about the duplicity of the image that at once lures towards the other night and assails a gaze delivered up to 'the madness of the day': J., in *Death Sentence*, figure of a Eurydice returning to the one who gazes upon her only another gaze, a gaze that isn't hers and which he cannot see. Gazed upon, the image gazes, with no symmetry able to make of this returned gaze the abyssal projection of the actual gaze. The point is not a point, but at once the lure and the impossibility of a unified vision: 'for the image, as image, can never be attained, and it . . . conceals, moreover, the unity of which it is the image' (p.92).

The shying away of the image, born of the gaze *and* dispersing the gaze, thereby eludes the perspectivist logic of Lacan and the blinding force of Derrida.[17] The experience of sight does not, in Blanchot, engage with the split (*schize*) in the gaze, where the one recognizes himself in misrecognizing himself in the other: the eye is not in the painting, where it would divide itself as it turned around; the eye is the actual withdrawal of the image, where exile disavows the possibility of centring the subject. And fascination, where 'what one sees seizes the gaze' (p.26), does not lead to the blinding of the gaze but to the emptying of vision, the singularity and strangeness of this void deriving from the fact that it never reveals itself as such, since it depends on the movement of the approach, which bears within it its own exclusion.

Put to the test by the image, the 'seeing that one doesn't see' never will have the allure of a unique revelation; and the tears of joy that, in *The Writing of the Disaster*, accompany the discovery of the void through the gaze can only intervene through the repetition of the same scene – the same sky – that would offer both the ordinariness of everyday vision (for which the pane is transparent) and the vertigo of a vision suddenly precipitated, by the breaking of the pane, from the outside.

Let us bring together briefly the threads of imaging duplicity, in which is played out, from *The Space of Literature* onwards, the relation between the writing-process and unworking. The image both attracts and arrests the image; the image unveils the void, but without giving it the consistency of a unitary vision; the image derives from the fact of seeing, but this seeing proposes the experience of a 'not seeing' or of a 'seeing that not'. This series of contradictory gestures never gives rise to a dialectical confrontation, in so far as duplicity cannot be thought in terms of duality: the specificity of the image is thus not to be as such, being only pure becoming-image, both duplicitous and unrealizable. A becoming that is manifest even in fixity: the image in Blanchot is not mobile – it doesn't take flight like Deleuze's image-movement; it acts within the very heart of the cessation (*arrêt*), which precisely does not arrest, because it must always deal with the turning round of the image in the renunciation of the gaze.

'To write is to make fascination rule over language . . . where the thing becomes image once again, where the image changes from being an allusion to a figure into an allusion to what is without figure' (p.27). Hence the detour is inherent in the image *in itself*, and unworking thereby depends on the experience of the image, interminable by definition. If, then, fascination can be called by Blanchot 'the passion of the image' (p.25), this passion should be understood in the contradictory sense it bears of desire and disaster. The passion of the image introduces, in fact, to *the space of the outside*, under the incessant attraction of which we write ceaselessly, because the one who writes cannot have done with the arrest of the image.

OUTSIDE: IMAGE SPACE

'The movement of writing may come, under the attraction of the outside': this is the reply that *The Infinite Conversation* awaits of the absent work.[18] 'Vague', 'without place or rest' (p.24), the outside constitutes the very essence of a writing-process that, by delivering itself up to space, would break with the realization of art by and through time. But the first characteristic of this outside, what makes its 'strangeness' uncontainable,[19] is that it depends on both intimacy and exteriority: always calling us outside of ourselves without allowing the constitution of a place, it refers us back to a familiarity that is all the more menacing in not allowing us to keep to it. In this sense, writing is only the movement of writing; and the lure of the outside, never resolved in any ascribable region, belongs both to exile from the inside and to the impossibility of the outside itself.

Certainly the image is not space, in so far as it still touches on figuration, while already belonging to the void. However, even when formed by the void, the image, by virtue of its paradoxical constitution (resemblance and splitting, attraction and turning away), keeps the termination of all figuration active within the heart of space. This is the image's essential role: to bring us to the unthinkable of the outside, where are combined, without confusion or conflict between them, the attraction of content and the absence of depth, distance and contact, envelopment and separation; operations experienced in the fascination of a gaze turning upon itself – 'seeing is contact at a distance' (p.25), as the double rises slowly 'from the depths to the surface'.[20] As generally understood, space is characterized by bringing multiple dimensions into play; this multiplicity becomes, with Blanchot, a questioning of dimensionality itself, by recourse to an imaging operator whose duplicity derives from the capacity to invoke both movement – that of the approach – and immobility – that of the arrest, where the image gazes.

Yet the image is not space, but is even opposed to space, when 'the presence of the space of writing' is affirmed in 'the absence of images'. While celebrating *The Poetics of Space* in *The Infinite Conversation*, Blanchot expresses a reservation regarding Bachelard's tying of the poetic image to an emergence of the image. There might have appeared to be a flagrant contradiction with those texts in *The Space of Literature* where, on the contrary, the image is approach to space, if Blanchot's analysis did not end up establishing an equivalence between the presence and absence of the image: a rotation wherein, with 'the enigma of the image', the *non-phenome-nological* relation it maintains with the imaginary is declared. If 'the imaginary speaks without speaking either of or through images',[21] it is because the imaginary disavows any sliding of perception towards imagination; but if the imaginary gives us access to 'the proper reality of the unreal',[22] then it concerns the actual 'place' of the image, allowing us to take on, by its absent presence, and by the presence of the absence it invokes, the conception of a space 'as vast as night', where immensity would be figured only by the impossibility of its figuration. The image is then a 'figure of the unfigurable', not because it would give on to some always interiorized immensity of the invisible, but because, being visible, it defies its own visibility.

I shall come back to the interest for theory of a conception that engages simultaneously with the evidence of visibility and the fracture of an invisibility operating at the very heart of the visible and for it alone. First, however, I should like to bring out a final paradox of the image, discernible in its contradictory relation to space. If the image is both a symptom and a mask of space, if it figures the attraction of the void while denying it any figurable form, it is because it invokes one last attribute that explains its persistence throughout Blanchot's work. The image has a relation to the gaze and, through the gaze, to the attraction of death: this is what was at stake in the Casares story evoked above. But the image's relation to death is not one that could be underwritten by too hurried a reading of the second version of the imaginary or even of the gaze of Orpheus. If the image reveals itself in the corpse, where man is undone in his own image, this revelation of death will still remain strange to the experience of the subject, who is never the subject of his death, since I can never say that I die. *I* never die, and the death of Eurydice that Orpheus knows when he looks upon her signifies also 'the loss of the ability to die' (p.330), which is also the impossibility of beginning, and hence of living in time: this is the lesson of a key text in *The Space of*

Literature, where Blanchot returns to the myth of Orpheus via a commentary on Rilke's *Sonnets to Orpheus*. This network of dying's impossibility governs the whole of Blanchot's reflection upon the writing-process and upon unworking. Dying is the task of the writing-process: I can only write if 'death writes in me', 'makes of me the empty point where the impersonal is affirmed' (p.195). The writing-process gives itself up thereby to the attraction of the image, where death works towards the exile of the subject, but the writing-process inscribes itself thereby in a logic of the unrealizable. The task of dying will be without end, for the image – this is the meaning of the myth of Narcissus – is 'incorruptible';[23] and the dying Narcissus does not die, but becomes immortal, having seen, in the image that he does not recognize, 'the divine part, the non-living part of eternity'.

If, then, death 'is never accomplished once and for all',[24] it is because the image in which death recognizes itself defies the possibility of its being figured. The image proposes thereby 'the unfigurability of death', and through it passes the inextricable network connecting the interminability of writing and the unrealizability of dying: a child always to be killed and always already dead, Narcissus dying of immortality, Orpheus ceaselessly dying in Eurydice. Doubtless *The Writing of the Disaster*, by attaching itself to the relation between dying and writing without end, situates itself in the 'step not beyond' of *The Space of Literature*, which is still preoccupied by the necessity of making the detour emerge in the work, and the second version of the imaginary emerge in the first. But despite the distance between the two books, from one to the other there seems to be a constant that makes of the image the point of extreme distortion, which, in offering both dying and the impossibility of dying – the ghostly and the incorruptible – would inscribe the impossible realization of time in the attraction of the outside.

Pure becoming, and yet inalterable, designating death as it disavows it: the image is a defeat and an undoing, since in undoing the living it does not make come about – it makes not come about – the event of death. In this the image seems like the vector of a negativity without negation: figuring the *not* of death in figuring the incompatibility of death and figuration.

AN IMAGE-LANGUAGE?

In combining exile and attraction, depth and surface, the event and the impossibility of coming about, so far the image has seemed to be a mediator in the thought of the writing-process: its duplicity illumines the double play of unworking and the unconstitutability of the outside. In this respect, it could be asked if the image did not simply serve in Blanchot's thought as a metaphor for writing, adding a tangible experience to the theoretical paradox engaged in the relation to the writing-process. However, the insistence of this doubling, its recurrence in those texts most concerned with the abstraction of thought, suggests that we examine the intervention of the image in the act of writing itself.

Removed from the logic of affirming and denying, the image alone would not be able to work towards that internal effacement of negation evoked above; but, in so far as it accompanies the work of language, the image could play the role of double acting negatively in the heart of speech. In a note to *The Space of Literature*, Blanchot himself reflects upon the eventuality of an *image-language*: not, of course, a language of the image – and in this he situates himself at the furthest remove from any semiotic consideration of the image – or an image-making language – in this sense, no aesthetic concession is made in the recourse to the image – but a language 'that would still be no more than its image', and where speaking would engage 'only the shadow of speech' (p.48). This 'step not this side' (*pas endeça*) of speech, where the ghost image would precipitate the ghostly becoming of language, could, in syntactical terms, be specified as a factor of internal disjunction coextensive with the use of the sign; the image would participate in a double step (*pas*) of syntax that, in deploying within the order of the sentence the contrary movement of a saying ceaselessly turned away from itself, would suggest a consideration, on the plane of verticality, of that shadow cast whereby language would transform itself, without thereby becoming another language. As imperceptible fissure, attraction of the other night within night, the image would then be both condition and erosion of language: doubling it, without being present, and making it speak solely by recalling the impossibility of the negation that directs it. In the manner of 'he who didn't accompany me', the image figures the *step/not* (*pas*) of the writing-process, which we hear, going on from Derrida, as the detour of the negative in the passage of the sign.

This is the first conclusion I would come to. Far from being solely a mediator of the thought of unworking, the image intervenes in Blanchot's writing-process and as factor of writing, maintaining with writing this 'relation of the third kind'[25] that eludes the horizon of the One: neither conflict nor confusion, but indeed insinuation of the Other, defined by Blanchot as 'pure interval between man and man',[26] and which I would gloss as an interval operating in the heart of language. That the image tends no longer to appear as such in the work of Blanchot alters nothing in the exigency of this recourse: if the image seems more and more to absent itself, it is according to the logic of an acceptation whereby the idea of image carries absence within it; not necessarily the absence of image, but above all the absence to itself of the image, that is, the image's ability to absent itself from itself: an internal gap, a gesture of torsion, the 'first turning'[27] to which Blanchot returns the writing-process in restoring to it the buried trace of this obscure double. So the image becomes the only figure of *detour*, both attraction and a deflection that constitutes attraction; but the singularity of this detour derives from its simultaneously invoking the indication of another sign – here, iconic figuration – and deciding not to give place to this sign.

For Blanchot it is not, then, a matter of thinking the image in itself, but of bringing the thought of the image into the unworking of language. This gesture is to be measured in terms of its most radical consequence: the sign, in its linguistic abstraction, on its own would never be able to break with the power of signifying invoked by discourse; and the plural speech suggested by *The Infinite Conversation* cannot have done with the semantic plenitude of the utterance without injecting into it the attraction of another sign, which in no circumstances could itself give a sign, not even to point to the ineffable. The image is a supplement, but one that subtracts; hence it works only towards the withdrawal of the linguistic sign, with no symbolic remainder; but the image acts in this way only because it eludes its own seizure, playing thereby, on the syntactic plane, the role of a negative that would prevent even its own negation.

'A thought that doesn't let itself be thought'; it is this 'suspicion' – this 'less than a thought'[28] – that the shadow of the image – or rather the image as shadow – brings into Blanchot's more speculative narratives or texts. The image's task would then be not to compensate for but indeed to increase the sign's insufficiency, to open the way to the unknown of language, which defies equally the tangible effusion and the assertive utterance: another dimension, but without fixable form; a rhythm, but beyond scansion; a movement that both sustains and suspends the flow of syntax. Through the difficult relation that ties the sign to the absence of image can be heard the 'murmur' or the 'rustling' of a language, which would no longer quite be and would never entirely become a language; and which in this respect would be removed, by the fact of its speaking, from unity and hence from the truth that trusts in it. If unworked speech disavows the being of truth, it is by means of the fracture introduced therein by the imaging shadow: not the avowal of a beyond, but the retraction of the being-there. Taken up in terms of the torsion of the image, Blanchot's unworking does not propose a poetics, but it recalls us to the aporetic necessity of the writing-process, and hence to critical vigilance, in analysis as in the enterprise of writing.

THE INVISIBILITY OF THE VISIBLE

A second consequence should be emphasized, this time concerning the theoretical approach to the notion of image, which Blanchot helps to undermine even when he is not directly dealing with it. It touches essentially on the relation of the visible to the invisible, a relation that is destroyed by a paradoxical thinking about the image.

To bring together the two components of the paradox: on one side the imaginary is concerned with the presence of the image, not with its repercussions in subjective imagination; and on the other the image derives from a gaze given over to not seeing, that is, to seeing that it doesn't see. We should not misunderstand the sense of this detour: the thought of the image brings us back to sight, even if only to experience the turning away that is intrinsic to the gaze and the effusion of loss of sight; not seeing is internal to the act of seeing, and dissimulation acts *through* figurability itself.

A double expropriation thus comes together by means of the double contradictory insertion of the image, belonging at once to the gaze and to representation: in being perceptive, the image divides the subject, but by exiling the subject and without refiguring it abyssally; in being mimetic, the image divests the object, while keeping it as body of a representation, simply cut off from any reference to the model. So the double belonging of the image, which Blanchot never ceases to evoke obliquely, calls into question the apprehension of the subject and of the object, but without thereby restoring a phenomenological objective that would eventually authorize their reciprocal reinstatement: the image is not in front of but in the gaze, where it provokes the collapse of vision in sight; thereby, visual experience proposes both a revealing of the visible, which is materially demonstrable, and the failure of visibility, operating at the heart of the visible and imputable to it alone. Calling thus into question its own visibility, the visible does not make room for the 'double of invisibility' noted by Merleau-Ponty in the gaze's crossed relation to the image. Through the dialectic of the seeing and the visible, the veil projected by vision on to the real contributes to the unveiling of Being in its 'dehiscence';[29] and aesthetic experience makes us sensitive to the internal reserve of the invisible inhabiting the visible. But with Blanchot the aesthetic is brought into the sphere of the writing-process, and hence of unworking, where the relation between art and being is undone; and the retraction that affects visibility refers us back to the necessity and, at the same time, to the impossibility of seizing the void at work in the work itself of figuration.

The invisibility of the image belongs specifically to the visible, as Foucault has shown:[30] without making room for the shying away or the forgetting of being, this invisibility accepts no other double than that of the unreal revealing itself in the reality of imaging experience. And if some aesthetic reference subsists in Blanchot, it is at play neither on the side of the veil unveiled, whereby Derrida rejoins Merleau-Ponty and perhaps Lacan,[31] nor on the side of a 'visuality' that would double figuration and liberate therein the forces of dream and thought, as proposed by Pontalis in his re-reading of Valéry with Freud.[32] Blanchot's aesthesis refers us first to the unsustainability of the idea of image: a literal image, and yet never given; actual yet without virtuality; offering itself to sight yet defying vision; an image that would be incapable of sustaining its own presence other than by an expansion of the gesture whereby it absents itself. If this is an aesthetic, it is because it touches on the gaze, while proposing the removal of the gazing subject; and if it remains figuring, it is in so far as it shows the retraction of representation under the attraction of the image, which embodies itself in this aesthetic without substituting itself for it. Blanchot invites us to gaze directly upon this disfiguring logic of the image, even of modernity's most mechanical images: if such images seduce us, is it not because they dissimulate the turning away of sight in the offer of vision? Calling us to turn around to see the interval opened up by the image in the heart of the image's own works.

The last word belongs to *The Writing of the Disaster*: 'The image exerts the attraction of the void, and of death in its falsity (*leurre*).'[33]

Translated by Roland-François Lack

NOTES

1 In her versions of *L'Espace littéraire* and *L'Ecriture du désastre*, Ann Smock translates *désœuvrement* as 'inertia' and *désœuvré* as 'idled'. Despite the awkwardness of 'unworking', I use it to translate Blanchot's

term because it preserves the essential reference to the 'work' (*œuvre*). What is lost is the familiar sense of 'being idle', or 'at a loose end' (translator's note).

2 Maurice Blanchot, *The Infinite Conversation*, trans. Susan Hanson (Minneapolis and London: University of Minnesota Press, 1993), p. 30.

3 Ibid., p. 32.

4 Maurice Blanchot, *The Writing of the Disaster*, trans. Ann Smock (Lincoln and London: University of Nebraska Press, 1986), p. 5.

5 Blanchot, *The Infinite Conversation*, p. 32.

6 Ibid., p. 79.

7 Maurice Blanchot, *L'Espace littéraire* (Paris: Gallimard, 1955). Though *L'Espace littéraire* has been translated as *The Space of Literature* (Lincoln and London: University of Nebraska Press, 1982), all page references are to this French edition and all translations mine. Further references are cited in the text.

8 See Maurice Blanchot, *Le Livre à venir* (Paris: Gallimard, 1959), pp. 136–8. Translations mine.

9 Ibid., p. 136.

10 See Maurice Blanchot, *L'Amitié* (Paris: Gallimard, 1971).

11 Blanchot, *The Writing of the Disaster*, p. 125.

12 Blanchot, *The Infinite Conversation*, p. 386.

13 Ibid.

14 Blanchot, *L'Amitié*, p. 167.

15 Blanchot, *Le Livre à venir*, pp. 135–6.

16 Ibid.

17 See Jacques Lacan, 'The split between the eye and the gaze' and 'The line and light', in *The Four Fundamental Concepts of Psycho-Analysis* (London: Hogarth Press, 1977) and Jacques Derrida, *Mémoires d'aveugle* (Paris: Réunion des musés nationaux, 1990), pp. 64–5.

18 Blanchot, *The Infinite Conversation*, p. 32.

19 Ibid., p. 462.

20 Blanchot, *L'Amitié*, p. 168.

21 Blanchot, *The Infinite Conversation*, p. 324.

22 Ibid., p. 325.

23 Blanchot, *The Writing of the Disaster*, p. 128.

24 Ibid., p. 69.

25 Blanchot, *The Infinite Conversation*, p. 66.

26 Ibid., p. 69.

27 Ibid., p. 30.

28 Maurice Blanchot, *Le Dernier Homme* (Paris: Gallimard, 1957), pp. 20–1.

29 Maurice Merleau-Ponty, *L'Œil et l'esprit* (Paris: Folio, 1964), p. 85.

30 Michel Foucault, 'La Pensée du dehors', *Critique*, 229 (1966).

31 Derrida, *Mémoires d'aveugle*, pp. 56–7.

32 J.-B. Pontalis, *La Force d'attraction* (Paris: Seuil, 1990), pp. 32–56.

33 Blanchot, *The Writing of the Disaster*, p. 125.

9 The trace of trauma
Blindness, testimony and the gaze in Blanchot and Derrida

Michael Newman

> There is always, however, something not to see.
>
> (Maurice Blanchot)

> What I look at is never what I wish to see.
>
> (Jacques Lacan)

> I write without seeing . . .
>
> (Jacques Derrida, after Diderot)

THE IMAGE OF NARCISSUS

In the last of the fragments of the *The Writing of the Disaster* headed, between parentheses and in the interrogative, '(A primal scene?)', Maurice Blanchot proposes a reinterpretation of the myth of Narcissus. He suggests that the aspect of the myth that Ovid forgets is that Narcissus does not recognize *himself*, but rather falls in love with the *image* which 'exerts the attraction of the void, and of death in its falsity'.[1] It is not, for Blanchot, that Narcissus is closed up in his reflection, but rather that 'he lacks, by decree (you shall not see yourself), that reflected presence – identity, the self-same – the basis upon which a living relation with life, which is other, can be ventured.' It is for this reason that the voice of Echo 'gives him nothing *other* to love'.[2] What Narcissus sees, without recognizing it, is 'the nonliving, eternal part', namely that in him which is death. If, in the myth, 'the prohibition upon seeing sounds once more', it is because Narcissus, lost speechless in presence and therefore unable to respond to the other, misrecognizes that withdrawing point at the heart of appearances where death and alterity coincide.

Narcissus falls in love with his image because he is oblivious to that otherness in himself which cannot be seen. The blind spot of vision is associated here with that place where the subject is touched by both death and the other. A question which might pose itself is which comes first: does the non-relational confrontation with death – finitude – make possible the relation with the other person, or is it through the other person that one encounters death? Whatever the case may be, Blanchot's extraordinary claim here is that Narcissus is not narcissistic, at least in the sense in which the term is understood in common parlance: it is not because he loves himself that Narcissus cannot love another, but rather that, not recognizing his image as his own, he cannot relate to the other, since he has no relation to himself. But this also implies the inverse: that Narcissus has no self-relation because it is only through the other that he would have been able to recognize his image as his own. To have a direct – that is to say, fascinated – relation to the image is to seek to by-pass mediation – time, space, the other – for the sake of an unlimited, instantaneous and fully present enjoyment, a vision without lack, without a blind spot. Forgetting his blind spot, the image for Narcissus becomes all. But how can the blind spot be remembered without being reduced? Is its occlusion not in some sense unavoidable? Do we not necessarily live in the untruth, or in, as Heidegger would put it, *Irre*, errancy, the oblivion of forgetfulness?

Within a philosophical context the blind spot has tended to be thought in transcendental terms: the condition for the possibility of vision cannot itself be considered to fall within the visible. Thus the relation to this condition, if considered in phenomenological rather than purely formal terms, will be either through a special kind of higher vision, or through a certain blinding. Jacques Derrida describes this economy as transcendental and sacrificial in *Memoirs of the Blind*, where he finds it to be exceeded – not only on the outside, but indeed *within* its own (failed) project of narcissistic self-closure – by tears which are associated with women and with a non-specular relation to alterity.[3] It is tempting to read those texts of Blanchot that concern the entwinement of vision and blindness in precisely these terms. This reading would involve a movement whereby the deconstruction of the transcendental yields an ethical claim, such that the condition of possibility itself depends upon an alterity that it cannot recuperate and that leaves an unassimilable remainder. In *Memoirs of the Blind* Derrida contrasts the blindness where empirical vision is sacrificed for a higher, spiritual insight with another 'essence' of the eyes figured by those tears of response – upon which, of course, vision itself also depends. Thus the determinations of the eye or eyes would, according to this account, appear to be thought according to the difference or intertwinement of the transcendental-sacrificial and the ethical. Applied to the figure of blindness in Blanchot, such an approach would tend to occlude an aspect of his treatment of vision which can be properly associated with neither the transcendental nor the ethical, even if it has implications for both.

The motif of vision and blindness in Blanchot is fundamentally concerned with the relation to desire and enjoyment. We shall find that in its absolute character, enjoyment (or *jouissance*[4]) is connected on the one hand with death, and on the other with the indeterminate or *apeiron* which Blanchot calls the *il y a*, the 'there is . . .' that is un-negatable being. Furthermore, this enjoyment would infect the ethical purity of any witness to the relation with the other as absolutely, irreducibly other. In other words, to begin to account more fully for Blanchot's concern with vision and blindness, we need to supplement the philosophical account – whether transcendental or ethical, or both – with one nuanced by the distinction between vision and the gaze. Only in this way can we hope to understand what it might mean to take the gaze as an object, and indeed what may be covered over by such a gesture.

REVELATION OF NOTHING: BLANCHOT'S DOUBLE VISION

If Narcissus sees without seeing, the child of the first of the fragments following the words '(A primal scene?)' sees nothing. After what may be its title – and we must never forget that question mark – the fragment continues, in italics, '*You who live later, close to a heart that beats no more, suppose, suppose this*: . . .'[5] The reader is asked to identify with the 'you' addressed as, in effect, dying. We are to suppose '*the child – is he seven years old, or eight perhaps? – standing by the window, drawing the curtain and, through the pane, looking*'. Not one, but two accounts follow, the first introduced by '*What he sees*: . . .', and the second by '*What happens then*: . . .'. The testimony thus splits apart into the description in the third person of a thing or representation seen, and the account of an event which occurs or, one might say, 'befalls', an occurrence without a subject or which does not involve the intentional act of the subject.

What the child initially sees is '*the garden, the wintry trees, the wall of a house*'. What '*happens then*' is not some*thing* different from that which is seen: it is

> *the sky, the same sky, suddenly open, absolutely black and absolutely empty, revealing (as though the pane had broken) such an absence that all has since always and forevermore been lost therein – so lost that therein is affirmed and dissolved the vertiginous knowledge that*

nothing is what there is, and first of all nothing beyond (que rien est ce qu'il y a, et d'abord rien au-delà).

So, finally, what is the effect of this 'scene'?

The unexpected aspect of this scene (its interminable feature) is the feeling of happiness (bonheur) *that straightaway submerges the child, the ravaging joy to which he can bear witness only by tears, an endless flood of tears. He is thought to suffer a childish sorrow: attempts are made to console him. He says nothing. He will live henceforth in the secret. He will weep no more.*

In a sense the child sees *through* the representation, yet there is no other world behind the represented world of the first part of the fragment. Behind the sky is nothing – or is it the nothing that is behind the sky? Not the dialectical negativity put to work by the subject, but the nothingness of a pure exteriority. The leaden day has become something like that which Blanchot elsewhere calls 'the other night', the night not of refreshing sleep to prepare for the work of day, but the restless night of insomnia, of passivity and indeterminacy, a night without stars, without orientation, without limits.

But far from the anxiety provoked by insomnia, not only can the child bear this absence, but it is for him bliss, *bonheur*. Does the disaster, etymologically the star of evil omen, signal for him good fortune? Or will this happiness *as lost* mark his life with melancholy? This moment of enjoyment can, like death, according to Blanchot, be related to nothing else: it is ab-solute, absolved from relations, incomparable, and at the same time the response – weeping – is as immediate and physical as can be. It is worth noting that this structure of a non-relational immediacy is also that of trauma – unmasterable unbound endogenous excitation, in the Freudian account – and of Lacan's Real, which is non-relational as excluded from the Symbolic Order, and thus a kind of 'nothing', while also being experienced as the immediate and nauseous proximity of life-substance.

Subject to interpretation – '*He is* thought *to suffer a childish sorrow*' (my emphasis) – this experience of '*rien*', of nothing, becomes a secret, in effect the secret that there is no secret, which means also that the secret – the nothing, impossible death, absolute enjoyment – may be everywhere.[6] '*He will weep no more.*' The secret can neither be told nor not told, and this is the paradox of testimony: as Blanchot writes in the second 'primal scene' fragment, '– *The secret alluded to is that there is none, except for those who refuse to tell. – But it is unutterable inasmuch as narrated, proferred.*" The very telling, in other words, obscures what is to be told.

The 'primal scene' of *The Writing of the Disaster* implies that vision is not a neutral registration of light and shade, but rather has as its cause an absence, a loss or a secret. Does the subject, then, want to see again that lost nothingness, or is it that the gaze, as object, is put in the place of an absence, in answer to some primordial anxiety?

Perhaps both. The 'primal scene' of Blanchot's child could, in psychoanalytic terms, be said to involve two moments: a primal scene of origin or genesis, and a further scene in which maternal castration is simultaneously witnessed and disavowed. Both would converge upon the 'nothing'. If such a scene were, in the first place, that of an impossible witnessing of the very origin of the subject who is doing the looking, the subject identifying with a gaze present at its origin, it is not, in Blanchot's 'primal scene', the sight or phantasm of parental copulation that is the object here, but rather nothing: *this* subject is created from nothing, *ex nihilo*. Were we to take the scene as one of fetishism, if the structure of the child who is looking for something and finds nothing could be taken to refer to the desire to see the maternal phallus,[8] or not to see the mother's lack, the outcome here in the fragment would not be – or at least not obviously – the substitution of a fetish-*object*, but a bliss which comes from seeing that there is nothing, a jubilation of nothingness. However, far from acknowledging sexual difference, the fact that the 'nothing' becomes total and absolute means, in effect, that nothingness itself would conceal lack and difference. In this case nothingness, whether experienced in joy or in anxiety, becomes the ultimate defence.[9]

Would not the *double* character of vision – that it always wants at once to see and not to see, whereby the visible becomes a screen revealing and concealing a non-visible alterity – account for the possibility that vision here is ready to tip into trauma, as it does when it goes over the edge in the 'event' of a near-blinding recounted in Blanchot's récit *The Madness of the Day*?[10] The duplicity of vision in Blanchot becomes all the more apparent when these texts are read alongside Derrida's avowal, *Memoirs of the Blind*, where this duplicity is at once echoed – in blindness and tears – yet turned in the direction of an affirmation of the other, an affirmation that Blanchot does not seem to have allowed himself.

THE GAZE IN THE NIGHT: ORPHEUS' DOUBLE TURN

Both 'Orpheus' gaze'[11] and *The Madness of the Day* turn on the duplicity of vision: that the eye both wants to see and not to see, to see – or not to see – that which lies behind the visible. This duplicity is manifested in Orpheus' double turn – away from and towards Eurydice – which figures at the same time the paradox of the work of art, which is necessarily both work – the sacrifice of the absolute object of enjoyment – and *insouciance*, the sacrifice of work for the glimpse into 'the other night'. According to Blanchot, Eurydice 'is the profoundly obscure point toward which art and desire, death and night, seem to tend. She is the instant when the essence of night approaches as the *other* night.'[12] By Blanchot's 'other night' we may understand the night which withdraws from the dialectical opposition of day and night and which, as the murmur of un-negatable being, is linked with the *il y a*.

Blanchot goes on to elaborate a paradox. Orpheus' *work*, his labour, consists in bringing the 'other night', the 'obscure point', back to the light of day. The art*work* is to grasp and bring to light – if we can still use these terms – the origin or cause of representation: in this case we could say that what art's 'autonomy' means is the desire of the work to attain and identify with the origin or source – the cause – of desire itself. However, the only way to approach this point, and to make a work of it, is to turn away. To make a work is to produce a representation or a signifier or a thing, it is to produce something which will be related to other signifiers and to other things within a horizon of meaning, even if that horizon is to be generated by the work itself (which is strictly the determination of a work of genius). This implies that the work is necessarily *relational*, as representation or thing that relates to a horizon, and as a complex of signifiers that are in an oppositional or negative relation with other signifiers. In other words, to make a work is to bind the object-cause of desire to a world or symbolic order. But if what desire desires is to grasp its own origin, and if the origin of desire were absolute or unconditioned – were, in other words, *without relation* – then this would be to relate to other things and to other signifiers that which is not to be so related. In other words, precisely that which is to be brought forth in the work of art would be lost through the very activity of work, of production. Thus, if Orpheus would have failed by succeeding, by bringing the object of his desire to the light of day precisely as an object produced by work, according to Blanchot he in a certain sense succeeds by failing, or more specifically by *forgetting*. Orpheus, we are told,

forgets the work he is to achieve, and he forgets it necessarily, for the ultimate demand which his movement makes is not that there be a work, but that someone face this point, grasp its essence, grasp it where it appears, where it is essential and essentially appearance: at the heart of night.[13]

By losing the object (Eurydice, who is drawn back to Hades according to the law or contract) Orpheus is able to capture, or at least intimate, the 'impossible' *relation* as one of loss or withdrawal, the experience of the absence which is in excess of any act of negation, the experience of the 'other night'. Through a forgetting which is not really an *act* of transgression, but rather a kind of *passivity* or 'inspiration', Orpheus, while remaining subject to law – he loses Eurydice – is able to bring the essence of desire – Eurydice *as lost* – to the work. What Orpheus wants is not the appearance so much as the appear*ing* 'itself' , with the *dis*-appearing that conditions it.

In effect, Orpheus wants to *see the blind spot*, or that point of withdrawal which makes manifestation possible. To develop the figure of vision, this would involve three sightings: the object, the gaze-as-object, and that which the gaze covers up. Progressively the active intentionality of the subject is undermined. The congruence of these three sightings – a paradoxical or impossible conjunction – would be the point 'where the work endures its measurelessness': that is, Orpheus wants to grasp the vanishing point in its non-relational, non-horizontal character, in its intimate exteriority. What Orpheus wants is 'to look in the night at what the night hides, the *other* night, the dissimulation that appears'.[14] For dissimulation 'as such' – the dissimulation which destroys the possibility of the 'as such' – to appear would be for the nothingness that makes possible the image, the groundlessness or void behind the phantasm, to be itself visible.

Orpheus desires the impossible – and is not all desire desire for the impossible? He wants to *see* the presence of Eurydice's '*infinite absence.*' Blanchot elaborates the paradox:

Had he not looked at her, he would not have drawn her toward him; and doubtless she is not there, but in this glance back he himself is absent. He is no less dead than she – dead, not of that tranquil worldly death which is rest, silence, and end, but of that other death which is death without end (*cette autre mort qui est mort sans fin*), the ordeal of the end's absence.[15]

Orpheus' desire for Eurydice is a *desire without limits*. It is an infinite, unlimited desire, unlimited by anything else, whether the relational structure of the signifier or Apollonian measure and limits: 'he desires her beyond the measured limits of the song'.[16] But this unlimited desire is, Blanchot tells us, equally necessary to the song, to the work as work of *art*. In disobeying the law, the law of limits, of the signifier (in a psychoanalytic register this would be the law of symbolic castration), 'Orpheus had only obeyed the deep demand of the work'. Inspiration is, according to Blanchot, '*desire which forgets the law*':

> The work is everything to Orpheus except that desired look where it is lost. Thus it is only in that look that the work can surpass itself, be united with its origin and consecrated in impossibility.[17]

Orpheus sacrifices work, and thus in a sense the work, to the measureless movement of desire, but – and here is the paradox – 'unknowingly he still moves toward the work, toward the origin of the work'.

In Blanchot's recasting of the myth, Eurydice comes to figure the 'object' that is between the subject and that alterity, identified by Blanchot with the 'other night', which exceeds dialectic. The object of desire withdraws into the void or nothingness which Blanchot calls 'the other night', and he also implies that such an object of desire in a certain sense *is* this 'other night'. The 'object' here is both the term *and the relation*, hence its ungraspability.[18] What Orpheus really wants is not just Eurydice but Eurydice-*as-lost*. This movement – of appropriation and disappropriation at once – involves an encounter with the absolutely other, and a turning away from this other in an impossible but unavoidable attempt to approach it through the *loss* of the object of desire, to mediate it through signifiers or through a work, to tell or to say it. In order to bring Eurydice to the light of day Orpheus must not look at her directly. Turning to look at her, he loses her; the singular other cannot fall within the horizon of the day without losing its alterity. But by looking at Eurydice, and thus losing her, Orpheus intimates an alterity beyond that of the object and the other person, an alterity connected with horror, with an enjoyment beyond sexuality, and with sublimation.[19] The paradox is that only by turning away from the absolutely other can one mediate this other, but then if one has turned away, how does one know that it is the absolutely other that one has mediated? What, we may now ask, is the relation between the blinding-effect of the other, and testimony?

THE TRAUMA OF THE GAZE

By taking the medium of vision, the light that is one of the founding metaphors of both the philosophical and theological traditions, as itself an object of desire, Blanchot leads the reader into a paralogism: to grasp the condition in terms of that which it conditions in such a way that the condition suffers an inversion, from, for example, light to darkness. If description is predicated on presence or re-presentation, in this case that which is to be described subverts the condition of possibility of description. Vision implodes into a state of being blinded; description turns into a self-cancelling testimony.

The central paradox of *The Madness of the Day* recalls that of 'Orpheus' gaze', but takes it further into a self-cancelling of the work, in this case the *récit*: while the narration is supposed to be of the unmediated event, it has to sacrifice the very event it is to narrate, rendering the narration impossible. All that can be presented, then, is the impossibility of narrating the event. The *récit* is thus *both* about the impossibility of the *récit* – this is its protective moment – and *also* about the necessity of sacrificing in turn this very impossibility, that is, the necessity of turning away from a sheltering in the impossibility in order to *write*, to make a work, thus necessarily submitting to the law of the signifier (or, in psychoanalytic terms, to symbolic castration, the acceptance of the necessity of detour – deferment – with respect to absolute enjoyment, and thus, to return to the Heideggerian register, the acknowledgement of finitude). If, as Blanchot tells us in 'Speaking is not seeing' in *The Infinite Conversation*, writing is indeed a 'cutting' with a 'stylet',[20] this is because it breaks or severs the immediate relation or 'contact' suggested by the way Blanchot diverts the traditional metaphor of light[21] to describe the relation with the other.

In *La Folie du jour* (*The Madness of the Day*) Blanchot has the narrator state, '*Je faillis perdre la vue, quelqu'un ayant écrasé du verre sur mes yeux. Ce coup m'ébranla, je le reconnais*', which is translated as 'I nearly lost my sight, because someone crushed glass in my eyes. That blow unnerved me, I must admit.'[22] The use of the verb *faillir* indicates lack in a way which undermines the opposition of positive and negative, and of active and passive, in other words, the basis for the structure of the intentional act. Can such an event, in which I neither lost my sight nor did not lose my sight, be said to have happened, let alone be described? The problem raised here is the same as that alluded to by Blanchot in *The Writing of the*

Disaster when he considers the appropriateness of the term 'scene':

> – *This term is ill-chosen, for what it supposedly names is unrepresentable, and escapes fiction as well; yet 'scene' is pertinent in that it allows one at least not to speak as if of an event taking place at a moment in time – A scene: a shadow, a faint gleam, an 'almost' with the characteristics of 'too much', of excessiveness, in sum.*[23]

Now, *verre* can mean both glass and lens, emphasizing that it is that which one normally sees through, which loses itself in transparency, which is pushed, in this case, into the eyes. In what may therefore still be called – since it involves an 'event' that cannot be said to have happened, and an excess, or 'outside' – the 'scene' of almost-blinding in *The Madness of the Day*, the glass that is supposed to have been crushed into the eye of the narrator recalls the apparently transparent medium through which light passes to reach the eye, as figured, for example, by the window of perspectival representation.

The connection between the 'primal scene' of *The Writing of the Disaster* and the almost-blinding of *The Madness of the Day* is made quite explicit in the second 'primal scene' fragment, where the breaking of the window of representation is placed in the broader metaphysical context of the loss of a meaningful cosmic order of being:

> – *Exactly, it has to be the* same. *Nothing has changed. – Except the overwhelming overturning of nothing. – Which breaks, by the smashing of a pane (behind which one rests assured of perfect, or protected, visibility), the finite–infinite space of the cosmos – ordinary order – the better to substitute the knowing vertigo of the deserted outside . . . the revelation of the outside by absence, loss and the lack of any beyond.*[24]

The happiness of the child becomes a painful cut for the adult. In the first 'primal scene' fragment the child is at once anterior to the law, has access to an il-legal *jouissance* which will persist, perhaps, as Blanchot will himself imply in a passage from *The Madness of the Day*, not for the man but for the woman. In the second fragment identified with the law as a totalized 'nothing'. In neither case is the boy acknowledged as being subject to the law in the sense of finite, limited, castrated.

In the 'primal scene' of *The Writing of the Disaster* the boy 'sees' the 'nothing'; in the traumatic moment of *The Madness of the Day* the man could be said (almost) to have had a revelation of the condition of vision. The latter, however, is not presented as a primal scene, even suspended by a question mark, since the episode with the character of a screen memory of a primal scene – the man and the woman with a stroller entering a doorway[25] – is split off from it. In *The Writing of the Disaster*, the light, as object, turns in effect into the gaze which, as 'seen', is blinding. That which reveals, the light, once it becomes itself an object, is blinding, and yet that blinding-effect in turn reveals vision as desire – the gaze as object of the drive[26] – which is disavowed in the supposedly neutral medium of everyday visibility. The 'almost-blinding' could be taken as the moment when, through the loss of sight, the gaze is manifested as visibility – which is why it cannot simply be said to be a blinding. This experience would thus involve an identification with the gaze and thereby with the enjoyment in the other,[27] simultaneously a step beyond the law and a punishment for this transgression.

In this way being blinded by the gaze manifests the duplicity of vision implied by the 'primal scene' of the child at the window: the gaze is a vision which almost blinds. If the gaze is to make objects visible to the eye, the almost–blinding of the eye by the gaze suggests a second role of the gaze as concealment. The gaze, it could be suggested, is the object which covers – thus revealing – the 'nothing' at which the child weeps with joy. Thus the blinding by the glass – by the gaze itself – analogous to a cut with a stylet, marks the enjoyment (the 'ravaging joy' of the 'primal scene') for which it is at the same time a punishment.[28] This would be the moment when desire, intrinsically linked to transgression of the law as it is in the phrase *le pas au-delà*, becomes a *defence* against an unlimited enjoyment.[29]

If the other is interpreted in ethical terms as the other person (*autrui*), then the implication of Blanchot's articulation is that the ethical relation – the relation with a singularity, and hence an absolute relation – is inseparable from an enjoyment connected with the *apeiron*, the state of indeterminacy prior to the law, the *il y a*. In other words, ethical questions are inextricably intertwined with those of desire, and an ethics of the singular, traumatic other with the horror and enjoyment of the Real. If Levinas writes concerning the dimension of testimony to the trauma in *The Madness of the Day*, 'Madness of now, madness of the day. Madness of Auschwitz which has not been able to pass' ('Folie du maintenant, folie du jour. Folie d'Auschwitz qui n'arrive pas à passer'),[30] to take seriously the structure of the trauma of blinding in *The Madness of the Day* would be to acknowledge in a most disturbing way the enjoyment it provokes; the *il y a* is explicitly linked with the enjoyment of the child in the second 'primal scene' fragment of *The Writing of the Disaster*, where the il y a is what the sentence '*can contain*' not by negation but '*only by bursting* (or rupturing: en éclatant)'.[31] Thus the ending of the *récit* becomes ambiguous, to say the least: 'Un récit? Non, pas de récit, plus jamais.' Is there to be no *récit* because the traumatic event exceeds any possibility of description, as literally unrepresentable and for that matter un-negatable since it was never 'present' in the first place – was, as Levinas might put it, 'immemorial'? Such would be the standard reading of this self-cancelling gesture. On the other hand perhaps there *must* be no *récit*, either to protect an illicit enjoyment, or as a punishment for such an enjoyment, or as simultaneously punishment and preservation. This would be a much more troubling conclusion, since it would implicate the reader as witness in the guilty *enjoyment* of a trauma.

This would seem to be far from the reason we might adduce why *Memoirs of the Blind* draws to a conclusion with the imploration or asking for pardon of the weeping eye.[32] The different senses of the eye, of its relation to weeping, memory and blindness that we have derived from Blanchot and from Derrida relate to a difference in their respective conceptions of the trace. For Derrida the *trait* or mark points two ways: towards unpresentable singularity, and towards the repetition that is the condition of ideality and representation. Thus the trace links the moment of blindness with the interruptive temporality of the blink; and it is this interval – repetition – which is occluded in the unblinking stare of the metaphysical eye expressive of the desire for pure presence. If revelation reveals the light, the condition of phenomenality, the catastrophe which is its originary supplement intimates the 'outside', the other.

In *The Madness of the Day* the structure appears to be similar: the medium of visibility, of transparency (almost) blinds the seer. However, if Derrida's conversation ends on a note of affirmation – 'one has to believe . . .', circling back to the epigraph, 'I write without seeing' – Blanchot's story ends with a performative self-denial of the text that we are reading: 'A story? No. No stories, never again.' ('Un récit? Non, pas de récit, plus jamais.') To put it baldly, we might say that the *récit* is impossible in so far as the event that is to be described or narrated was never present, and it was never present because – as is claimed in *The Step Not Beyond* through a reading of Nietzsche's thought of eternal recurrence – there simply is no present.[33]

TRACES OF BEING AND NOTHINGNESS

In the Introduction to her translation of Blanchot's *Le pas au-delà* (*The Step Not Beyond*), Lycette Nelson points out that Blanchot distinguishes the mark from the trace, citing the following passage:

> The mark (*La marque*), it is to be missing from the present and to make the present lack. And the trace (*la trace*), being always traces, does not refer to any initial presence that would still be there as remainder or vestige, there where it has disappeared.[34]

Contrary to Derrida's determination of the trace (of *différance*) as constitutive of the present, for Blanchot it is entailed by Nietzsche's thought of eternal recurrence that there is simply no present to be constituted: the present is a limit that is effaced, and therefore not present, since it is crossed always too late or too soon.[35] This conception of the non-present temporality of the present affects Blanchot's conception of the trace. 'Writing marks and leaves traces, but the traces do not depend on the mark, and, at the limit, are not in relation to it.'[36] Blanchot's point seems to be that the mark – the mark that is marked, we might say naïvely, in an 'act' – cannot be said to be the *origin* of the trace, since for Blanchot there is no present in which such a moment or act of origination could occur. The marks are effaced because there is no present in which they can be present; and the traces are 'forever cut off from that of which they would be the traces'.[37] Thus for Blanchot not only are not all marks traces, but there is a radical rupture between the mark and the trace; whereas for Derrida it is the alterity of the trace, that it is the *trace of the other*, that would disturb or disrupt any notion of the mark – say the mark made with the pencil of the one who draws – as visible and present origin or phenomenon. The implication is that for Derrida there cannot be any pure, autochthonous origin, and all marks must bear the trace of the other, must be *in memoriam*.

In *Memoirs of the Blind* the drawing of the mark is temporally Janus-faced: both a deferral of contact, and its memorial. It is this ambiguity which is in turn effaced by the transcendental revelation, the higher, spiritual vision which is supposed to be attained by the sacrifice of natural sight. What Derrida is refusing to go along with is the absorption of the sacrifice by the compensation that is offered for it. He shows how for a certain tradition blinding becomes a sacrificial event which makes possible the transition from a physical to a spiritual eye. That which is excluded in the substitution and process of exchange involved in this sacrificial 'event' is then concealed by that which it makes possible, in this case a higher or transcendental vision of the condition for natural vision.

If in the onto-theological tradition the natural eye is sacrificed for the sake of a higher, spiritual vision, Blanchot's *The Madness of the Day* recounts what happens when this spiritualizing sacrifice runs in reverse, when the spiritual light is rendered literal as glass in the eye. Since there is, for Blanchot, no presence, this intrusion can change nothing, or else it changes everything: in the second 'primal scene' of *The Writing of the Disaster*, the experience of the child is explicitly linked with the '*inevitability of* there is (*il y a*)' as the '*hearing of strangeness*' in response to an '*initial summons* (l'interpellation initiale) *which proposes the fictive supposition*' without which

> *to speak of the child who has never spoken would be to insert into history, into experience, or reality, as an episode or a tableau, that which has ruined them (history, experience, reality), leaving them intact. – The generous effect of the disaster.*[38]

History, conceived as representation, truth or a telos towards absolute knowing, is in effect ruined by the non-presence of the fiction required to speak of it. While Blanchot writes of nothing being changed by the disaster – how can there be determinate change without a present, which fiction and eternal recurrence vacate? – Derrida insists on a remainder or residue as a reminder of the non-present *in the very presencing of the present*. In the act of transcendence – as is stressed over and over again by Derrida – sacrifice does not join, make possible a certain economy, without an excluded, forgotten remainder, even if that remainder is less than nothing, ash, *cendres* (cinders).[39]

In the word *aveugle* in the French title of the book, *Mémoires d'aveugle*, we may hear another word, *aveu*, meaning acknowledgement, admission, confession and avowal. As confession, *Memoirs of the Blind* is, just as Derrida elucidates the necessary failure of the circle of self-reflection, a self-portrait in ruins, and indeed, the book is subtitled *The Self-Portrait and Other Ruins*. It is the other who comes to ruin – and make possible – the self-relation of the self-portrait, at once ruined and made possible by the other person and by the alterity of the law, and beyond the law the *pleurantes* – a ruin which in turn makes possible the breakout from self enclosure, the exposure to the other, the pledge of faith, the witness given and the avowal, the *aveu*. In witness as avowal or response, Derrida moves towards an affirmation that Blanchot does not allow himself, except in the form of the enjoyment, in tears, of the 'primal scene', always already lost since it occurs even the first time as an absence, to be remembered in an Orphic art which, by a paradoxical double movement, seeks to grasp the lost object in its very withdrawal.

There are other points on which we can discern a difference between Derrida and Blanchot over the significance of blindness. In Derrida we find two approaches, neither of which quite corresponds to the structure we have found in Blanchot. According to Derrida's reading of *The Madness of the Day* in *Parages*, Blanchot's *récit* is a story of the madness which consists in seeing the day itself, in seeing vision or visibility, the condition of seeing which should not itself be visible, hence the blinding effect of this experience.[40] This would be precisely the transcendental blinding which, towards the end of *Memoirs of the Blind*, Derrida distinguishes from a response of the eye to the other which is neither vision nor blindness, but rather tears.[41] Through the eyes that weep is invoked an outside to the economy according to which the sacrifice of empirical sight is repaid with a higher, transcendental vision. The move here is from the transcendental-sacrificial economy to an acknowledgement of the ethical moment – in this case a response to the loss of the other – involved in, but at the same time concealed by, the economy underwriting the transcendental gesture: the movement of *Memoirs of the Blind* is from vision to visibility, and then on to an 'outside' of both, as it touches the inside of the economy of vision through the sensible response of weeping, associated with the *pleurantes*, weeping women, rather than the 'great blind men' of the tradition from Homer to Milton and beyond.[42]

It should be clear by now that this structure is quite different from what we have found in Blanchot by reading *The Madness of the Day* alongside 'Orpheus' gaze': the move in Blanchot is not simply from vision to visibility so much as from vision to the gaze, which *both* has a transcendental relation to vision *and* is itself an object of the drive. Blanchot is thus in one respect at least closer to Lacan's account of the gaze in its distinction from the look[43] than he is to Derrida's treatment of vision. If the blinding in *The Madness of the Day* can be said to be due in part to a vision of the condition of visibility, that condition needs in turn to be related to desire, and therefore to prohibition and the law. Rather than a law of genre, concerning the 're-marking' of the *récit*, its non-closure (which is thereby identical to the law of the self-portrait which Derrida articulates in *Memoirs of the Blind*), this law concerns the prohibition of seeing what the subject wants to see, namely the 'absolute' object or 'Thing' of enjoyment which would lie beyond the dialectic of desire.[44]

The episode in *The Madness of the Day* when the law is personified as the lover of the narrator, crediting the narrator with the power to, literally, touch the law implies an attempt on the part of the narrator to identify in an unmediated way with the enjoyment of the law. Traditionally, though, the role of the law is supposed to be, precisely, to prohibit access to unmediated – immediate, unsublimated – enjoyment. Thus the identification with the place (manifest as a spot or stain in the field of the visible) of the gaze condenses both access to and prohibition of an enjoyment beyond the law. This is suggested – and given a gendered inflection – by one of the games the law plays with the narrator:

> She would show me a part of space, between the top of the window and the ceiling. 'You are there', she said. I looked hard at that point. 'Are you there?' I looked at it with all my might. 'Well?' I felt the scars fly off my eyes, my sight was a wound, my head a hole, a bull disembowelled. Suddenly she cried out, 'Oh, I see the day, oh God', etc. I protested that this game was tiring me out enormously, but she was insatiably intent upon my glory.[45]

The identification which would lead to omnipotence and omnipresence ('glory') turns out to be castrating ('a wound . . . a bull disembowelled' – images reminiscent of Bataille[46]) through its inscription in a difference involving a position which 'he' cannot occupy, that of women's pleasure – she sees the day, but his vision is wounded. It may be possible to discern here a gendering of the difference in the relation to enjoyment which serves to delimit the Orphic conception of art as a figure of masculine, Oedipal desire – desire, in short, as a defence against the anxiety of enjoyment and the impossible Real.

That which is (almost) blinding in Blanchot is thus not simply visibility, but rather the gaze as object of the drive in relation to a forbidden absolute enjoyment. It follows that the injunction with which *The Madness of the Day* ends – 'A story? No. No stories, never again' (*'Un récit? Non, pas de récit, plus jamais'*) – cannot simply be read as an ethical prohibition, that the representation of the event would be its betrayal, or a reflexive performance confounding the relations between inside and outside, between truth and fiction, both of which can go under the name *récit*. Rather, the phrase 'pas de récit' can be read as *both* imperative, a prohibition on narration or description, *and* as refusal: a refusal, precisely, to give up an enjoyment which would have to be sacrificed for the sake of writing the *récit*; the deferment of immediate enjoyment would be the condition of writing. The refusal to testify, coupled with the fantasy of the law being personified as a lover, suggests an unwillingness to take up a place as a subject of the law and, indeed, the necessity of transgression. But, in another twist to the paradox, this is a place that has always already been taken up in so far as what we are reading is a *récit* that has been written. Being blinded is related to writing: the writing is the blinding, cutting into the immediacy of vision and the absolute enjoyment associated with the gaze. If in Derrida the mark of drawing is also the re-mark of the impossibility of closure, for Blanchot the stroke of the stylus is more closely related to the entwinement of desire and prohibition.

If there is affirmation in Blanchot, it can only be of loss, of absence, of the 'nothing' that circumscribes a void that is not itself nothing but rather something unspeakable. For Blanchot, faithful in a certain way, although not entirely, to the Heideggerian irreducibility of Being,[47] economy is exceeded by the ceaseless murmur of the *il y a* which is linked in turn to enjoyment and (the impossibility of) dying;[48] while for Derrida, who is at least in this closer to Levinas, economy is exceeded rather by the gift of the other whose touch is the blind-spot and the blink of the eye. One might say that as *lethe* is to *aletheia* for Heidegger,[49] so *aveu* is to *aveuglement* for Derrida: if for Heidegger truth as disclosure is conditioned by a forgetting given by Being, for Derrida the blind-spot at the heart of vision – and the notion of truth conditioned by vision, including disclosure – is the locus where the subject bears witness to (always already) having been touched by the other.

And for Blanchot, different again this time from Heidegger as much as from Derrida, the traumatic moment is where the work encounters the impossibility of its origin in the absence of any present. This must be, for Blanchot, the sense of the Judaic prohibition of images which is the very condition for a vigilance without expectation, living on, to all intents and purposes in a vigilant blindness or blind vigilance, '*expecting nothing*' and '*– Consequently, waiting and watching* (attendant et veillant), *for suddenly awakened and, knowing this full well henceforth, never wakeful enough* (jamais assez éveillé)'.[50] With no mediation of past and future through the present, writing, the ruin of 'history, experience, reality', of retrospective and projective vision, becomes the ascetic discipline of a pure awaiting, a perpetual messianism.[51] Writing is, according to a passage from *The Step Not Beyond*,

> Effaced before being written. If the word trace can be admitted, it is
> as the mark that would indicate as erased what was, however, never

traced. All our writing – for everyone and if it were ever writing of everyone – would be this: the anxious search for what was never written in the present, but in a past to come.[52]

NOTES

1 Maurice Blanchot, *The Writing of the Disaster*, trans. Ann Smock (Lincoln and London: University of Nebraska Press, 1986), p. 125.

2 Ibid., p. 127.

3 See Jacques Derrida, *Memoirs of the Blind: The Self-Portrait and Other Ruins*, trans. Pascale-Anne Brault and Michael Naas (Chicago and London: University of Chicago Press, 1993), pp. 92–4 and 127. For a more detailed discussion of this and other issues raised by Derrida's *Memoirs of the Blind*, see my essay 'Derrida and the scene of drawing,' *Research in Phenomenology*, 24 (Fall 1994).

4 In line with Lacanian thought, I use the term *jouissance* to indicate an enjoyment that goes beyond the limit of the dialectic of desire, the latter conditioned by negativity or lack. Thus it becomes possible to see desire as a defence, linked with anxiety, against an enjoyment that would involve the extinction of the subject. See Jacques Lacan, 'The subversion of the subject and the dialectic of desire,' in *Ecrits: A Selection*, trans. Alan Sheridan (New York: W. W. Norton, 1977). In his Seminar 20 of 1972–3, *Encore* (Paris: Seuil, 1975), Lacan makes the further distinction between phallic and feminine *jouissance*.

5 Blanchot, *The Writing of the Disaster*, p. 72.

6 See also ibid., pp. 137–8.

7 Ibid., p. 114.

8 See Helene Cixous, *Readings: The Poetics of Blanchot, Joyce, Kafka, Kleist, Lispector and Tsvetayeva*, trans. Verena Andermatt Conley (Hemel Hempstead: Harvester Wheatsheaf, 1992), p. 20. See also her discussion of the scene in *The Madness of the Day*, which has the structure of a screen memory, in *Readings*, p. 104.

9 Lacan, writing on the 'cut' (*coupure*) that delimits the erogenous zone of the drive from the metabolism of its function, includes 'the nothing' among the list of objects of the drive 'which have no specular image': 'Observe that this mark of the cut is no less obviously present in the object described by analytic theory: the mamilla, faeces, the phallus (imaginary object), the urinary flow. (An unthinkable list, if one adds, as I do, the phoneme, the gaze, the voice – the nothing.)' *Ecrits: A Selection*, p. 315. To say that the nothing is an object in this sense is to suggest that it is already a substitute for something else, which it both indicates and defends against. Thus rather than being a cause of anxiety, as a certain philosophical tradition would have it, the nothing is already a defence.

10 Blanchot's *The Madness of the Day* was first published in *Empédocle*, 2 (May 1949), under the title *Un récit?*, then in 1973 by Fata Morgana as *La Folie du jour*. For a discussion of the issues raised by this publishing history and the change in title, see Jacques Derrida, *Parages* (Paris: Galilee, 1986), pp. 130ff. References in this chapter will be to the bilingual edition, *The Madness of the Day*, trans. Lydia Davies

(Barrytown, N.Y.: Station Hill Press, 1981). Both the 'primal scene' from *The Writing of the Disaster* and the blinding scene from *The Madness of the Day* receive perceptive discussions in Cixous, *Readings*, pp. 19–27 and 95–108 respectively.

11 Maurice Blanchot, 'Orpheus' gaze', in *The Space of Literature* (1955), trans. Ann Smock (Lincoln and London: University of Nebraska Press, 1982).

12 Ibid., p. 171.

13 Ibid.

14 Ibid., p. 172.

15 Ibid.

16 Ibid., p. 173.

17 Ibid., p. 174.

18 In Lacanian terms, the question here is that of the relation of the *objet a* to the 'impossible Real'. See Jacques Lacan, *The Four Fundamental Concepts of Psycho-analysis* (London: Penguin, 1979).

19 Sublimation, according to Lacan, 'raises an object to the dignity of the Thing'. *The Seminar of Jacques Lacan, Book VII, The Ethics of Psychoanalysis 1959–1960*, ed. Jacques-Alain Miller, trans. Dennis Porter (New York: W. W. Norton, 1992), p. 112. The Thing (*das Ding, la Chose*) of which the *objet a* is a substitute is that which is beyond qualities, having the dignity of being the *absolute* other of the subject (p. 52), and thereby being connected with the *jouissance* and horror of the Real as the 'beyond-of-the-signified' (p. 54).

20 Maurice Blanchot, *The Infinite Conversation*, trans. Susan Hanson (Minneapolis and London: University of Minnesota Press, 1993), p. 28. 'Stylet' is defined as: a probe, graving tool, writing instrument, piercing part of an insect's jaws, a stiletto. This is a metaphor frequently used by Nietzsche.

21 For analyses of vision and its dominance as a paradigm, see *Vision and Visuality*, ed. Hal Foster, Dia Art Foundation Discussions in Contemporary Culture 2 (Seattle: Bay Press, 1988); *Modernity and the Hegemony of Vision*, ed. David Michael Levin (Berkeley, Los Angeles and London: University of California Press, 1993); Martin Jay, *Downcast Eyes: The Denigration of Vision in Twentieth-Century French Thought* (Berkeley, Los Angeles and London: University of California Press, 1993). A key analysis of the metaphor of light in philosophy is of course Jacques Derrida, 'White mythology: metaphor in the text of philosophy', in *Margins of Philosophy*, trans. Alan Bass (Brighton: The Harvester Press, 1982).

22 Blanchot, *The Madness of the Day*, p. 11.

23 Blanchot, *The Writing of the Disaster*, p. 114.

24 Ibid., p. 115.

25 Blanchot, *The Madness of the Day*, p. 10.

26 Cf. Lacan, *The Four Fundamental Concepts of Psycho-analysis*, pp. 67–119.

27 See Antonio Quinet, 'The Gaze as an Object' in *Reading Seminar XI: Lacan's Four Fundamental Concepts of Psychoanalysis*, ed. Richard Feldstein, Bruce Fink and Maire Jaanus (Albany: State University of New York Press, 1995), p. 146.

172 *Michael Newman*

28 It is also possible that the glass may be taken as that of a mirror, as in Hans Christian Andersen's tale 'The Snow Queen', where the shard from a bad goblin's smashed mirror which makes everything good and beautiful shrink to nothing enters a little boy's eye, blinding him to the worth of his girl companion: the boy's heart is frozen, and he becomes the colour of a corpse, until, touched by the tears of the little girl, his feelings awaken once again. This would make a nice link between the near-blinding of *The Madness of the Day*, the 'primal scenes' of *The Writing of the Disaster*, the 'heart that beats no more' and Narcissus, and the *pleurantes* of Derrida's *Memoirs of the Blind*. I thank my mother, Hana Newman, for suggesting the connection with this tale.

29 'For desire is a defence (*défense*), a prohibition (*défense*) against going beyond a certain limit in *jouissance*.' Jacques Lacan, *Ecrits: A Selection*, p. 322.

30 Emmanuel Levinas, *Sur Maurice Blanchot* (Paris: Fata Morgana, 1975), p. 60, translation mine.

31 Blanchot, *The Writing of the Disaster*, p. 116.

32 Derrida, *Memoirs of the Blind*, p. 127.

33 Derrida's analysis of this passage concerns the question of the limit of the text, the relation between inside and outside, text and context, such that, rather than one determining or conditioning the other, they are abyssally, mutually enfolded through, in this case, the self-citation of the text two paragraphs above. Is this self-reference, this re-marking, inside or outside the *récit* just read? And if the *récit* is thus cancelled, can we be said to have read it? (See *Parages* (Paris: Galilée, 1986), pp. 142–8, 243–5, 269–77; and 'The law of genre', in Jacques Derrida, *Acts of Literature*, ed. Derek Attridge (London: Routledge, 1992), pp. 235–43.) If Derrida is concerned here with the 'law of genre', my topic is rather the relation of the law of/in Blanchot's text to desire and enjoyment. This gives a different sense of the relation of vision and blindness to testimony.

34 Blanchot, *The Step Not Beyond*, trans. Lycette Nelson (Albany: State University of New York Press, 1982), p. 54. The trace always refers to other traces and therefore is the plural 'traces' of difference.

35 See also the discussion of time in chapters 6 and 7 of the excellent study of Blanchot by Annelies Schulte Nordholt, 'L'Expérience de l'écriture dans l'œuvre de Maurice Blanchot', Ph.D. thesis, University of Amsterdam, 1993.

36 Blanchot, *The Step Not Beyond*, p. 53.

37 Ibid., p. 54.

38 Blanchot, *The Writing of the Disaster*, p. 116.

39 Derrida states in an interview broadcast in 1986 and published under the title 'Il n'y a pas *le* narcissism' in 1987 that 'Cinders is the destruction of memory itself; it is an absolutely radical forgetting . . .' And he adds, 'the experience of cinders communicated with the experience of the gift, of the non-keeping, of the relation with the other as the interruption of economy, this experience of cinders is also the possibility of the relation to the other, of the gift, of affirmation, of benediction, of prayer . . .' Jacques Derrida, *Points; Interviews, 1974–1994*, ed. E. Wetes and trans. P. Kamuf et al. (Stanford: Stanford University Press, 1995), pp. 208–9.

40 Derrida *Parages*, p. 137.

41 Derrida, *Memoirs of the Blind*, pp. 127–8.

42 For the attempt on the part of the Greek *polis* to control through legislation the excess of women's mourning, see Nicole Loraux, *Les Mères en deuil* (Paris: Seuil, 1990). The refusal of a limit on mourning, associated with women's behaviour at funerals, is seen as a threat to the order of the city.

43 Cf. Lacan, *The Four Fundamental Concepts*, pp. 182–4.

44 For Lacan's discussion of the Thing (*das Ding*) see *The Ethics of Psychoanalysis*, pp. 43–70.

45 Blanchot, *The Madness of the Day*, p. 17.

46 Cf. Georges Bataille, *Story of the Eye*, Hans Joachim Neugroschal (London: Marion Boyars, 1979), p. 53.

47 Blanchot's displacement of Heidegger is perfectly captured in the fragment of *The Writing of the Disaster* which reads: '*Ereignis*, thought's "final" word, does not, perhaps, put into play anything but the play of the idiom of desire' (p. 104).

48 Whereas discourse is for Blanchot based on the movement of negation and the possibility of death, or death as possibility, writing tends not towards nothingness but towards un-negatable being (sheer 'existence' or the *il y a*), and consequently dying as impossibility (see Maurice Blanchot, 'Literature and the right to death', in *The Work of Fire*, trans. Charlotte Mandell (Stanford: Stanford University Press, 1995), pp. 300-44). If the *il y a* may be associated with the Lacanian Real as formless life–substance, this may suggest why the impossibility of dying has the implication of something terrible. See also Mark Cousins, 'The ugly', *AA Files* (The Annals of the Architectural Association School of Architecture), No. 28 (Autumn 1994), pp. 61–4, where the claim is made that 'the ugly object is existence itself' (p. 64), a punitive force in response to which the subject seeks to destroy the object or to abandon its position as subject.

49 Cf. Martin Heidegger, 'Vom Wesen der Wahrheit' (1930) in *Wegmarken*, 2nd edn (Frankfurt am Main: Vittorio Klostermann, 1978), pp. 175–99; 'On the essence of truth', in *Martin Heidegger: Basic Writings*, ed. David Farrell Krell (New York and London: Harper & Row, 1977), pp. 115–41. See also Martin Heidegger, *Gesamtausgabe*, vol. 54 (Frankfurt am Main: Vittorio Klostermann, 1982); *Parmenides*, trans. André Schuwer and Richard Rojcewicz (Bloomington and Indiana: Indiana University Press, 1992).

50 Blanchot, *The Writing of the Disaster*, p. 116.

51 Cf. ibid., pp. 141–2, where Blanchot claims that in Judaism the coming of the Messiah 'does not correspond to any presence at all'.

52 Blanchot, *The Step Not Beyond*, p. 17.

10 'A wound to thought'

Michael Holland

At the beginning of the 1980s, well before the 'Heidegger affair' blew up, Maurice Blanchot solemnly denounced Heidegger's Nazi past in an article of homage to his friend Emmanuel Levinas:

> Heidegger's Nazism is a wound to thought, each of us wounded intimately.[1]

Reading that, his readers could only be reminded of what remains for many of them the painful reality of Blanchot's own political writing in the 1930s, namely its violence. Not simply its verbal violence, or even the real violence that its language occasionally invokes, but its formulation of a doctrine of violence considered as the means of taking thought (political reflection) beyond language and into direct action. Blanchot's 'revolutionary' writing came to a head in 1937 as a violent language preparing itself logically to overspill into violent action.[2] Even today, the reader of these early writings can only recoil at what appears in its turn as a wound to thought.

It would thus seem that the question posed by Philippe Lacoue-Labarthe in 1981, 'What was it in Heidegger's thinking that made possible – or rather: *did not prevent* – his political involvement?',[3] could equally well be applied to Blanchot. In fact, however, it can be reversed: something *did* prevent his involvement at a decisive stage. By 1937, as is indicated by the title of his first piece of literary criticism, 'From revolution to literature', Blanchot had begun to turn away from the politics of violence towards another outlet for what there is in thought that overspills it, namely literature.[4]

However, if it can be said that literature deflected Blanchot's thought away from the brink of what, by 1940, would become unredeemable, the question immediately arises: how can that be possible? By providing a retreat from politics, surely literature merely leaves the political in suspense. The answer is that it *became* possible, but only over a long period of time. By 1940, literature *had* become a retreat for Blanchot: a condition of political non-involvement which endured for about twenty years. Initially, while providing the basis for an attitude and a response to the Occupant that remained consistently honourable,[5] this retreat left the political *position* Blanchot had occupied intact. Politically, he can be said to have remained in a state of tragic fixation on the catastrophic moment in history (the collapse of France) from which he retreated in anticipation, *as if* it had already happened. *Death Sentence*, written in 1948, attests to that fixation, but reveals also that 'literature' was no secure retreat for the tragic subject, but rather the scene of its undoing.[6] Then in two stages, the turn from politics became a return to politics. In 1958, putting the past behind him,[7] Blanchot emerged from his retreat and joined the movement opposed to the Algerian War and the return of de Gaulle to power. Ten years later, in May 1968, he was involved in the student revolt against the Gaullist state. During those ten years, in the *récits* forming the sequel to *Death Sentence* and in his critical writing, the *cover* provided by literature for his retreat from politics was progressively questioned and dismantled. This process culminated in 1969, with the publication of *The Infinite Conversation*,[8] which, with its prefatory claim that 'writing is the greatest violence', the way to which 'passes through the advent of communism',[9] signals that Blanchot's relationship as a writer to politics had come full circle. There is now *no greater* violence than writing: what overspills thought, be it 'action' or 'literature', remains confined to language as writing. The following year, Blanchot made his first direct reference to the Holocaust.[10]

In retrospect, the decade of writing encompassed by *The Infinite Conversation* can be seen as a gradual and sometimes difficult confrontation with the wound opened up in Blanchot's own thought by his political involvement in the 1930s – what he alludes to himself, in 1984, as 'the most vulnerable area of my memory'[11] – and reopened with his return to politics in 1958. Inevitably, what he wrote in this period reflects the tensions and conflicts generated in the process. A prime site for this is the name Heidegger. Associated in 1937 with 'the dregs of German philosophy',[12] then hailed in 1938 as one of the most important contemporary thinkers,[13] Heidegger surfaces again, in all his ambivalence for Blanchot, in an article written in 1958, 'Nietzsche, today', which forms the first part of the sixth chapter of Section II of *The Infinite Conversation*, 'Reflections on nihilism'.[14] By examining the role played by Heidegger in this article, it is possible both to identify symptoms of the wound that has been reopened and observe the way Blanchot sets about the task of overcoming it through writing.

*

Between 1958, when it appeared as an article, and 1968, when *The Infinite Conversation* was being put together, the argument of 'Nietzsche, today' develops in a decisive way. Its basic thesis is a simple one and remains the same: Nietzsche's philosophy of the Will to Power and the Superman is irreducible to the ideological interpretation placed upon it by the Nazis, because Nietzsche is an essentially contradictory thinker. Between these two dates, however, the way Heidegger's philosophy is presented changes fundamentally: first it is cited in defence of Nietzsche against Nazi ideology; then it is discredited for its defence of that ideology. In the process, Blanchot looks back for the first time in his post-war career to the pre-war period when he himself became involved with extreme nationalist ideology. It is thus that the history of the writing of this chapter of *The Infinite Conversation* becomes the scene of a confrontation between Blanchot and his own history as a writer.

This confrontation is both tentative and oblique, however. 'Nietzsche, today' is, on the surface, a response to the publication by Karl Schlechta of an edition of Nietzsche's works in 1956. It opens, however, with a clear reference back to the 1930s: to 1934, when Karl Schlechta gained access to the Nietzsche Archive; and to Elisabeth Förster-Nietzsche's death in 1935. Never quite, it may be noted, to 1933 – at least, not yet, not in 1958. In so referring back, Blanchot's purpose would appear to be to identify and locate the origin of the knowledge which allows us to say today: '*The Will to Power* is therefore not Nietzsche's book' (p.137) – knowledge which would appear to originate with Schlechta. At the same time, he is referring back to what that emergent knowledge failed to prevent:

> Nietzsche had been delivered over to lies; lies that were conscious, resolute, at times refined, and that went from the use of a free thought for anti-Semitic ends to the fabrication of a weighty mythology organized by a pseudo-religious ambition.

(p.136)

It is noteworthy that anti-Semitism is here simply one mode of the historically traceable falsification suffered by Nietzsche's thinking: it is not evoked for *its* history, or for what history became because of it. In fact, despite appearances, Blanchot's perspective here is not primarily historical at all. True, the opening words of the chapter do present the question 'What about Nietzsche, today?' as a historical one: 'it concerns history and the petty details of history' (p.136). But history, it turns out, is the history of 'the old lioness', 'Nietzsche's fatal sister' (p.137), and of her exploitation of her brother's work so as to illustrate the Nietzsche name. In other words, history is in fact nothing *but* 'the petty details of history'. And this trivializing conflation of the two is confirmed when Blanchot continues:

> This sinister but simplistic and superficial falsification, like all political falsification (Hitler had not the least notion of Nietzsche and cared very little about him), would be of only mediocre interest, had it not been the sequel to a falsification more serious bearing upon the work itself, and that had been evolving for more than thirty years.
>
> (p.137)

And he goes on: 'As early as 1895, Frau Förster-Nietzsche . . .'.

A double displacement can be seen to be operating here in relation to history. First, the moment when Nietzsche's thinking became *politically* most significant (the coming to power of Nazism and anti-Semitism) is a moment whose significance lies primarily in the history of *thinking*; it is thus merely one phase of a period in history going back to the end of the nineteenth century, when Nazism had still to emerge on to the scene, and anti-Semitism had not ye acquired its ultimate political significance. Second, the *politica.* history of that lengthy period is entirely hidden beneath Nietzsche's family history in Blanchot's account. And as if to underscore this downgrading of history to 'the petty details of history', Blanchot ends the section with a lengthy footnote, relating more anecdotal evidence of Elisabeth Förster-Nietzsche's misdeeds, which are less serious than the act of violence by which she forged 'the false great work', he says, but more sordid (p.138, n. 2). In short, it is quite clear that the issue for him – the issue raised by Nietzsche 'today' – is not historical but philosophical, or rather: historical only in so far as it is philosophical.

Having thus established the historical perspective within which Nietzsche should be discussed 'today', Blanchot goes on, in the following section of the article, to consider whether there was anything in Nietzsche's own philosophy that allowed the falsification to occur. In effect, he asks the same question Lacoue-Labarthe will ask concerning Heidegger: 'What was it, in Nietzsche's thinking, that did not prevent . . .'. In other words, he raises the question of responsibility, and it is at this point that he brings Heidegger into his argument in 1958:

> Where does the sort of trickery that permitted (not without good faith) an editor's compilation to impose itself as the essential work [the Hauptwerk, as Heidegger still calls it][15] arise from?
>
> (p.138)

The trickery, he acknowledges, can be traced to a sister's prejudices and a publisher's unscrupulousness. Historically speaking, between them they are responsible for creating a work which provided the Nazis with a philosophical basis for their politics of racism. There are mitigating circumstances, however:

> at times, Nietzsche himself also yielded to the common prejudice and . . . seems to have been tempted . . . to express himself in a more traditional language and a more systematic form. At least so he stated, and he was taken at his word. This is his responsibility.
>
> (p.139)

In other words, Nietzsche was not the book's author, 'but [it was] authorized by him' (p.139). There is, in short, a political responsibility and a philosophical one in his case. The philosophical one (Nietzsche's) predates the political one (theirs), and so it would appear historically to authorize the latter to some extent. In fact, however, history has once again been reduced to 'the petty details of history' in Blanchot's argument: responsibility in history, which is always ultimately a political question, has been shifted not only back in time, but out of political history entirely, and relocated in the domain of philosophy.

But to return to Heidegger, his entry at this point in Blanchot's argument in 1958 is a curious one. This is because in a footnote to the words 'the *Hauptwerk*, as Heidegger still calls it', Blanchot points out that in 1953, when Heidegger does indeed use the term *das Hauptwerk* to describe *The Will to Power*, he is nevertheless 'careful to point out that this book is merely a compilation of posthumous writings "to which the title *Will to Power* was given"'.[16] Why, then, what can be no more than a quibble? Why is Heidegger, in effect, wrong-footed on entering Blanchot's argument? The question is all the more pressing given that, once Blanchot has established the historical perspective on 'Nietzsche, today' as that of philosophy and not that of politics, it is upon Heidegger that he calls, the

Heidegger of 'today', to defend Nietzsche against philosophical falsification (that is, against Jaspers) and against political falsification (that is, against Lukács). Against Jaspers, he quotes Heidegger's view that: "'to link Nietzsche with Kierkegaard is to misread him essentially. . . . Nietzsche *never* thought existentially, he thought metaphysically'" (p.141). Rather, he must be placed in the mainstream of philosophy and read with the same rigour with which we read Aristotle.[17] Against Lukács, for whom the contradictions in Nietzsche's thought merely reflect those of European capitalism as it enters its imperialist phase, he quotes what he calls Heidegger's moving description of Nietzsche as 'one of the most silent and timid of men', painfully obliged to cry out, in what he terms "'the written cry" of his thought' (p.143),[18] and condemned either not to be heard or to be misheard by his age. In short, though Heidegger is *still* calling 'the false major work' a *Hauptwerk today*, and thus helping to perpetuate the political falsification of Nietzsche, *today* he would seem to be the only person capable of defending a true philosophical reading of Nietzsche's work, and therefore of sustaining the priority of the philosophical over the political in Nietzsche's case.

Yet Blanchot feels it necessary, in 1958, to quibble, to wrong-foot him over a word, *das Hauptwerk*. And not to do it just once, but to follow it up a few pages later, and reiterate what he previously said about the 'false major work' by saying 'no *Hauptwerk* at all' (p.140). But what a *faux pas* this wrong-footing turns out to be in 1969, when the article comes to be included in *The Infinite Conversation*! In between, Heidegger has published his *Nietzsche* (in 1961), a book consisting of lectures given in the 1930s. And there, Blanchot discovers, Heidegger calls *The Will to Power* not *das Hauptwerk* at all, but 'das *sogenannte* "Hauptwerk"', 'the *so-called* "major work"'. And does so in a lecture first given in 1939.[19] Inevitably, then, in 1969 the reference to him *still* calling it a *Hauptwerk* 'today' has to go, and along with it the footnote in which he says that notwithstanding Heidegger's use of the word, he is careful to point out, etc. . . . In its place, but in a different place, comes a new footnote, a very long one, written in 1969, and which begins:

I think it still needs to be recalled (*Je crois nécessaire de rappeler encore*)[20] that, well before Schlechta, and at least from 1936 on . . . Heidegger questioned in the firmest and most authoritative manner, if not the editors, at least the publication of the text of Nietzsche for which they were responsible. Under the heading (which in itself is significant) 'das sogenannte "Hauptwerk"', Nietzsche's 'so-called "major work"', Heidegger denounces . . . the arbitrariness in choice and classification of the notes borrowed from the years 1884–88 and published under the title *The Will to Power*.

(p.449, n. 4)

What, then, could possibly be the point, in 1958, of sniping at Heidegger for what he says in 1953? Particularly since the tone of authority of the above passage not only appears to place Blanchot resolutely on Heidegger's side, but implies that he has long been there. The answer, it seems to me, lies precisely in the common cause Blanchot needs to make with Heidegger in 1958, so as to rescue Nietzsche from the political and its history. More precisely, instrumental in his historical displacement of Nietzsche's case from the domain of the political to that of the philosophical is the establishment of a community of *those who know*, with its own history, and thanks to which the priority of the time of philosophy over the time of politics can be seen to have inserted itself ahistorically into history at a decisive moment, and to have had historical effect.

From the outset, this community is invoked in its exclusivity:

In publishing a new edition of Nietzsche and in revealing the conditions under which it had come about, Karl Schlechta created a great stir. He said nothing that had not been known in a vague sort of way, but he said it with the proof [we were][21] lacking (*qui nous manquaient*).

(p.136)

This opening reference to a state of vague knowledge about the falsification of Nietzsche's thought, on the part of an unspecified community which includes Maurice Blanchot (as is clear from the *we*), but appears to exclude Karl Schlechta, seeks to establish clearly from the outset both the historical priority of that knowledge over Schlechta's precisely documented proofs and also its absolute independence of such proofs. It is followed, in the 1958 footnote containing the quibble, by a much firmer assertion of the priority of such knowledge over mere proof:

It must be pointed out here that before Schlechta's publication, Nietzsche's readers were perfectly aware that this work was the work of a publisher, and that, in its order, it was constituted by a disorder of writings from every sort of source.

The historical dimension of this priority of knowledge remains vague in 1958, however. Given its vagueness, it is tempting, in an article entitled 'Nietzsche, today', to understand this 'before' as simply an extension of the precise reference to Heidegger in 1953 that immediately precedes it. The knowledge Schlechta gained in 1934 is thus effectively glossed over, his state of ignorance *prior* to 1934 seemingly of greater significance than what he discovered in the Archive, since his knowledge, once acquired, remained that of the mere historian: destined solely to be corroborated by documentary proof, and otherwise without effect (since it could not prevent the falsification from happening). According to the 1969 note, however, the vaguer but superior knowledge that the article is referring to can be traced much further back, to Heidegger in 1936. It is thus almost, though still not quite, contemporaneous with Schlechta's own acquisition of knowledge. It seems clear from this that, in rectifying his account of Heidegger's knowledge of Nietzsche's work, Blanchot is doing much more than simply eliminating an unjustified and even petty quibble. Ten years after first writing the article, owing to the need to acknowledge what Heidegger wrote as early as 1936, he finds himself obliged both to open up and to clarify the historical perspective within which the question of knowledge was originally examined in 'Nietzsche, today'. But although he is thereby replacing the unavowed wariness about *Heidegger* 'today', expressed in the quibble, with an acknowledgement that both he and Blanchot have long been kindred spirits as far as knowledge of the falsification of Nietzsche's philosophy is concerned, something continues to affect Blanchot's ability to acknowledge and define the role he is giving Heidegger in his examination of Nietzsche today.

Further light is shed on this continuing wariness by a 1969 addition to the earlier footnote concerning Elisabeth's sordid misdeeds. On the surface, this addition opens up the historical perspective of Blanchot's argument, by extending back the knowledge shared by the community to which Heidegger and he belong, so as to give it priority even over Schlechta's own. Prior to 1934, when he gained access to the Archive, the main text says, 'Schlechta . . . scarcely foresaw what awaited him' (p.136). In the terms of the 1958 article, where Schlechta's acquisition of knowledge retains its simple historical priority over anyone else's, this move from ignorance to knowledge is irrelevant, as I have suggested: the knowledge Blanchot is interested in is that of the philosopher, not that of the historian. In 1969, however, the footnote I am referring to is extended as follows:

What to my mind remains decisive is that, for those who were subject to Hitler's advent, the use of Nietzsche's name does not belong to a history that is conjectural; it was rather a part of everyday political experience. It could be read in the newspapers. Some of us, on November 4, 1933, were made aware of the following information, which appeared in the press [there follows a report, from an unnamed newspaper, of a visit by Hitler to Elisabeth, during which she presented him with a sword-stick that had belonged to her brother]. That same day, November 2, 1933, in Weimar, Hitler has a photograph taken of himself next to a statue of Nietzsche.

(p.448, n. 2)

With this addition, what remains an *attitude* to Schlechta in the 1958 article (and one tinged with a churlishness uncharacteristic of Blanchot) is developed into a full-scale demotion of both his knowledge and his publication of that knowledge: by 1934 there were those (of *us*) who knew already, and 'our' knowledge, which has throughout had priority 'today', because it is that of 'Nietzsche's readers', has at last acquired historical priority also.

Significantly, however, this extended footnote does not extend *Heidegger's* knowledge back to give it priority over Schlechta's. According to the footnote added in 1969, in place of the quibble, in both 1953 and 1936 Blanchot includes himself and Heidegger in the same community of knowledge (which, in each case, derives from and accords priority to the expression Heidegger gives to it in his writing): they belong to the same *us*. And this footnote draws substantially on the Nietzsche lectures to assert the truth about Nietzsche against those who, 'through an unreasonable attachment to the past' (p.449, n. 4) (those, in other words, for whom it is politics, not philosophy, that determines history), continue to oppose the publication of a complete critical edition of Nietzsche's writings. However, when the earlier footnote is extended so as to extend knowledge back, historically, beyond even Schlechta's – to 1933 – that *us*, which is always an exclusive one, now, as '*some* of us', excludes not only Karl Schlechta (the historian) but also Martin Heidegger (the philosopher). Though the words Blanchot quotes Heidegger as uttering in 1939 'should have rung out clearly, as a warning and as a call, to the ears of some of the listeners in the audience', in November 1933, at the level of 'everyday political experience', Heidegger was not *subject* or *submitting* to Hitler: he was following up and acting upon his endorsement of Hitler and hence of racist ideology in the *Rektoratsrede* of May 1933, as Blanchot makes clear at the end of the long 1969 footnote with which he rectifies his quibble over the term *Hauptwerk*, and which refers directly to 'Heidegger's principal "political" text of [November] 1933', namely the 'Declaration of support for Adolf Hitler and the National Socialist state'.[22]

Though no direct explanation has been found, it is perhaps clearer now why Blanchot quibbled so over the term *Hauptwerk* in 1958. As the extensive footnote additions in 1969 reveal, 'Nietzsche, today' was originally the site of a complex and unstable strategy, which consisted in using Heidegger to establish the historical priority of the philosophical over the political for an understanding of 'Nietzsche, today', without acknowledging Heidegger's own implication in the political history whose significance he was being used to suppress. The quibble, I would argue, is a superficial sign of the tensions present, for Blanchot, in such a strategy in 1958 – the year, precisely, when he sought to put the past behind him and emerge from twenty years of political silence.[23] In 1969, with the elimination of the quibble and the acknowledgement of Heidegger's responsibility, those tensions would seem to have disappeared.

They have not, however. The quibble in the 1958 text may have been stabilized and opened up so as to disentangle the philosophical and the political in the history of knowledge concerning Nietzsche. Though absent from the 1969 text, it nevertheless remains embedded there, its *still* echoed ironically by the *still* of the 1969 footnote, and acting as a pointer towards what remains glaringly the problem with the section of footnote quoted above: namely Blanchot's omission, in 1969, by which time Heidegger's responsibilities are being forensically set out, of any reference whatsoever to his own political past, to what constituted 'everyday political experience' for him in November 1933, and which was the very opposite of *reading* the newspapers, since by then, in the *Journal des débats*, but above all in *Le Rempart* (from April to October), he had begun writing extremist articles in response to the 'ordeal' being undergone (*subi*) by France (both internally and externally) following 'the advent of Hitler'. In 1958, I would suggest, that issue amounts to a veritable ordeal for Blanchot, as he begins to look back on the period in history when what he will eventually call 'a wound to thought' actually occurred, but in his own thinking, not in Heidegger's. To talk about 'Nietzsche, today' in 1958 is, for Blanchot, to open up a 'yesterday' which, until this point, has been shrouded by him in a very particular form of silence: the silence of literature. On the surface, this 'yesterday' remains a German one, represented by Schlechta and Heidegger, the difference between France and Germany remaining blurred by the vague community of Nietzsche's philosophical readers, to which both Heidegger and Blanchot belong. Even then, however, there is something in this community that is *unavowable*, and in 1969, when 'some of us' finally excludes Heidegger and thus separates Germany and France,[24] what it is comes starkly into view.

*

To read 'Nietzsche, today' historically is thus to witness an author being drawn back reluctantly towards the very past which he initially sought to put behind him at the time of writing it. In a way which is never fully controlled, Blanchot finds himself obliged to recall his own 'everyday political experience' in 1933 not only at the end of a decade of very different political involvement, but in a way which deprives him of what, throughout that decade, has determined his political activity: the subordination of the time of politics to the time of philosophy. The political experience (which is also an experiment) extending from the Manifesto of 121, by way of the *International Review*[25] to May 1968, has effectively failed. It was, essentially, a utopia, as Blanchot seemed aware when he wrote, in the preparatory documents for the *International Review*: 'if it is a utopia, we must be willing to fail utopianly' (*Lignes*, p.180). Furthermore, philosophy considered, in its ahistorical historicity, as a way of being in time through language has been discredited historically. As he wrote in 1984, referring again to Heidegger's political activity: 'what took place was a falsification of writing, an abuse, a travesty and a misappropriation of language. Over the latter, from then on, there will hang a suspicion.'[26] By 1969, with the publication of *The Infinite Conversation*, Blanchot can thus be said to stand exposed: not morally (in the eyes of others), but in relation to himself and his history. The future he refers to in his letter to Mascolo has now been and gone. The present has opened up to reveal the memory of a past whose reality can no longer be comprehended either politically or philosophically, and which he evokes in the following terms in 1986, in a letter to Salomon Malka entitled '"Do not forget"':

Heidegger himself, in the posthumous testament in *Der Spiegel*, admits that in the advent of Hitler he had hailed the grandeur and the splendour of a new beginning. What begins is always what is most important for him: it is the upsurge of absolute renewal, the interruption that suspends our relation to established laws and values, perhaps even to the 'gods'. And in a sense, this was true. But that interruption, which was for Heidegger the promise of a Germany heir to the excellence of Greece, and as such, at whatever price, called on to enlighten the world by dominating it, was also for us, and first of all for the Jews, the interregnum where all rights and all redress ceased, where friendship became unsure, where the silence on the part of the highest spiritual authorities left us without assurance, not only under threat, but uneasy at being unable to respond in the way we should have to the silent appeal of others.[27]

The last lines of this extract appear to come closer than anything Blanchot has ever written to an acknowledgement of responsibility for his own past. In fact, however, this is less a 'confession' (he has nothing to confess to) than a reminder of what, from 1969 onwards, he remains exposed to in his own writing and to which henceforth in writing (in *The Step Not Beyond* and *The Writing of the Disaster*) he will never cease to respond: the violence that history itself became when events and actions escaped both political and philosophical control, and the peculiar responsibility shared by all who were the contemporaries of such overspill, which wounded more than thought.

NOTES

1 'Our clandestine companion', trans. David B. Allison, in *Face to Face with Levinas*, ed. Richard A. Cohen (New York: State University of New York Press, 1986), pp. 41–52 (p. 42).

2 In *L'Insurgé*, which appeared weekly from January to October 1937, Blanchot at first wrote two articles, one political, the other literary. His political column ceased appearing in July, save for a final piece in October. His literary column appeared until the newspaper folded. The political pieces consistently make use of a language of violence that is disturbing. It has been repeatedly cited, and I shall not cite it here. (For a recent rehearsal of examples of this language, see Philippe Mesnard, 'Maurice Blanchot, le sujet de l'engagement', *L'Infini*, 48 (Winter 1994), pp. 103–28.) In fact, it is in the literary column that the doctrine of violence I am referring to is put forward. Julien Benda is dismissed as someone 'totally incapable of forming a real thought, that is to say the beginning of a true act' (*L'Insurgé*, 5, 10 February 1937, p. 5); in a review of Denis de Rougement's *Penser avec les mains* Blanchot writes: 'to become involved, for thought, is to encounter the real, to strike it with the violence of its creative force' (*L'Insurgé*, 3, 27 January 1937, p. 5); finally, in response to Alphonse Séché's *Réflexions sur la force*, he argues: 'Is not physical force also moral, in fact morality itself, and such

that it can accept no epithet, no specification?' (*L'Insurgé*, 10 bis, 17 March 1937, p. 5) (my translations). To me, the relationship between thought and violence reflected in these assertions is the greatest cause for concern in Blanchot's pre-war writing.

3 Philippe Lacoue-Labarthe, 'La Transcendance finie/t dans la politique', in *L'Imitation des modernes* (Paris: Galilée, 1986), pp. 135–74 (p. 136). This is a version of a lecture given in 1981. It first appeared with a simpler title ('finit' for 'finie/t') in Luc Ferry, Jean-Luc Nancy, Jean-François Lyotard, Etienne Balibar and Philippe Lacoue-Labarthe, *Rejouer le politique* (Paris: Editions Galilée, 1981), pp. 171–214 (p. 173).

4 'De la révolution à la littérature', *L'Insurgé*, 1, 13 January 1937, p. 3. According to Blanchot, he began writing *Thomas the Obscure* (1941) as early as 1932; the *récits* that make up *Vicious Circles* (1951) were written in 1935 and 1936 respectively.

5 It is not possible to broach this issue here, though as one of Blanchot's most recent published texts recalls, it has become a crucial one (see '*Pré-texte*: pour l'amitié' ['*Pre-text*: for friendship'], in Dionys Mascolo, *A la recherche d'un communisme de pensée* (Paris: Editions Fourbis, 1993), pp. 5–16)). Simply as a contribution to a clearer under-standing of Maurice Blanchot's position during the Occupation, I offer the following two quotations (my translations):

(1) My mind then went back to November 1940, one of the most perilous months in my life. I had received a letter from the sister of the editor of *Aux Ecoutes* [i.e. Maurice Blanchot], informing me that I was about to be arrested. Because of the origin of that letter, I could be in no doubt as to the threat that hung over me. . . . It was the period when the German French-language papers were engaged in a campaign against me. *La Gerbe* and *Je suis partout* stood out in the front rank of the informers.

(Paul Lévy, *Journal d'un exilé* (Paris: Grasset, 1949), pp. 29–30)
(2) Maurice Blanchot, who used to be the editor-in-chief of the Jew Lévy, has made his debut in what he calls the novel, just as he made his debut in what he no doubt used to call a political newspaper. In exactly the way he once used to refuse to see reality, preferring to submit to the ethic of those who employed him, today he refuses to recognize what the art of story-telling and the art of writing are. . . . On top of his other charms, [his Thomas] possesses that of being as outmoded as the Jewish art he is identified with.

(R[ebatet?]., in *Je suis partout*, 534, 18 October 1941, p. 8)
6 The first part of *Death Sentence* is a complex allegory, in which history (the Munich crisis), literature (*Thomas the Obscure*) and (narrative) subjectivity ('Je', 'I') are brought into alignment with the uncertain borderline which separates fiction and reality once disaster has struck the world, and in the process gradually undone. In the second part, all that remains – narrative itself, *le récit* – is disengaged from the empty generic frame left behind once this process is complete, and turned into a language of impersonality existing between what are no longer indi-vidual persons. (I have attempted to examine the processes at work in the first part in 'Towards a new literary idiom: the fiction and criticism of Maurice Blanchot from 1941 to 1955' (unpublished D.Phil. thesis,

University of Oxford, 1981), Part I, 'L'Arrêt de mort', pp. 35–109. For a study of the second part in terms of the emptying of the frame of existing narrative, see my 'Rencontre piégée: "Nadja" dans *L'Arrêt de mort* de Maurice Blanchot', in *Violence, théorie, surréalisme*, ed. Jacqueline Chénieux-Gendron and Timothy Mathews, Collection Pleine Marge 3 (Paris: Lachenal & Ritter, 1994), pp. 117–38.

7 See Dionys Mascolo, 'Un itinéraire politique' ('A political itinerary'), in *Le Magazine littéraire*, 278 (June 1990), pp. 36–40:
   In 1958, de Gaulle seized power. With Jean Schuster – from the Surrealist group – I founded an anti-Gaullist journal with the title *Le 14 juillet*. As soon as the first number appeared, Maurice Blanchot, who since before the war had not said a word politically, sent me a letter which I found stunning: 'I want you to know that I am in agreement with you. I refuse all the past and accept nothing of the present.'
   (p. 40 (my translation))

8 Maurice Blanchot, *The Infinite Conversation*, trans. Susan Hanson (Minneapolis and London: University of Minnesota Press, 1993).

9 Ibid., p. xii.

10 In 'Fragmentaires', *L'Ephémère*, 16 (Winter 1970), pp. 376–99. The fragment is included in *The Step Not Beyond*, trans. Lycette Nelson (Albany: State University of New York Press, 1992), p. 114:
   That the fact of the concentration camps, the extermination of the Jews and the death camps where death continued its work, are for history an absolute which interrupted history, this one *must* say, without, however, being able to say anything else. Discourse cannot be developed from this point. Those who would need proofs will not get any, even in the assent and the friendship of those who have the same thought, there is almost no affirmation possible, because any affirmation is already shattered and friendship sustains itself with difficulty in it. All has collapsed, all collapses, no present resists it.

11 'Les Intellectuels en question', *Le Débat*, 29 (March 1984), pp. 3–28 (p. 28). Translated by Michael Holland as 'Intellectuals under scrutiny', in *The Blanchot Reader* (Oxford: Blackwell, 1995), pp. 206–27.

12 In his review of Denis de Rougement's *Penser avec les mains* in 1937 (see n. 2 above), Blanchot says of its author's philosophy: 'It sometimes appears to draw on the dregs of German philosophy, in particular that of Heidegger.'

13 In a review of Jean-Paul Sartre's *Nausea*, significantly entitled 'L'Ebauche d'un roman' ('The beginnings of a novel'), Blanchot wrote:
   This novel is visibly inspired by a philosophical movement that is little known in France, and yet is of the utmost importance: that of Edmund Husserl and especially Martin Heidegger. Some extracts from the work of Heidegger have just been translated into French. They reveal the force and the creative will behind this thought which, in the infinite dispute between laws, intelligence and chance, offers art a new standpoint from which to contemplate its own necessity.
   (*Aux Ecoutes*, 30 July 1938, p. 31. Translated by Michael Holland in *The Blanchot Reader*, pp. 33–4)

14 Blanchot, *The Infinite Conversation*, pp. 136–51. Further page references will be given in the text.

188 *Michael Holland*

15 The section between square brackets is omitted in the 1969 version.
16 See 'Nietzsche, aujourd'hui', *Nouvelle Revue française*, 68 (August 1958), pp. 284–95 (p. 287).
17 See Martin Heidegger, *What is Called Thinking?* trans. J. Glenn Gray (New York: Harper & Row, 1968 (1954)), p. 70.
18 Ibid., pp. 48–9. However, I prefer 'written cry' to Gray's 'written scream'.
19 Martin Heidegger, *Nietzsche* (Pfullingen: Neske, 1961). See the two-volume English edition by David Farrell Krell (San Francisco: Harper & Row, 1979–87). The second volume (Volumes 3 and 4) contains the text of the 1939 lecture 'The will to power as knowledge', whose second chapter is entitled 'Nietzsche's so-called major work' (pp. 10–14).
20 *The Infinite Conversation* omits the 'encore', subsuming it under 'recall'. The precise sense of Blanchot's formula is ambivalent, however. Though the *encore* could simply mean 'again', it has nothing to refer back to in either 'Nietzsche, today', or *The Infinite Conversation*: Blanchot has not previously 'recalled' or 'pointed out' the facts he is referring to. The words 'Je crois nécessaire de rappeler encore . . .' could also be translated 'I feel that it is *still* necessary to point out . . .'. This could be seen as a repetition of the *still* of 'as Heidegger *still* calls it', and so have the effect of cancelling it out, ten years on, by means of a sort of *mea culpa*.
21 *The Infinite Conversation* has 'the proof that had been lacking', which omits the feature (*nous*, 'we') that I wish to focus on.
22 And not, as Susan Hanson suggests, *Die Selbstbehauptung der deutschen Universität* (*The Self-Affirmation of the German University*), which dates from *May* 1933. Both this piece and the 'Declaration of support for Adolf Hitler and the National Socialist state' which is dated 11 November 1933 were first made public by Guido Schneeberger in his *Ergänzungen zu einer Heidegger Bibliographie* (Bern: Suhr, 1960) and *Nachlese zu Heidegger* (Bern: Suhr, 1960). English versions can be found in *The Heidegger Controversy* ed. Richard Wolin (Cambridge, Mass.: MIT Press, 1993).
23 A postscript to the second part of 'Reflections on Nihilism', 'Crossing the line', when it appeared in the *Nouvelle Revue française* in September 1958, explicitly links Blanchot's reflections on Nietzsche 'today' to the renewal of his political activity (translation mine):
    P.S. – Having read the commentary on the current situation on page 346 of the last number of the *N.R.F.*, I am unable to endorse it. In my view, it is to despair of this people and this country, to place all of one's hope for them in an episodic individual [i.e. de Gaulle].
    See also n. 7 above.
24 Another perspective on this wish to separate Germany and France, as far as Nietzsche is concerned, is provided by an addition to the footnote on the first page of 'Nietzsche, today' in *The Infinite Conversation*. It begins: 'I might note that these reflections go back more than a dozen years' (p.448, n. 1). Such references to the history of the texts that make up his books are rare in Blanchot. However, despite the tensions present, historically, in 'Nietzsche, today', his sole purpose in evoking history is to point out that, since Schlechta, another edition of Nietzsche's works

'in their entirety and their integrity' has been undertaken, 'notably by the publisher Gallimard' ('notamment par les éditions Gallimard'). This curious presentation of a German-language edition of Nietzsche, whose editors (Colli and Montinari) are Italians, as primarily a French undertaking would seem to be a further sign of the historical tensions present, even in 1969, in Blanchot's attempt to rescue Nietzsche from politics and restore him to philosophy: Nietzsche does not belong to Germany; he is not a German author. Many of Blanchot's reservations about Schlechta, both in 1958 and in 1969, may also be read in the same light. (I am grateful to Leslie Hill for clarifying this point for me.)

25 See 'Le Dossier de "La Revue internationale", 1960–1964', *Lignes*, 11 (September 1990), pp. 161–301. For a discussion of the project for a new review, see my introduction to Part IV of *The Blanchot Reader*, 'The step beyond', pp. 253–65.
26 'Intellectuals under scrutiny', in *The Blanchot Reader*, pp. 206–27 (p. 226, n. 3).
27 '"Do not forget"', in *The Blanchot Reader*, pp. 244–9 (p. 247).

11 Potter's Field
Death worked and unworked

Gillian Rose

When morning was come, all the chief priests and elders of the people took counsel against Jesus to put him to death:
And when they had bound him, they led *him* away, and delivered him to Pontius Pilate the governor.
Then Judas, which had betrayed him, when he saw that he was condemned, repented himself, and brought again the thirty pieces of silver to the chief priests and elders,
Saying, I have sinned in that I have betrayed the innocent blood. And they said, What *is that* to us? see thou *to that*.
And he cast down the pieces of silver in the temple, and went and hanged himself.
And the chief priests took the silver pieces, and said, It is not lawful to put them into the treasury, because it is the price of blood.
And they took counsel, and bought with them the potter's field, to bury strangers in.
Wherefore that field was called, The field of blood, unto this day.
Then was fulfilled that which was spoken by Jeremiah the prophet, saying, And they took the thirty pieces of silver, the price of him that was valued, whom they of the children of Israel did value;
And gave them for the potter's field, as the Lord appointed me.

(Matthew 27:1–10)

I

Today, in the middle of the Atlantic Ocean, lies an island called Potter's Field. There, on fresh winds, the foul blood of New York City is transported. For that acre of blood affords the only *columbarium* for the ashes of the unclaimed, derelict dead of the city – for unidentified murdered bodies, for paupers, and now, for the new category of destitution: those who die of AIDS in the *triage* wards of the city hospitals.

New York City, 16 May 1992: the body of my love has been taken to Potter's Field, taken outside the walls of the city; beyond the ramparts, his ungodly ashes will have been scattered upon that collective grave for the unreprieved – without community, without commemoration and hence without end.

Yet, by decreeing this merciless disposal, the city reclaims his soul – and mine. Without proper burial and mourning, he cannot rest, and I cannot recommence. He belonged body and soul, in his manner of living and in his manner of dying, to the *polis*. According to Plato, the tripartite soul, which consists of reason, appetite and *thumos*, the principle of high spirits, ally or enemy of reason and desire, corresponds to the inner constitution and inner warfare of the city. We always knew we owed the purity *and* the contamination of our love to the splendour and the misery of that city – to its laws and to its anarchies.

Since mourning refuses to become me, should I then follow the wife of Phocion,[1] and, with a trusted woman companion to keep guard, steal away from the city to that abominable and abominated island, abyss of the city itself, there to gather the cursed ashes of my love, to give them a tomb, a resting place in my own body, to release his soul, and mine, too, from the agon of interminable wandering? To inaugurate by consuming his ashes the long-overdue work of mourning, in a pitiable reversal of that work which, in the normal course of events, takes place within the city? Then to incorporate the dead one into one's own body and soul is to refuse the work of mourning, to refuse, in melancholy, to let go.

If all meaning is mourning, and mourning (or absence) must become our norm (or presence) for there to be morning (dawning or future), and *not* interminable dying, then all meaning and all mourning belong to the city, to the *polis*.

In Poussin's painting *Gathering the Ashes of Phocion*, Phocion's wife bends down outside the boundary wall of Athens to scoop up his ashes, in an integral *gestus* which gathers her own soul and body into this act of perfect devotion. The tension of political defiance and the fear of being discovered appear only in the taut *contrapposto* of the woman servant, which is juxtaposed to the utter vulnerability of the stooping wife. Arising above the two foregrounded figures is a combined land- and townscape of classical magnificence with gleaming temples and municipal buildings, perfect displays of the architectural orders, which convey no hint of malign intent. Yet Phocion's condemnation and manner of dying were the result of tyranny temporarily usurping good rule in the city. Does Poussin's representation, taken from Plutarch's *Life of Phocion* oppose pure, individual love to impure, worldly injustice?[2]

To participate body and soul in our relationships and in our self-identity in the work and in the undoing of the city and yet to be deprived of, or to refuse, the work of mourning has *political consequences*. It tempts us to oppose pure, gratuitous love to the injustice of the world; to see ourselves as suffering but good, and the city as evil. As a result, we are no longer able to chant with Antigone: 'Because we suffer we acknowledge we have erred.' This opposing of our cherished good to public ill denies the third term which gives meaning to both judgements – the just city and the just act, the just woman and the just man. In Poussin's painting *this transcendent but mournable justice* is configured, its absence given presence, in the architectural perspective which frames and focuses the enacted justice of Phocion's wife, her response to the implied act of injustice by the City. To see the built forms themselves as ciphers of the unjust city would be to perpetuate endless dying and endless tyranny – unending disaster.

In Blanchot's *œuvre* death and dying are interminable; he invents a new mode of mourning, which does not involve working through, or acceptance of, the inevitable negation by which meaning is secured against an always absent world. Mourning in Blanchot becomes *poiesis* or 'making', which is the elegy to Orpheus, hymn and witness to incessant *désœuvrement* – Being without work. For Blanchot, the letting go of mourning is not for morning or dawning, for commencing, but for the endless reality of ending, which our workful beginnings can only, and must always, violate.

Blanchot's immense and multiform elegy to death as *désœuvrement* not only takes place outside the city walls, but takes place beyond the cosmos: it is the writing of the disaster – *dés-astres*: the stars torn out – beyond the music of the intelligent, ordered heavenly spheres, and hence beyond any conceivable, intramundane political order. Even less does it concern the tripartite soul, analogue of the city, whose reason, appetite and high spirit (*thumos*), engaged in work and in mourning, have no access to unbounded, incessant dying.

No work, no city, no soul – this *aberrant* mourning of endless ending is, nevertheless, *a work of the city and of the soul*. It is a mourning which, like mine, has been banished beyond the city walls; there it has substituted its pain, its agon, its barren and lyrical gestures, its reflections in poetry and prose, *its writing*, for *the justice which it has vowed to renounce*.

II

Lazare, veni foras (Lazarus, come forth)[3]

(John 11:43)

This rebirth of Lazarus, this miracle of faith – Christ's and Lazarus' – this difficult return to difficult life, is presented by Blanchot as the quintessence of 'the murder', 'the immense hecatomb', which summons 'the dark cadaverous reality from its primordial depths and in exchange gave it only the life of the mind . . . and not the intimacy of the unrevealed'.[4] Language, according to Blanchot, brings into being by negation, but 'the torment of language is what it lacks because of the necessity that it be the lack of precisely this. It cannot even name it.' It can be no accident that Blanchot selects Lazarus' return *from* death as a return *to* death, in two senses: by being named, something is murdered; by coming forth, Lazarus returns to 'the impossibility of dying'. In these two senses, Blanchot focuses on what Lazarus loses and to what he is restored, but not on the difficulty to which he miraculously, *non-naturally*, accedes: the supernatural difficulty of natural life.

What is this *impossibility* of dying – in living, in language and in literature?

The proverbial formula: 'as soon as someone begins to live, he is old enough to die', is indeed impressive in as much as it distributes mortal possibility uncertainly the whole length of life, in an unexpected relation with duration. All the same, through this formula, there is still a facile relation between life and death: dying remains a possibility – a power that life attributes to itself or that is verified in it and confirms itself in death – determined in this way between two terms (one begins to die with this beginning that is life's debut – the expulsion of birth being metaphorically recovered as an overwhelming encounter with a sort of death –, and one ends by that which finishes life, cadaveric equality or, to go further to the ultimate repose, the entropic equality of the universe). But perhaps dying has no determined relation to living, to the reality, the presence of 'life'. A pure fantasy perhaps, a mockery that no trace would make material in the present, or again a madness that would overwhelm being from top to bottom and, at the same time, would only reach us as an imperceptible neurosis, escaping any observation, invisible because too visible. Thus perhaps to write: a writing that would not be a possibility of speech (no more than dying is a possibility of life) – a murmur nonetheless, a madness nonetheless that would play at the silent surface of language).[5]

If to die (*mourir*) is not a *possibility*, facility or power, then to propose that to die is *impossible* is to rejoin and reaffirm the metaphysical opposition of possibility and actuality which is putatively under erasure. To propose that to die is *repetition* falls to the totalizing, numerical, serial connotation of 'repetition' which Blanchot discerns even in Nietzsche's Eternal Return.[6] To hear that it is *forbidden* to die is to hear 'constantly in us, not as a call of obligation to live, but as the voice itself breaking each time the commandment'. The horror of the death camps and of the millions dying 'makes each dying guilty even when never more innocent'. 'Possibility', 'repetition', 'commandment', 'event' – language is dissolved in the attempt to name this one thing on which it depends, and which it therefore cannot name or describe.[7]

In italics: *'To die – dying in the cold and dissolution of the Outside: always outside oneself as outside life'*.[8] Can this discourse of *externality* escape any more than any other the twin paradoxes, one, of collapsing back into its metaphysical partner (the Inside, warmth, immanence) so that, once again, dying becomes the logical and existential double of living; or two, the destruction of actuality which must take place for the name to arise? In addition to the difficulty of naming and situating *dying*, the difficulty of thinking *dying* appertains to its temporality, its futurity, or the tense of its verb, since it cannot be simply past or perfected – that would be 'to be dead (*être-mort*)'.[9] All verb tenses are gathered in the impossibility of this thinking of return: 'that which has happened without traces and which it would be always necessary to wait for from the empty infinity of the future'.[10] This formula could equally well be taken as a parable of *the kingdom of God*, for the kingdom, too, has happened, is happening and is always yet to happen. Or, as John Henry Newman proposed, in an alleviation of verb tension that distinguishes the Saints from Christ: 'The Saints are ever failing from the earth and Christ is all but coming'.

Death delivers from death – Perhaps only from dying. – Dying is this lightness within any liberty from which nothing can liberate. – It is this no doubt that is frightening in death, contrary to the analyses of antiquity: death does not have within it that with which to allay death; it is thus as if it survived itself, in the powerlessness of being that it disperses, without this powerlessness assuming the task of incompletion – unaccomplishment – proper or improper to dying. – The exteriority of being, whether it takes the name of death, of dying, of the relation to the other, or perhaps of speech when it has not folded itself up in speaking ways, does not allow any relation (either of identity or of alterity) with itself. – With exteriority, speech perhaps gives itself absolutely and as absolutely multiple, but in such a way that it cannot develop itself in words: always already lost, without use and even such that that which loses itself in it (the essence of loss that it would measure) does not claim, by a reversal, that something – a gift, an absolute gift: the gift of speech – is magnified or designated in the loss itself. – I do not have therefore the right to say anything. – Certainly, no right at all.[11]

The second half of this paragraph provides guidance for the first – unappeased, ever-surviving, impotent, dispersing, the being of death is captured by epithets which are normally employed as its contraries (death is appeasement, non-survival, capacity, concentration of an event of nothingness) in order to erase the logic of relationship with itself, of identity and alterity, which must be implied in any idea of self-relation by which something is identified. Yet sharing the marker of 'exteriority', speech (but not death or the relation to the other), is only given absolutely (that is, without relation or self-identity), not as something which will be developed in speech, but instead as an absolute loss in relation to which speech cannot be understood as the contrary – as the magnified gain. This prompts the abrupt, intrusive, first-person confession in italics that therefore 'I' do not have the right to say anything (for nothing can be claimed by right or developed in speech – it can only be hymned in writing), emphasized by the insistent '*Certainly, no right*'.

Two crimes are indicated by the strange incursion of litigious terms: murder and illegitimate right. The use of a dialectic of *terms* in a double negation – *not* the magnified contrary of loss and gift – cannot be justified as the expression of the in*termi*nable, hence the exclamation '*I do not have therefore the right to say anything.*' The idea of death can only be insinuated by referring to its contrary characteristics – unappeasement, survival, impotence – and in so doing advertising *the murder*. For we could not understand even inappropriate epithets and the substantive to which they point without the logic of self-alterity and identity, without, that is, committing the murder which bestowed on Lazarus 'only the life of the mind and . . . not the intimacy of the unrevealed'. Dying and death, even in the guarded ratiocination and lyricism of this writing, have been usurped by spurious right in being spoken of, and murdered by being thematized. Moreover, these crimes are committed in an active and reflexive labour of form.

'Exteriority' is hymned under many names in *The Space of Literature*: 'the gaze of Orpheus', 'the original experience', and several sets of non-contrary doubles: 'the other night', 'the other day', 'the other death', 'two versions of the imaginary'. All these *murders*, these illegitimate *rights*, presuppose *the disaster* – they evince the disturbed, gnostic (I use *gnostic* and not *mystical* advisedly), the *gnostic* relation to law and to the idea of law which comes with perennial expulsion from the city, and now with contemporaneous destruction in the death-camps, from surviving and not surviving outside the city; at the same time, the inconsistent introduction of litigious terms, such as 'murder' and 'right', shows that the memory of the law of the city has not faded so completely that its juridical actions cannot be invoked.

III

Orpheus is not Dionysus.[12] Orphism was 'a reformulation and reformation of Dionysiac religion', even while it returned to a type of religion more primitive than prevailing Olympianism. Orphism and Dionysian religion involve two different types of immortality and of individuation. Dionysian immortality focuses on the annual recurrence of earthly life; Orphic immortality focuses on the periodicity of the heavens from which the individual soul descends: it is preoccupied with the purification and the salvation of the individual soul throughout the round of incarnations. Dionysian faith has a sense of 'easily and perpetually renewed communion'; Orphism knows dualism, the separation of the bounded and solitary soul in a difficult relation to its others – its body, God, nature, the cosmos. Above all, Orphic immortality of the individual soul has forgotten the Dionysian knowledge of there being no life without death, 'that there is only one life which dies and is reborn in every shape of existence'.

The untitled preface to *The Space of Literature* directs the reader to the piece entitled 'The gaze of Orpheus', the centrifuge of the work. *Metaphysically*, Orpheus' turning to gaze at Eurydice is his advent to 'the other death' – not the worldly death of rest, silence and end, but death without end, the ordeal of the end's absence, which is the meaning of Eurydice.[13] *Existentially*, this piece commends Orpheus' 'mistake' in gazing at Eurydice, that is, to risk everything, to ruin the work, 'to interrupt the incessant by discovering it'.[14] It is this sacrifice of the work which makes the work, not as a dialectical gamble, but as the risk that cannot be written without returning to logism, and removing the risk. *For writing*, this experience of 'the other death' can only be approached through art which it consecrates: ruins and makes. 'In this contrarity are situated the essence of writing, the difficulty in the experience and inspiration's leap.'[15] This inadvertently captures the meaning of the Holy – beyond contraries and their dialectic. *For Blanchot* to chose Orphic death as the emblem of 'the other death' is not neutral: it conveys an otherness which is the original separation of the individual soul. Although Orpheus descends into the womb of the earth, and although animals and even trees follow his subsequent song, all seek immortality which, singular and salvific, pertains to the individual soul. If Orphic immortality is to stand for 'the impossibility of dying', ineluctably it bears with it the contours of the separate, solitary, difficult soul, searching for the elixir of life.

'The original experience' would seem to deny this individual Orphic immortality by stressing the anonymity and impersonality of 'the other death'.[16] Death as ending, civilization, achievement, the risk of the day, is contrasted with the call or command to lose death as power and possibility, to die 'other than [oneself], at the level of the neutrality and impersonality of the eternal They'.[17] To embrace a failure which is not no success, but, in beginning all over again, is 'precisely the *impossibility* of being for the first time'.[18] The work of art begins – not in the worldly sense of negating to signify or form – but by ruining the kingdom: 'It ruins the origin by returning to it the errant immensity of directionless eternity.'[19] The work is a leap by virtue of its suspension: 'it hovers between death as the possibility of understanding and death as the horror of impossibility'.[20]

Yet the use of existential terms such as 'leap', 'risk', 'ruin' and 'hovering' brings in Orphic connotations of individual salvation. The image of hovering between the two deaths is comparable to Kierkegaard's *teleological suspension of the ethical*. In *Fear and Trembling*, the ethical is bracketed for the sake of the test of faith, the test of the risk: if the leap is taken, then the ethical is instantaneously resumed – this is the meaning of 'the knight of faith', who lives the sublime in the pedestrian. If the leap is not taken because of the preference for infinite pain and resignation, then the ethical is lost to the suspended soul – this is the meaning of 'the knight of resignation', who dwells in the romance of the non-ethical. Blanchot's use of 'hovering' implies suspension in the sense of *wavering* rather than in the sense of *the return to the ethical*. This is why he employs contraries whose dialectical relation he must constantly deny: two deaths; not two deaths. There is no return to the ethical in Blanchot; there is only the endless distress of the poet, who 'dwells in God's default'.[21] Yet the ethical is there, or he could not assert that his contraries are not contraries. Blanchot's double negations display the distraught soul of loss and resignation, who will not return from 'the other death' to the city or to its work of mourning.

IV

For men it is hard not to look at dead bodies.[22]

(Plato, *Republic* IV.439e–440e)

Let us look death in the face. In Plato's *Republic* the desire to look at dead bodies lying outside the city wall illustrates the relation of *thumos*, the principle of high spirit, the third part of the soul, that with which we feel anger, to reason and appetite or desire. Socrates recalls the case of Leontius, son of Aglaion, who could not, as he came up from Piraeus, resist looking at the corpses lying outside the North Wall, the place of public execution. Leontius felt both desire and

> repugnance and aversion, and . . . for a time he resisted and veiled his head, but overpowered . . . by his desire, with wide staring eyes, he rushed up to the corpses and cried [to his eyes] 'There, you wretches, take your fill of the fine spectacle!'

Socrates and Glaucon confront the dilemma whether the principle of anger (*thumos*) fights against desire and forms a third to reason and desire, or whether it is indistinguishable from one of them. The case selected for the debate by Socrates involves the most extreme desecration of death in the shameless gaze reported, which occurs, equally, in shame. The gaze arouses the most acute struggle between the three parts of the soul: *thumos* does not constrain the desire or aid rational scruple, but accentuates all three to a pitch of internecine warfare. Plato offers this battle within the soul as the analogy of the city – its constitution and its disharmonies.

In 'The two versions of the imaginary', Blanchot contrasts the image as cadaverous remains, 'the absolute neutrality of death',[23] with the image as 'life-giving negation, the ideal operation by which man, capable of negating nature, raises it to signification'.[24] The cadaverous 'resemblance' is an image without difference, that is, without an otherness to itself which is self-identity: therefore, 'he resembles *himself*'.[25] This is the corpse apart from its being mourned, its being-in-mourning: 'our mourning, the care we take of the dead and *all the prerogatives of our former passions*, since they can no longer know their direction, fall back upon us, return towards us' (my italic).[26] This response to the cadaver outside mourning is equally without passion; it approaches Stoic *apatheia* – passionless-ness – in a world understood as cosmic, not political, beyond the warfare within and between cities. 'Eventually we have to put a term to the interminable. We do not cohabit with the dead for fear of seeing *here* collapse into the unfathomable *nowhere*. . . . And so the dear departed is conveyed into another place'; this 'unsituatable' *'here lies'* is 'the anonymous and impersonal place par excellence'.[27]

Between Plato's interested, highest spirit, aroused by the desire to gaze at dead bodies on the boundary of the city, and Blanchot's indif-ferent, least spirit, drained of passion at the image of the imposing cadaver in unsituatable space, *the disaster* has taken place – the disaster which has made Blanchot vow to renounce all passion, all feeling, all suffering, at the sight of the beloved dead. This leads him to banish the city to the discourse of the *term* – the measure and the monument – yet the term is voided of the difficulty of justice in the city. This 'worldly place' is said to afford a 'level of ambiguity', the third level to the image qua power to control things in their absence through fiction and image, and the image qua passivity, what he calls 'the passion of indifference'.[28] This passionless gazing at the strange beauty of the dead bodies of those beloved and murdered is *the aber-rant mourning*, the mourning *désœuvré*, of this hymn to death.

V

Banished from the city – in exile, hovering, errant – the law of Blanchot's hymn to death has, however, a name: *the absence of the book*. This absence of the book is introduced by contrast with 'the civilization of the book', and approached via the Bible, in which the logos is inscribed as law *and* language is taken back to its origin.[29] This would give the idea of the absence of the book a transcendental structure and argument, according to which the absence of the book is 'the prior deterioration of the book . . . with reference to the space in which it is inscribed; the preliminary dying of the book'.[30] This disin-tegrating a priori is radicalized so that it does not express a transcen-dental condition but *a transcendent gnosis of the book* – that is, a transcendence which is not the contrary of instance or of immanence, but which, beyond those contraries, is Godhead, white and invisible flame,[31] holy and apart writing, from which the demiurgic emanation of the law '*saves us . . . A salvation* that introduces us to knowledge.'[32]

This Kabbalistic understanding of the breaking of the first tablets of the law is made explicit: it inaugurates the distinction between the oral Torah and the written Torah, both given to Moses on Sinai in the Rabbinic tradition, which the Kabbalah appropriates antinomically by claiming that the written law itself is an oral commentary on the mystical letters of the original, inaccessible writing: 'Writing, (pure) exteriority, alien to every relationship of presence and to all legality'.[33] Blanchot refers to this Kabbalistic tradition of the invisible writing and its visible interpretation, colourless flame and black fire, by proposing to conduct 'a future experiment of writing',[34] which would tempt us to approach 'an exteriority without limitation', to contact 'otherness itself', 'a severity', 'an austerity', 'the burning of a parching breeze'.[35] This theurgic *gnosis* opposed to the law, which it sees as idolatrous, tempts us to be consumed by the fire of the Godhead.

Blanchot concludes or halts his monumental, interminable *The Infinite Conversation* with this gnostic transcendence *without the prophets*, this antinomian gaze into divine invisibility *without prophetic justice*. He has presented a mimesis of the *Trauerspiel*, the mourning play, of Jewish exilic history: those periods of expulsion, pogrom and holocaust when even the prophetic justice of the Bible, the portable fatherland, rediscovered whenever the normal insecurities of Rabbinic Jewish life are intensified, can offer no consolation. Under these traumatized conditions, forsaken by the city and in turn forsaking the Torah, Jewish communities have seen the law itself and its traditional commentary as idolatry. In Blanchot, the covenant between God and Israel becomes an unavowable community, for both have succumbed to the disaster.

VI

The disaster ruins everything while leaving everything intact.[36]

Through patience, I take upon myself the relation to the Other of the disaster which does not allow me to assume it, or even to remain myself in order to undergo it. Through patience, all relation between myself and a patient self is lost.[37]

Passivity, the contrary of activity; such is the ever-restricted field of our reflections.[38]

Passivity, 'the hidden face of humanity',[39] advent of, access and response to, the disaster, can be seen as having been prepared philosophically by Blanchot in the long essay in italics which concludes *La Part du feu* (1949): 'Literature and the right to death'. This preparation takes the form of an engagement with activity, consciousness, learning and objectivity in Hegel's *Phenomenology of Spirit*. Blanchot sets the engagement in the context of the section of the *Phenomenology* called 'The Spiritual-animal kingdom, deceit or the matter in hand' ('Das geistige Tierreich und der Betrug oder die Sache selbst'). In this section, Hegel expounds the violence of business and affairs when the apparently communal universality of action ('the matter in hand' or 'the thing itself') serves solely ruthless, individual ends, a deception which is not truly ethical but is the way ethical substance is approached and learnt. Blanchot contrasts the meaning of the thing itself (*la chose même*) as 'civilizing power' with the meaning of meaning, 'the absolute concern for truth' which depends on 'an incapacity to act in a real way'.[40] Blanchot's movement from the civil to the absolute may be discerned, therefore, as the movement from the historically structured injustice of the spiritual-animal kingdom to the unworked passivity, sublime and non-sublimated, which is developed in *The Writing of the Disaster*. His *œuvre* may be shown to be in the grasp of impersonal meanings and powers in a sense which he is unable to acknowledge within his own transcendent reduction of the meaning of meaning.

The engagement with Hegel's notion of experience cannot, in effect, take place. In Hegel 'the *disparity* between concept and actuality which lies in [the] essence [of the action of the individual consciousness] is *learnt* by consciousness in its work' (second italic mine),[41] that is, there is objectivity or objective reality which is learnt by the way in which work as the matter in hand, the thing itself, emerges as *initially* the concern of the individual – her business or affair – and so deceives others who become involved that they too may participate in it.[42] First, deceived, others hurry 'along like flies to freshly poured milk', only to discover that the individual is concerned with the matter or thing itself, 'not as an *object* but as his own *affair*'.[43] Subsequently, all parties learn that they are affected and are invited to participate. It is the coming together of these two experiences that make the thing itself *ethical substance* and the consciousness of it *ethical consciousness*.[44]

Hegel distinguishes this learning of the actuality and objectivity of ethical substance by means of the work, or the thing itself, from 'the Thing of sense certainty and perception' – the thing which emerged from the sheer negating and distancing power of naming and language. The work 'now acquires its significance through self-consciousness and through it alone; on this rests the distinction between a Thing and a cause of the Thing itself. A movement corresponding to that from [sense-] certainty to perception will run its course here.'[45] Blanchot's argument covers *the same two contrasted movements, but in reverse order.* Where Hegel moves from naming to action to ethical substance, Blanchot moves from action and the thing itself (*la chose même*) to the name (*la chose*) and its ungraspable remnant, and thence to the absolute meaning of meaning.

Blanchot starts from Hegel's exposition of the work as conscious action, but he presents *the deception* as the worldliness of the work *per se*,[46] and not as learning the outcome of the originally individual concern when others become involved in it as their work. The work is 'no business but [the writer's] own . . . its indifference mingles hypocritically with everyone's passion'.[47] Here the flies have hallucinated the freshly poured milk according to their own, individual affairs. The work is not universal in actuality or deception; it is impersonal – it is substituted for the inability to act, the ruin of action in the guise of the negative act of transformation.[48] 'Stoicism', 'scepticism' and the 'unhappy consciousness', which in Hegel stand for various kinds of misrecognition of the work and desire of others thematized as negative relations to 'the world', are here various forms of submission to the unworking of the world which is the work.[49] Action remains solely as the temptation to move back from the unreality of the work to realizing it; from the space outside history and civilization to revolutionary action in history (the state, law, etc.); to claim the absolute freedom of the Revolution, 'revolutionary action is in every respect analogous to action as embodied in literature'.[50]

For Blanchot, the challenge is to move from revolutionary death, described by Hegel as 'the coldest and meanest of all deaths with no more significance than cutting off the head of a cabbage or swallowing a mouthful of water',[51] to the impossibility of dying which is the real dread of man; to move from a frenzy of revolutionary control, through the life which endures death and maintains itself in it,[52] that is, the murder of naming, to the death 'which does not end anything', the meaning of meaning.[53] To effect this movement, Blanchot turns from expounding the work of literature according to the analogy of revolutionary action to the *status* of language itself as naming, to the analogies of destroying 'woman', 'flower', 'Lazarus'. He turns from *the thing itself* to *the thing*:

When we speak, we gain control over things with satisfying ease. I say, 'This woman', and she is immediately available to me, I push her away, I bring her close, she is everything I want her to be, she becomes the place in which the most surprising of transformations occur and actions unfold: speech is life's ease and security. We can't do anything with an object that has no name.[54]

To whom is Blanchot speaking? Does she not speak too? She serves the contrast between language as manipulation and words as things (*la chose*), as 'one moment in the universal anonymity'. Nothing, however, can be learnt from the disparity between the evocation of her name and her actuality, *her desire and work*, because she is not a self-relation whose middle term is equally the other's self-relation, his desire and work. The ruin of love, with its always attendant risk of loss, follows from the ruin of action and the impossibility of death in Blanchot. 'Literature and the right to death' yields loveless, endless dying, which remains within the fixed history of the spiritual-animal kingdom, with no disparity and hence no actuality of the spiritual-political kingdom.

VII

> However, to watch and to keep awake, over the immeasurable absence, is necessary, it is necessary unceasingly, because what has recommenced from this end (Israel, all of us), is marked by this end from which we will not finish awakening.[55]

The disaster is both 'imminent' and 'immemorial';[56] our access to it demands patience and passivity,[57] which 'separate us from all forms of daily activity',[58] *and* the disaster is 'the concentration camp, annihilation camp, figures where the invisible is forever made visible'.[59] A third meaning of the disaster is announced, justified and fixed in this writing: the devastation of knowledge by responsibility.

> Concentration camps, annihilation camps, figures where the invisible is forever made visible. All the features of a civilization laid bare. . . . The meaning of work (*travail*) is the destruction of work in and through work/ work ceasing to be [the] manner of living and becoming [the] manner of dying. Knowledge which goes so far as to accept the horrible in order to know it reveals the horror of knowledge, the squalor of coming to know, the discrete complicity which maintains it in a relation with what is insupportable in power. I think of this young prisoner of Auschwitz (he

suffered the worst, led his family to the crematorium, hanged himself; *saved* – how can one say: *saved*? – at the last moment – he was exempted from contact with dead bodies, but when the SS shot someone, he was obliged to hold the head of the victim so that the bullet could be more easily lodged in the neck). When asked how he had been able to bear it, he is said to have answered that he 'had observed the bearing of men before death'. I will not believe it. As Lewenthal wrote to us whose notes were found buried near a crematorium: 'The truth was always more atrocious, more tragic than what will be said about it.' Saved at the last instant that young man of whom I speak was every time forced to live and relive, each time frustrated of his own death, exchanging it for the death of everyone. His response ('I observed the bearing of men . . .') was not a response; he could not respond. What remains is that, constrained by an impossible question, he could find no other alibi than in the search for knowledge, the claimed dignity of knowledge: that ultimate propriety which we believe will be accorded us by knowledge. And how, in effect, can one accept not to know? We read books on Auschwitz. The wish of all in the camps, the last wish: know what has happened, do not forget, and at the same time, never will you know.[60]

I will not believe it. In this passage, knowledge is said to have been offered in place of response, in place of responsibility. The dignity of knowledge is thereby shown to be obscene. First, Blanchot blames the victim: he should compare the story reconstructed by Christopher Browning of the reserve German policemen, who accepted the commission to shoot Jews, men, women and children, in the neck without any compulsion or prior suffering.[61] Second, the statement, 'I observed the bearing of men before death' can be heard as the pathos of an unbearable witness. 'Observing' is the pure passivity which is pure activity; 'the bearing' is the one moment of possible dignity witnessed *before* that dying: how the men held themselves, mind and body and soul, in the face of certain destruction. Third, the last wish of the victims, 'know what has happened, do not forget, and at the same time, never will you know', does not command a contradiction, but it requires a *work*, a working through, that combination of self-knowledge and action which will not blanch before its complicities in power – *activity beyond activity*, not passivity beyond passivity. For power is not necessarily tyranny, but that can only be discovered by taking the risk of coming to learn it – by acting, reflecting on the outcome, and then initiating further action.

What is this response Blanchot would oppose to knowledge?

Responsible: that qualifies in general . . . the man of action and success. But now responsibility – my responsibility for others, for everyone, without reciprocity – is displaced, belongs no longer to conscience, is not an activating reflection put to work, not even a duty which imposes from without and from within. My responsibility for the Other presupposes an overturning such that it can only be marked by a change in status of me, a change in time and perhaps a change in language. Responsibility which withdraws me from my order – perhaps from all orders and from order itself – and, separating me from myself (from the me that is master, power, from the free, speaking subject) discovers the other *in place* of me, requires that I answer for absence, for passivity, for the impossibility of being responsible – to which this responsibility without measure has already devoted me by making me accountable and by discounting me.[62]

This paradox destroys the integrity of the subject, subjectivity, the person, will, resolution, reflective action, and even involuntary action, any relation of positing.[63] It exposes me to 'the passivity without name', by disengaging 'the me from me, the singular from the individual, the subjective from the subject, the non-conscious from the conscious and unconscious'.[64] 'Declared responsible for dying (for all dying), I can no longer appeal to any ethics, to any experience, to any practice whatsoever', but to

(perhaps) a word of writing . . . in order that this incomprehensible word be understood in its disastrous heaviness without either understanding it or bearing it. That is why responsibility is disastrous – the responsibility never relieves the other (never relieves me of him) and makes us mute of the word which we owe him.[65]

This hyperbole amounts to the refusal of the work of mourning – refusal of entering into any experience which *comes to learn* that will, action, reflection and passivity have consequences for others and for oneself which may not be anticipated and can never be completely anticipated; which *comes to learn* its unintended complicity in the use and abuse of power; and hence to redraw, *again and again*, the measures, the bonding and boundaries between me and me, subject and subjectivity, singular and individual, non-conscious and unconscious. This is *activity beyond activity* in three senses: activity emergent from reassessment of the actions of the *initially* abstract person; activity initiated subsequent to the act of imposing *initially* a pure and hence destructive, totalitarian universal. The *work* of these experiences bears the meaning of meaning – the relinquishing *and taking up again* of activity which requires the fullest acknowledgement of active complicity. The work of mourning is difficult but not interminable; beginnings may be made in the middle.

This work of mourning is the spiritual-political kingdom – the difficulty sustained, the transcendence of *actual* justice. Though tyrants rule the city, we understand that we, too, must constantly negotiate the *actuality* of being tyrannical. As I search for the ashes on Potter's Field, as I follow the urgent and haunting voice of our dead from Auschwitz, to know and yet not to know, to be known, to mourn, I incorporate that actual justice in *activity beyond activity*. I would not ruin it for ever.

NOTES

1 Phocion was a virtuous Athenian general and statesman, who, like Socrates, was sentenced to die by drinking hemlock, and, in addition, refused burial within the walls of Athens.
2 See *The Age of Alexander: Nine Greek Lives*, trans. Ian Scott-Kilvert (London: Penguin, 1973), pp. 218–51; and Walter Friedlander, *Poussin: A New Approach* (London: Thames & Hudson, 1970), p. 176, fig. 74, plate 39.
3 Maurice Blanchot, 'Literature and the right to death', in *The Gaze of Orpheus and Other Literary Essays*, trans. Lydia Davis, ed. and with an Afterword by P. Adams Sitney (Barrytown, N.Y.: Station Hill Press, 1981), p. 45.
4 Ibid., pp. 42, 45.
5 Maurice Blanchot, *The Step Not Beyond,* trans. and with an Introduction by Lycette Nelson (Albany: State University of New York Press, 1992), p. 95.
6 Ibid., pp. 12, 21, 37, 96, 110.
7 Ibid., pp. 5–6.
8 Ibid., p. 97.
9 Ibid., p. 110.
10 Ibid. Translation amended.
11 Ibid., p. 132. Translation amended.
12 The comparison of Orphic and Dionysian religion developed in this paragraph is taken from F. M. Cornford, *From Religion to Philosophy: A Study of the Origins of Western Speculation* (1912) (Brighton: Harvester, 1980), pp. 163, 195, 179, 180, 196.
13 Maurice Blanchot, *The Space of Literature*, trans. and with an Introduction by Ann Smock (Lincoln and London: University of Nebraska Press, 1982), p. 172.
14 Ibid., p. 175.
15 Ibid., p. 176. Translation amended.

16 Ibid., p. 241.
17 Ibid., pp. 237–42.
18 Ibid., p. 243.
19 Ibid., p. 244.
20 Ibid.
21 Ibid., p. 246.
22 Compare Michael Platt, 'Looking at bodies', *International Journal of Philosophy*, 3 (1979), pp. 87–90.
23 Blanchot, *The Space of Literature*, p. 259.
24 Ibid., p. 260. Translation amended.
25 Ibid., p. 258.
26 Ibid., p. 257.
27 Ibid., p. 259.
28 Ibid., p. 263.
29 Blanchot, *The Gaze of Orpheus*, p. 151.
30 Ibid.
31 Ibid., p. 155.
32 Ibid., p. 158.
33 Ibid., p. 156.
34 Ibid., p. 153.
35 Ibid., pp. 157–8.
36 Blanchot, *The Writing of the Disaster*, trans. Ann Smock (Lincoln and London: University of Nebraska Press, 1986), p. 1. Translation amended.
37 Ibid., p. 14. Translation amended.
38 Ibid., p. 15.
39 Ibid., p. 31.
40 Blanchot, *The Gaze of Orpheus*, p. 62.
41 G.W.F. Hegel, *Phenomenology of Spirit*, trans. A.V. Miller (Oxford: Clarendon Press, 1977), p. 244.
42 Ibid., p. 250.
43 Ibid., p. 251.
44 Ibid., p. 253.
45 Ibid., p. 246.
46 Blanchot, *The Gaze of Orpheus*, p. 28.
47 Ibid., p. 30.
48 Ibid., pp. 35–6.
49 Ibid., p. 37
50 Ibid., p. 38.
51 Ibid., p. 39, citing Hegel, *Phenomenology*, p. 360.
52 Ibid., p. 59, also citing Hegel.
53 Ibid., p. 58.
54 Ibid., p. 41.
55 Blanchot, *The Writing of the Disaster*, p. 58. Translation amended.
56 Ibid., pp. 1, 3.
57 Ibid., p. 14.
58 Blanchot, *The Space of Literature*, p. 127.
59 Blanchot, *The Writing of the Disaster*, p. 81.
60 Ibid., pp. 81–2. Translation amended.
61 'German memory, judicial interrogation, and historical reconstruction:

writing perpetrator history from postwar testimony', in *Probing the Limits of Representation: Nazism and the 'Final Solution'*, ed. Saul Friedlander (Cambridge, Mass.: Harvard University Press, 1992), pp. 22–36.

62 Blanchot, *The Writing of the Disaster*, p. 25. Translation amended.
63 Ibid., pp. 25–6.
64 Ibid., p. 26. Translation amended.
65 Ibid., p. 27. Translation amended.

12 A Letter

Maurice Blanchot

24 décembre 92

Cher Roger Laporte,

Merci de m'avoir envoyé ce texte (et merci de l'avoir retrouvé). Je n'en avais gardé aucun souvenir et doutais qu'il eût jamais été écrit.

Je vais tout de suite au pire. Qu'en mars 1942, on nomme Maurras (alors, en plus, que rien n'appelle ici un tel nom), c'est détestable et sans excuse. Je sais bien qu'il ne s'agit pas du personnage malfaisant de l'époque, mais du lointain disciple d'Auguste Comte, qui – trente ans plus tôt – se recommande, à l'imitation de son maître, d'une observation des faits sociaux, étrangère à tout dogmatisme, et proche de la science ou d'une certaine science.

Il reste que le nom de Maurras est une tache indélébile et l'expres-sion du déshonneur. Je ne me suis jamais approché de cet homme, à quelque époque que ce soit, et toujours tenu à l'écart de l'Action Française, même quand Gide par curiosité allait le voir.

Que dire encore? Ce texte, non simple, voire embrouillé, a le mérite de rester en dehors du temps et en tout cas de n'apporter nul secours ni espérance au régime qui règne encore et déjà s'écroule.

Maurice Blanchot

P.S. On me suggère – vous connaissez la censure: celui qui est désigné ici, ce n'est pas le personnage encore puissant, c'est le posi-tiviste médiocre condamné par l'Eglise.

24 December 92

Dear Roger Laporte,

Thank you for having sent me the article (and thank you for locating it).[1] I had no memory of it and doubted whether it had ever been written.

Let me go immediately to the worst. That in March 1942 one pronounces the name of Maurras (particularly when nothing in the context demands a name such as this) is detestable and inexcusable.[2] Admittedly, the name is not a reference to the evil figure of those times, but the distant disciple of Auguste Comte, who, thirty years previously, recommends, imitating his master, the undogmatic observation of social reality, approximating to science or a certain kind of science.

The fact remains that the name of Maurras is an indelible stain and an expression of dishonour. I was never close to the man, during whatever period, and always kept my distance from Action Française, even when Gide out of curiosity would call to see him.

What else is there to say? This article, which is not straightforward, even confused, has the merit of remaining outside of time and at any event of giving neither comfort nor hope to the regime that is still in power and is already collapsing.

Maurice Blanchot

P.S. One suggestion made to me is this – you know what censorship is like: the man referred to here is not the figure who is still powerful, but the mediocre positivist condemned by the Church.

Translated by Leslie Hill

TRANSLATOR'S NOTES

1 It is worth recalling here the circumstances in which this letter came to be written. Some months prior to the International Conference on Blanchot held in London in January 1993, the draft programme for the conference was circulated, amongst others, to all intending contributors. In the programme, Jeffrey Mehlman had announced the title of his paper in the form of a cryptic summary: 'Pour Sainte-Beuve: Maurice Blanchot, March 10 1942'. The reference, as Mehlman's paper subsequently made clear, was to a little-known article by Blanchot, entitled 'La Politique de Sainte-Beuve', published in the *Journal des débats* for 10 March 1942, and never reprinted since. In the piece, Blanchot reviews Maxime Leroy's recent book, *La Politique de Sainte-Beuve*. Much of the article is in the form of a narrative summary recalling Sainte-Beuve's surprise at the July 1830 and February 1848 Revolutions and, despite his initial sympathy with them, his disappointment with the regimes they engendered; Blanchot ends with a critical evocation of Sainte-Beuve's endorsement of the coup d'état of Louis Napoleon in 1851 and his later profound disenchantment with politics. Shortly before the conference, intrigued by Mehlman's title, Roger Laporte contacted Blanchot for clarification. The letter printed here is part of the correspondence that ensued; written

before Mehlman's paper was delivered, it was read out by Laporte once Mehlman had finished speaking. Thanks are due to Maurice Blanchot for permission to publish the letter here and to Roger Laporte for supplying the text of the letter.

2 Charles Maurras (1868–1952), journalist, essayist and minor poet, was the most influential nationalist writer and polemicist of his generation; one of the founders of the French royalist movement, Action Française, he was probably best known as the editor of the daily paper of the same name from 1908. Though he was an early supporter of the positivism of Auguste Comte, Maurras's main political objective was to restore France to the values it had known before the French Revolution of 1789. In 1926 his works were placed on the Index by the Vatican for subordinating religion to politics. Anti-Semitic, anti-protestant, anti-democratic and anti-communist, Maurras was from 1940 till 1944 a staunch supporter of Vichy France and of Pétain; arrested in 1944, he was condemned in January 1945 to life imprisonment for collaboration.

13 Pour Sainte-Beuve

Maurice Blanchot, 10 March 1942

Jeffrey Mehlman

In response to a manuscript meditating his contributions to the 1930s fascist journal *Combat* and the distance he would have had to traverse from the margins of Action Française to the 'passivity beyond all passivity' of his later excursus on literature, Maurice Blanchot, in a letter of 1979, zeroed in on what he called an 'exemplary' error in the text I had sent him.[1] It turned on a footnote that quoted first Claude Roy on Blanchot's transition from 'Maurrassian nationalism' to the Resistance, then a passage from Léautaud's *Journal* in which Drieu la Rochelle – in May 1942 – is heard on the subject of the editorial assistance at the *NRF* (*Nouvelle Revue française*) he has received from Blanchot during a period in which he was overworked. Blanchot, in his letter to me, had eyes only for the Léautaud entry and insisted on setting the record straight. He recounted how he had in fact turned down an offer from Drieu to assume 'free' editorship of the journal (with Drieu himself retaining nominal authority as a safeguard). Blanchot, in consultation with Paulhan, first stalled, then came up with a list of 'great writers' for a new editorial committee. Given their anti-Nazi sympathies, Drieu declined. Thus Blanchot in his letter of 26 November 1979.

The most striking aspect of the letter was less the correction of Léautaud's second-hand account, about which I myself had expressed doubts, than its marginality to the principal subject of my essay. I wrote back to that effect, offering Blanchot a fantasy, whose vulgarity no doubt sealed the conclusion of our brief correspondence: a great work of fiction by Blanchot, which he would no doubt never write, registering the return of a 'phantasm' of February 1934 in the heart of May 1968. Its title, I suggested, might be *Les Evénements*. I have since come to the conclusion that Blanchot, in 1948, came quite close to having written just such a work – half in memory, half in anticipation – under the title of *Death Sentence*

(*L'Arrêt de mort*).² The principal elements of the demonstration are as follows: given the fact that *Le Très-haut* (1948) is, as Foucault intuited, Blanchot's idiosyncratic treatment of the Orestes myth, and given the fact that Louise, the Electra of that novel, reappears as the sister of J. in *Death Sentence*, mythological consistency would cast J. in the role of Iphigenia . . . condemned to death. Moreover, given the fact that the action of *Death Sentence* is said to coincide with the 'most sombre days of the Munich pact' in October 1938, the stalled mobilization of the French army at that time in anticipation of a bad war corresponds precisely to the situation of Agamemnon's army in the Greek myth. At which point the best candidate for superimposition on Iphigenia in 1938 would be precisely Blanchot's own investment in fascist ideology, embraced, no doubt, out of French nationalism, and now sacrificed, in the face of a looming fascist enemy, for the very same reason. Finally, if *Iphigenia at Aulis* is the subtext of the first (J.) segment of Blanchot's *récit*, one is hard put not to assign to the second (Nathalie) segment *Iphigenia Among the Taurians* as subtext. In 1948, Blanchot dreams a future return of Iphigenia 38, the receding fascist investment, in some ecstatic future encounter: Nathalie or May 1968. Philippe Ariès, moreover, has reported just such a fantasy – the anti-democratic right of the 1930s returning on the anti-parliamentarian left in May 1968.³

I recount my interpretation to underscore the oddity of its genesis: I had challenged Blanchot to write a book which I then proceeded to convince myself that he – thanks to my interpretation – had already written. My intention in these pages, however, is to return not to the utopian response I imagined my early text eliciting – *Les Evénements* or *Iphigenia 38* – but to the actual response it received: the zeroing in on the question of Blanchot's relations with Drieu and the spectre of collaboration Blanchot sought to dispel. It is remarkable that literary history has retained not Blanchot's account of declining Drieu's offer but rather the fact of his service with the wartime *NRF*. Thus Pascal Fouché writes: 'In April 1942, Maurice Blanchot came to assist Drieu, taking charge of the management of the journal.'⁴ And Pierre Hebey, in *La NRF des années sombres: 1940–1941*, refers to Paulhan's introduction of Blanchot on to the staff of the collaborationist *NRF* and quotes a Paulhan note to Drieu about increasing Blanchot's role: 'Perhaps we might ask Blanchot to organize the notes section. (But would he want to? From his writings, I find him rather intimidating . . .).'⁵

For Hebey, however, the collaborationist *NRF* was a shield or lightning rod whose collaborationism protected the (relative) independence of the Gallimard publishing house. That circumstance would make Blanchot the Resistance's ambassador to the Collaboration, a delicate situation indeed. Pierre Andreu and Frédéric Grover, whose biography of Drieu is a principal source for both Fouché and Hebey, refer, in the conditional, to the proposed new organisation of the review mentioned by Blanchot in his letter to me of 1979:

> Drieu agreed to be the nominal editor. . . . But it was agreed that the lion's share of the work would be done by a secretary (Maurice Blanchot), and by Paulhan, who would be officially charged with establishing communications between the editorial committee and Drieu.[6]

Once again we find Blanchot's projected role as that of liaison between the collaborationist Drieu and the *résistant* Paulhan, the vehicle of their collaboration with each other.[7]

But that eventuality, the official renewal of an independent *NRF* – conveyed by the conditional of Grover and Andreu's formulation – never materialized. Thus we are left with the past tense of Fouché's and Hebey's account: Blanchot's service for an *NRF* that remained Drieu's organ of collaboration, the intellectual pride of Abetz's and Heller's Paris.

One's sense of Blanchot being stranded in the collaborationist *NRF*, moreover, is confirmed by Paulhan's recently published wartime correspondence. On 9 June 1942, he sent a note to Drieu: 'At bottom, nothing leads me, or those I have asked, to believe that the time for reconciliation has come. Don't you think that the provisional situation that we are trying to set up with Blanchot might continue?'[8] That is: the Resistance writers will not work with you, but perhaps we can work out an arrangement with Maurice Blanchot, more or less in anticipation of a reconciliation which nonetheless seems unforeseeable. A day later, Paulhan writes to Drieu that in view of the failure of the newly projected *NRF*,

> the most 'prudent' course would no doubt be for you to take back the journal. . . . On that score, what might be done? Perhaps quite simply, for you and for me, to help Maurice Blanchot as best we can to edit the apolitical journal you gave over to him.[9]

Within a day, the future conditional has given way to the past tense. Blanchot appears to be stranded, the bearer of Paulhan's pipe dream of apoliticism, in an *NRF* fundamentally under the control of Drieu.

It is in this context of Blanchot between Drieu and Paulhan, the

Collaboration and the Resistance, that I should like to examine a text written by Blanchot for the resolutely Pétainist *Journal des débats*. Blanchot was a cultural critic for that paper, which had settled in Clermont-Ferrand, during much of the war. His column, which was called 'Chronique de la vie intellectuelle', first appeared on 16 April 1941, and seems, for the most part, supremely disengaged from the torment of the war in which much of the world was engaged. Many of the columns in the *Journal* appeared *tel quel* in *Faux pas* when that volume was published by Gallimard in 1943. Blanchot, that is, who was about fifteen years Paul de Man's senior, had a job during the war not all that different from the one Paul de Man had accepted with *Le Soir* in Brussels.[10]

Blanchot's articles, appearing regularly, at a few days' distance, in the *Journal*, were generally consigned to the third page of the abbreviated wartime newspaper. On 10 March 1942, however, Blanchot crafted a long first-page article headlined 'La Politique de Sainte-Beuve'. It was a review of Maxime Leroy's volume of the same name, which had been published by Gallimard in 1941, and was to all appearances a rousing endorsement of the book.[11]

For anyone interested in the role of politics in the life and work of Blanchot, arguably France's pre-eminent critic of the twentieth century, this article on the politics of France's pre-eminent critic of the nineteenth century cannot but be of central interest. But that circumstance cannot, of course, have accounted for the prominence accorded the Blanchot article. Such pride of place, I shall argue, may best be explained by the special opportunity an article on Sainte-Beuve's politics afforded its author to take a stand on the issue of intellectual collaboration with the Vichy regime. For Sainte-Beuve attained notoriety in the romantic generation as the one major figure from its ranks to have wholeheartedly embraced the 2 December *coup d'état* of Louis Bonaparte. Paul Guth, in his sprightly literary history, has captured the ignominy of Sainte-Beuve's career as the nineteenth century's nearest approximation to what the next century would call a collaborator: 'He sought to extract from the new regime everything that the previous ones had refused him.'[12] At a time when Marx was writing the *The Eighteenth Brumaire of Louis Bonaparte* and Victor Hugo, in exile, *Napoléon le Petit*, Sainte-Beuve was justifying the bloody December coup in these terms:

The fullness of the monarchical principle, in the free and national understanding of the term, is present when two restorers of society, at fifty years' distance, appear, two leaders of the people redressing France and, without having all that much in common, crowning her equally with glory.[13]

Worse yet, on 23 August 1852, Sainte-Beuve published a 'lundi' under the title 'Les Regrets'. Its subject was the foolishness of any intellectuals who chose to resist the regime whose brutal seizure of power was still fresh in all minds: 'I do not come here to advise anyone to embrace the government, but simply not to deny it obstinately, not to sulk at the society which has ratified it, the basis and truth of the society of our time.'[14] All resistance was assimilated to a variety of 'ressentiment'.[15]

> The danger, today, for a number of eminent minds, who feel assaulted in their habits, their political icons, and who have things to complain about, would be to fix themselves in a rancorous posture, one of petty hostility and sarcastic condemnation: the long-term result would be a deterioration of the very grounds of their thought and judgment.[16]

The central fact about the new regime for Sainte-Beuve was that it secured 'order and the guarantees of civilization'.[17] The issue of censorship was dismissed as a red herring.[18] All calls towards resistance were 'sentimental', appeals for pity on the part of men 'whom no other inconsolable misfortune has befallen than that of no longer governing me'.[19] In the face of such sentimentality, the critic writes, better to simply reset one's watch and commit oneself to living in the present.[20]

Sainte-Beuve's argument, then, sets up something of a primal scene of intellectual collaboration with an unpopular military regime. Sainte-Beuve nonetheless took wounded pride in his political incorrectness and referred to the scandal it provoked and above all to Cuvillier-Fleury's 'refutation' in *Le Journal des débats* as proof that it was on target.[21] The author of *Port-Royal* was being cast by the intelligentsia in the role of the complete opportunist – or conformist. Appointed professor of Latin poetry at the Collège de France in 1854, he was forced to resign his post because he was regularly jeered – as a collaborator – by his would-be students.[22] At the Ecole Normale, where he was subsequently appointed to a position in French literature, he was widely distrusted.[23] Even after entering into mild dissent vis-à-vis the orthodoxy of the regime, he would be characterized by the Goncourt brothers in their journal as: 'the regime's official supporter'. Moreover: 'courage came to him only with his pension and those senatorial *palmes* won by serving with a priest's bad faith all the petty rancors of 2 December'.[24] With the cartoon of the complete collaborator in place, it would not be long before a literary historian (Paul Guth) could feel authorized to risk the following comparison in his *Histoire de la littérature française* with reference to Sainte-Beuve's late dissidence towards the regime he had championed: 'In presenting the Empire with his limited opposition, he was preparing for the future, like those "collaborators" in the last war who, when the occupying power began to weaken, began helping the *résistants*'.[25]

Now lest the leap from 1852 ('Les Regrets') to 1942 (the date of Blanchot's 'La Politique de Sainte-Beuve') be regarded as too precipitous, we shall make a stop midway – at the Dreyfus Affair. Such a pause between Bonapartism and Nazism, at the anti-Semitic riots of the Affair, is, of course, a staple of the anti-fascist treatment of the genealogy of the Hitler phenomenon. Hannah Arendt saw the Dreyfus Affair as a 'dress rehearsal' for the ensuing genocide of the Jews, and evoked the abortive coup attempt of Jules Guérin, criminal hero of the subproletarian mob, in terms reminiscent of Marx's classic treatment of Louis Bonaparte.[26] Our own pause in the Affair, this time to observe the anti-Dreyfusard camp, will be to read Charles Maurras's 'capital' work of 1898, *Trois idées politiques: Chateaubriand, Michelet, Sainte-Beuve*.[27]

Maurras, Blanchot's early master, to whom he could not but make reference, as we shall see, in any discussion of Sainte-Beuve's politics, came up with an ingenious and artfully crafted argument. The right, he claimed, had made a grave error in thinking that Chateaubriand was its ideal standard-bearer, even as the left was completely mystified in promoting Michelet to ideological prominence. Moreover, once those errors were dispelled, a case could be made that the figure best suited to unite both (republican) left and (royalist) right would be (to general surprise) the (Bonapartist) Sainte-Beuve:

> If the parties of the right could forget his bouts of anti-clericalism; if, on the left, one knew what it means to speak, and where true freedom of thought lies . . . well, the work, the name, and the general course of thought of this great mind, without forgetting their natural sequel, their political consequences, would make the finest site imaginable in which to assemble in a day of general reconciliation.[28]

Maurras, in fact, proposed – in 1898 – a national *fête* consecrated to Sainte-Beuve, of the sort, no doubt, that Jeune France, the Vichy cultural machine on whose literary committee Blanchot served briefly during the war, would assiduously plan.[29]

Now before considering the substance of Maurras's argument, it should be observed that its conclusion, a reconciliation of right and left in a new political and cultural synthesis, was at the heart of fascism. *Ni droite ni gauche*, as Zeev Sternhell phrased it, in a study of fascism in the 1930s, which found its best definition in a programmatic political statement, perched between nationalism and socialism, by Blanchot himself.[30] If Maurras's 1898 text, moreover, concludes with a fascist gesture, superseding the division between extremes of left and right, it begins with an epigraph by Paul Bourget which is as chillingly and precisely anticipatory of fascist doctrine as anything in Maurras:

> We must search out what remains of old France and cling to it with our every fibre, rediscover the provinces of national and ancestral unity beneath the artificial and fragmented departments, administrative autonomy, local and fertile Universities beneath our lethal official University, reconstitute the land-based family through freedom to dispose of one's property, protect labour through the re-establishment of corporations, restore vigour and dignity to religious life by dismantling the budget for cults . . . in a word, on this point as on the others, systematically undo the murderous work of the French Revolution.[31]

Here, then, was an early call for the programme which would be attempted under Vichy's 'national revolution': reactionary corporatism or fascism intent on rolling back the political culture of the French Revolution. And the most remarkable feature of all, from our perspective, was that this reactionary revolution, according to Maurras, might well culminate in a national holiday or festival dedicated to Sainte-Beuve.

What, then, of the substance of Maurras's argument? For all his much-vaunted royalism, Chateaubriand was too much the romantic, devoted to an isolation in heroism substantially unrelated to the solidarities of the *ancien régime*. His royalism, moreover, was for the most part masochism: he may have been horrified by the advent of modern times, but the truth was that he loved his horror. No self-respecting monarchist, in brief, can have any truck with a man more interested in mourning monarchy, however elegiacally, than restoring it. On the left, Michelet, on the other hand, for all his interest in emancipation, is too weak a thinker to emancipate anyone: 'Michelet offered the scandal of a very great French writer, whose thought was shapeless, whose sense of order nugatory, and whose dialectic was without backbone.'[32] If education is the road to emancipation, Michelet, according to Maurras, is too intent on elevating every 'rudiment of a general idea' to the dignity of a divine principle to serve as anyone's mentor. Michelet, a man without nuance, and the cult his centenary in 1898 had become were as much an error on the left as the Chateaubriand cult, revived on the occasion of the fiftieth anniversary of his death in 1898, was on the right.

Enter Sainte-Beuve, whose 'empirisme organisateur' is seen by Maurras as the new left–right solution to the dilemma Chateaubriand's 'anarchy' and Michelet' 'democracy' had never come close to resolving. With Sainte-Beuve, according to Maurras, we are freed from the sentimental narcissism of his age: 'A day arrived when Charles-Augustin Sainte-Beuve succeeded in preferring truth to the stirrings of his heart. . . . When he considered writers of a century other than his own, he stopped looking for . . . his own semblance at the bottom of their works.'[33] No more self-dramatizing projection, then, but what Maurras calls the constitution of a museum of partial truth: 'un Musée de la vérité partielle'. And if a preference for the partial or component dimension over totalizing self-reflection seems precociously analytic, that is precisely the term chosen by Maurras for Sainte-Beuve: 'the most analytic of men' in the sense, we read, that analysis 'decomposes' in the interest of providing the 'elements of a recomposition'.[34]

Ultimately what characterizes Sainte-Beuve's thought is its refusal of sentimental utopianism, an empiricist's sensibility that has him 'organizing' tangents of ideality, *échappées sur l'idéal*, against what Maurras calls *l'imaginaire*, on the basis of the given. And it is that refusal of utopian rejection of empirical reality which dictated Sainte-Beuve's collaboration with the second Bonapartist regime.

> Although quite jealous of the liberties of the pen, Sainte-Beuve broke with the men of the Second Republic in order to submit to the constraints of the Empire. . . . Given that public order is the very condition of enduring science . . . how would science hesitate to yield to public order? One does not saw off the branch on which one is perched.[35]

To this thoroughgoing realism, Maurras opposes a 'scientific fanaticism' which threatens science itself. 'It would destroy a state in order to draw from the archives and bring to light an "interesting" document.'³⁶ The reference to the subversive curiosity of intellectuals is a reminder that Maurras was writing in the middle of the Dreyfus Affair, and lest anyone miss the point the founder of Action Française supplies us with a telling metaphor: what Sainte-Beuve (along with Maurras) is opposed to 'consists of replacing the god of the Jews by Curiosity, improperly dubbed Science, placed on an altar at the centre of the world, and graced with the same honours as Jehovah'.³⁷ Thus just as Sainte-Beuve, under Maurras's tutelage, is welcomed into the anti-revolutionary ranks of, first, Renan and Taine, then the ultra-Catholic de Maistre and Bonald, anti-Beuvianism is associated metaphorically with the Jews.

But let us now return to what Maurras would no doubt call our own fanatically searched out document, Blanchot's front-page column, in the *Journal des débats* of 10 March 1942, on the politics of Sainte-Beuve. What we have provided is a frame for that centre-piece, which it would be important not to turn into a frame-up. The frame consists of the established tradition which saw in Sainte-Beuve (by virtue of 'Les Regrets') the intellectual 'collaborator' par excellence with a dictatorial regime and (by way of Maurras) the anti-Semitic right's surprise choice, at the time of the Dreyfus Affair, as intellectual standard-bearer. The centrepiece was a test: Blanchot, we have seen, was to be – and, to a certain extent, was – Paulhan's man in Drieu's *NRF*, the Resistance's ambassador to the Collaboration. It is as though he, the ex-militant fascist, were being asked, in reviewing Leroy's *La Politique de Sainte-Beuve*, to take a stand in a literary code the Germans themselves may not have understood, on the whole vexed question of intellectual collaboration and/or resistance.³⁸

Leroy's *La Politique de Sainte-Beuve*, the subject of the Blanchot evocation or *tableau* we have just framed, offers itself as an apology for the political itinerary of the man Leroy calls, in 1941, 'our contemporary'.³⁹ For the famous critic was not only 'one of the two or three major intelligences of the nineteenth century',⁴⁰ according to Leroy, but a figure whom it would be an error to consider as fundamentally literary in his interests: 'his essence appears to me to lie elsewhere' – in a series of social preoccupations which would bring him closer to "us"'.

Now, the heart of any political apologia for Sainte-Beuve would of necessity lie in justifying his rallying, after the coup d'état of Louis Bonaparte, to the Second Empire. And this is in many ways the principal aim of the book. Leroy's is an effort to free Sainte-Beuve from the detestable epithet 'renegade', to restore a measure of integrity to a figure who, given his support for the insurgents of February 1848, was subsequently branded a traitor to their cause. Leroy, in 1941, confesses his 'astonishment' at the hatred provoked in 1852 by 'Les Regrets', Sainte-Beuve's broadside against the anti-imperial resistance. The critic's notorious humiliation and forced resignation under political pressure from his own students at the Collège de France in 1855 is characterized as 'a riot behind closed doors' and an exercise in 'cowardice' on the part of its perpetrators.[41]

How, then, does Leroy's defence proceed? The brief is pursued on two apparently contradictory fronts. On the one hand, we find an anti-utopian tendency in Sainte-Beuve which ultimately culminates in what might be called the Maurrassian defence. The rationalizing 'orgy' of the eighteenth century had led to a series of disappointing revolutions erupting every fifteen years in France. Sainte-Beuve appears to have had his fill of revolutions after 1830, which he supported, but which initiated a regime whose corruption he analysed with considerable venom and eloquence. By 1852, his position was one of 'organizing empiricism', a label of Maurras's that Leroy, who refers to Maurras only once, fully endorses. Better to reshape what is already there than to pretend to 'invent' a new regime. . . . The simple necessities of civilized life necessitate the minimum of order that Napoleon III alone can provide, or, in Sainte-Beuve's own words: 'The universal acclamation with which France saluted her president in 1852 and crowned him emperor was, among other things, an act of consummate good sense.'[42]

All of this, however, what might be called the sceptical, anti-utopian, incipiently Maurrassian side of Leroy's book, that is, of Blanchot's *subject*, is familiar to us as a motif from the ornate frame we have erected for Blanchot's *tableau*. (To clarify the painterly analogy: my earlier comments on Sainte-Beuve's notoriety in the nineteenth century and Maurras's effort to rehabilitate him at the time of the Dreyfus Affair constitute a *frame* for Blanchot's *tableau* or evocation, the March 1942 article, whose *subject* is Leroy's book *La Politique de Sainte-Beuve*.) We turn now to the other front in Leroy's apology for the critic's stance in 1852, one that is far more original, and which will undergo a curious displacement in Blanchot's own version of Sainte-Beuve. For Leroy devotes his longest and most substantial chapter to what might be called a left-wing defence of Sainte-Beuve. Around the time of the July Revolution, Sainte-Beuve served a year's stint as a Saint-Simonian fellow-traveller. Disillusionment with the theological and erotic antics of Saint-Simon's disciples was not long in coming, but Leroy leans particularly strongly on the critic's link to that productivist utopia in order to present his later rallying to the Second Empire as a residually Saint-Simonian outflanking of the Republican left *on its own left*. In Leroy's most succinct formulation: 'If [Sainte-Beuve] was a Caesarist, it was in so far as he was a socialist.'[43]

If, then (*côté Maurras*), there is a rightist evolution – from abortive revolution to abortive revolution – of Sainte-Beuve's thought towards support of the December coup, there is, on the left, something less in the order of an evolution than a surprise return of the repressed. For it should not be forgotten that the Saint-Simonian leader Enfantin greeted the advent of the Empire as 'providential', something in the order of what Maurras himself, in June 1940, would call a 'divine surprise'.[44] For Leroy, the belated return of the 'socialist' or Saint-Simonian in Sainte-Beuve was in fact of a piece with the critic's admiration for and interest in the work and person of Proudhon. Towards the end of his life Sainte-Beuve was at work on an unfinished biography of Proudhon, a 'masterpiece', and for Leroy it is as though the two nodes of Sainte-Beuve's leftward political itinerary were the early sojourn with the Saint-Simonians and the later work on Proudhon.

Now, concerning Proudhon, Leroy lays great emphasis on the fact that he was an early left supporter of the Empire. As a convinced anti-parliamentarian and anti-democrat, he was more concerned with social than political reality. And Sainte-Beuve's positions are said to be essentially those of Proudhon. In Leroy's words, '*La Révolution sociale démontrée par le coup d'État* by Proudhon is the exact counterpart of *Les Regrets* by Sainte-Beuve.'[45]

In the France of the young Blanchot, the name Proudhon was highly charged. In *Combat*, the journal for which Blanchot had written in the late 1930s, an effort was made to mythologize a pre-First World War movement, the Cercle Proudhon, as Europe's first authentic attempt at a fascist group. Under the name of (the rabidly anti-Semitic) Proudhon, (Maurrassian) royalists and (Sorelian) syndicalists had come together in their shared contempt for democracy.[46] It was in that context, no doubt, that Leroy felt comfortable anachronistically imagining Sainte-Beuve's 'disabused smile' at finding a 'striking justification for his own political empiricism' in a passage he proceeds to cite from Sorel.[47]

Leroy's 1941 apologia for Sainte-Beuve's collaboration with the Empire is thus twofold: Maurrassian on the right and Proudhonian-Sorelian on the left. As such it discreetly captured the two components of France's *ur*-fascist formation as mythologized in Blanchot's own milieu in the 1930s. But perhaps that extremist left–right fusion was already in germ in the Saint-Simonianism that Leroy seems so intent on assigning a formative role in Sainte-Beuve's political thought. For there is persistent reference to the paradoxical centrality of the thought of Joseph de Maistre (as well as Bonald and Ballanche) in the organic social vision of the Saint-Simonians. De Maistre, of course, was the reactionary ideologue whom Isaiah Berlin has discussed, most recently, as being at the wellspring of fascism. Berlin: 'He was the first theorist in the great and powerful tradition which culminated in Charles Maurras, a precursor of the Fascists.'[48] And for Sainte-Beuve, in his *Nouveaux lundis*,

> Saint-Simonianism performed for the French mind the eminent service of implanting within the camp of revolution and progress a number of the elevated thoughts of M. de Maistre and of naturalizing them there in fertile soil and in a vital fashion.[49]

Thus Leroy's Sainte-Beuve of 1941 moves from the extreme left–right fusion of Saint-Simon and de Maistre to that of Proudhon (or Sorel) and Maurras. *Ni droite ni gauche*, in Sternhell's phrase. Which is to say that no thinker could make as much claim to being 'our contemporary' during the Nazi Occupation – in a France intent on proving, in defeat, its own autonomy or centrality – as Leroy's Sainte-Beuve, who draws on an extreme left–right ideology in rallying to the brutal putsch of a military dictator.[50]

Thus far we have dealt with what I have called the frame of Blanchot's *tableau*: Sainte-Beuve's role as collaborationist bogeyman of the liberal intelligentsia and his coronation by Maurras during the Dreyfus Affair. And we have dealt with its subject: Leroy's two-pronged apologia for Sainte-Beuve's politics, 'empiricist' with Maurras, 'socialist' with Saint-Simon and Proudhon. But we have yet to read a word of Blanchot's piece. Which is to say, perhaps, that we have been engaging in a form of hyper-structuralism, sketching out the contours or even generating the only text, as yet unread, that might satisfy the various constraints – of frame and subject – we have adduced. Structuralist, indeed: were one to examine the space the *Journal des débats* accorded Blanchot's article – front page, double column, flush right – diachronically, one would find it was earmarked for cultural justifications for adhering to Pétain's policies. A week earlier (4 March 1942), Gaetan Sanvoisin, in the same space, issued a long and laudatory comparison between Richelieu and Pétain ('A parallel is called for. In so far as the dual concerns of national unity and nobility of vocabulary are concerned, Marshall Pétain, like Richelieu, has recourse to impeccable language in defining the

essential principles of our territorial security').[51] So much for
diachrony. Synchronically, Blanchot's article would appear to form a
diptych with a front-page editorial the same day hailing Pétain as 'the
only man able to lead us'.[52] Such at least must have been the expectation of Blanchot's editors. That those expectations were decisively
thwarted, even at the cost of a misreading of Leroy's argument,
strikes me as a precise gauge of Blanchot's political honour. It is to
that topic, as mediated by Blanchot's article, that we shall now turn.

The piece begins ominously enough with a statement of admiration for Leroy's identification with his subject. Leroy, we are told,
seems to have wanted to become 'just like' Sainte-Beuve. Indeed
Leroy's sympathetic insinuation into the critic's mind is compared to
Sainte-Beuve's own identification with the Catholic mystic and
monarchist Ballanche in an essay that so 'shocked' (Blanchot's
word) Sainte-Beuve's liberal friends that Leroy uses the word
'treason' to characterize their assessment of it.[53] At stake in
Blanchot's article, in brief, is an identification with the Sainte-Beuve
whose own political identifications opened him up to accusations of
treason on the part of the liberal intelligentsia. And that chain of
identifications, moreover, which admits no reservation, is what joins
the situation of Leroy in 1941 (and potentially of Blanchot in 1942)
to Sainte-Beuve at the time of the coup d'état of 1851. In Blanchot's
words: Leroy 'does not consent to any reservations. He finds the best
in the worst. And this apologetic posture, thanks to an extraordinary
harmony of hidden circumstances, only rarely gives the impression
of troubling the observer's perspicacity.' The extraordinary
'harmony' or affinity, concealed though it may be, and to which
Blanchot feels empowered to allude in the most discreet terms, is
precisely the one which I have attempted to shed some light on in my
preceding comments.

The subject, in brief, will at some level be, Blanchot suggests,
collaboration and its apologists in the France of 1941. And
Blanchot's tone in his first paragraph implies that Leroy's apology is
a remarkably impressive feat – without quite implying that it is a
politically or ethically justified one. At this point Blanchot turns to
the whole side of Sainte-Beuve's career which led Irving Babbitt to
suggest that the best motto for the critic might well have been
'Enthusiasm and repentance'.[54] In 1830 and in 1848, he was a
sympathizer with the insurgents, but one who soon found himself
disappointed and occasionally overwhelmed by the cause he had
championed. There is at times here a quite Blanchotian sense that the
repentance is so much stronger than the initial enthusiasm as to have

left nought but an extreme nihilism in its wake. Thus this quotation from Sainte-Beuve (in a letter to Adam Mickjewicz) as early as 1833: 'You call yourselves pilgrims and banished, and we too, we are banished from the revolution we have loved and waged: we are expelled from our hopes.' It is hard to imagine Blanchot, the ex-apologist for fascist terrorism, the ex-bureaucrat of Jeune France, not feeling addressed by the assessment.[55] Yet Leroy's Sainte-Beuve retained a certain positive wisdom of disillusionment, and it is precisely that dimension that brings Blanchot to Leroy's endorsement of Sainte-Beuve's rallying to the Empire:

> M. Maxime Leroy justifies at some length Sainte-Beuve for having accepted 2 December and having rallied to the Empire. He shows that his taste for authority, nurtured in the school of Saint-Simon, found more to praise than to blame in the new regime.

Yet curiously Blanchot does not approach the heart of Leroy's enthusiasm for what he regards as Sainte-Beuve's own enthusiasm for the Empire: the Saint-Simonian or 'socialist' heart of the programme, the possibility of outflanking the liberals on their left. Blanchot does all he can to mitigate Sainte-Beuve's enthusiasm, to inscribe the rallying to the Empire under the rubric of 'repentance' or disillusionment: 'There was a good deal of restraint and a certain contempt in his support.'

But this confronts Blanchot with a second embarrassment, the fact that the slope of repentance in Babbitt's imagined motto leads Blanchot precipitously to Maurras's own essay on Sainte-Beuve's 'empiricism'. For it would be more than a mere pun to read the authoritarian Second Empire back into Maurras's vision of the critic's empiricism. Now the paradox, in this chess game that Blanchot seems to be playing with Leroy (or his own editors) on the front page of the *Journal des débats*, is that the 'empiricist' culmination of Sainte-Beuve's disillusionment (or repentance) in the endorsement of Maurras forces Blanchot to confront, in Maurras, the very enthusiasm, on the margins of Action Française, he was then – in 1942 – desirous of shunting off if not repenting of.

At this point Blanchot appears to flinch. No sooner has he discussed the politically explosive precedent of rallying to the Empire than we read:

> It is known that M. Charles Maurras has given the name of *empirisme organisateur*, 'organizing empiricism', to the method of political observation applied by Sainte-Beuve and which led

him, in a century devoured by systems, ideology, abstract passions, and instinctual frenzy, to submit to the law of facts and results. Such is the principal lesson of this sinuous, unstable and – at bottom – religious mind, on whom intelligence, in agreement with a sensibility perpetually concerned with harmony, extended the broadest empire, one quite foreign to all limits.

Sainte-Beuve's itinerary in disillusionment or repentance, that is, has culminated in the object of Blanchot's enthusiasm, his endorsement of Maurras's analytic endorsement of Sainte-Beuve. That Blanchot's endorsement, moreover, all but repeats our pun, moving from 'empirisme organisateur' to 'empire', puts it in painful contiguity with the whole subject of collaboration, the presumed reason Blanchot's Pétainist editors had reserved pride of place on the first page of their newspaper for him. Blanchot would appear to have all but fallen into the trap.

Whereupon he performs an about-face, engages in his own palinode:

It goes without saying that the limits of such realism are bearable only with difficulty. Sainte-Beuve himself did not bear them. He ceasely broke free from their yoke and bore within himself dreams awakened by the movement of a stubborn will to believe.

Now, on the path to this shunting off of the Maurrassian reading that has just been endorsed, it is significant that the principal landmark is the critic's Saint-Simonianism: 'A Saint-Simonian in his youth, he devoted a fragment of his being to vague and consoling aspirations, to a kind of devout optimism which no disillusionment ever succeeded in dispelling.' Such is Blanchot's principal reference to Saint-Simon in the article, the starting point for a renunciation of what had been consolidated around the endorsement of Maurras. Yet we have seen that for Leroy, Sainte-Beuve's Saint-Simonianism (refracted through Proudhon) and his 'empiricism' or proto-Maurrassianism were not in conflict but in fact fused as the two strands – left and right – of what Blanchot's own generation had learnt to champion as fascism. So that the pitting of a dreamy Saint-Simonianism against a hard-nosed Maurrassianism is totally at odds with the Sainte-Beuve of whom Leroy writes: 'if he was a Caesarist, it was in so far as he was a socialist, like Enfantin or Proudhon, who also rallied to the Empire'.[56] In a flagrant and glorious misreading of Leroy's book, Blanchot has pitted the two ideological dimensions of what would fuse as fascism against each other in a patently anti-collaborationist move.

Where does this take him? The sole further reference to Sainte-Beuve's Saint-Simonianism is a quotation from the Goncourt *Journal*, denying the perpetuity of 'literary property'. Sainte-Beuve's Saint-Simonianism, that is, becomes the first step towards the domain of radical dispossession characteristic of what would later be called *l'espace littéraire*. The next anti-Maurrassian salvo is by way of the Abbé Brémond:

> The faith which the Abbé Brémond was intent on bestowing on Sainte-Beuve in his book *Roman et histoire d'une conversion* was thus refracted through a dark soul in which disquiet, disillusionment, the desire to love, and perpetually thwarted aspirations sustained a measure of dissatisfaction which fuelled his quest, but which brought him secretly to shatter the tranquil realism to which he felt attached.

The 'realism' or 'empiricism' or attachment to the Empire is again thwarted, shattered, by religious faith. The Brémond book is a curious tale of Sainte-Beuve's role as consoler and confessor in the conversion of his friend Ulrich Guttinguer.[57] It was an experience that saw both men writing novelistic versions – each named *Arthur* – of their joint ordeal and that brought Sainte-Beuve himself to the brink of religious conversion. What is most striking in the present context is that in Blanchot's article, Sainte-Beuve has moved from illustrious predecessor in the byways of collaboration with a reviled military dictatorship to confidant in an experience of conversion. But for anyone who has followed Blanchot's writing from the margins of Action Française to the extreme 'passivity' characteristic of 'literary space', is it not as though what were at stake were something in the order of a conversion? Blanchot, that is, would have written himself into the role of Sainte-Beuve's confidant and convert Guttinguer.

Consider, in that light, the fact that Guttinguer's conversion was in large part triggered by the flight of one of his mistresses, Rosalie, to a convent on the Rue Picpus, and was haunted by his desire to murder the woman he referred to in his correspondance (in italics) as 'the nun (*la religieuse*)'.[58] Guttinguer's conversion would at some level entail the sacrifice of 'la religieuse'. Let us pause to imagine that proposition, from the book adduced (against collaboration) by Blanchot, resonating in the critic's mind. Diderot's novel *La Religieuse*, he may have known, was said by its author to have been inspired by the myth of Iphigenia.[59] The fact becomes illuminating when one recalls, as evoked above, that Blanchot's own allegory of his sacrifice of an investment in fascism in 1938 was written up, after the war, as his own version of the myth of Iphigenia, *Death Sentence*. Here we find Blanchot, in flight from the spectre of collaboration, in flight from his own Maurrassian past, in concealed flight as well from Leroy's reading of Sainte-Beuve, inviting his readers to dream a tale of conversion informed, by implication, by the myth that would later haunt him, that of Iphigenia.

After Saint-Simon and the expropriation of the author, after the Abbé Brémond and his tale of conversion, Blanchot leaves us with a final marker for situating 'the politics of Sainte-Beuve', the Abbé Sieyès. Having gutted whatever positivity may have been left of Sainte-Beuve's proto-Maurrassian empiricism, having evoked the 'desperation' such a view would entail, he concludes:

> It is natural, when considering him, to evoke, as M. Leroy does, the strange retreat of Sieyès who, impelled by disillusionment, renounced his very self and withdrew into silence. Extreme disbelief, when it is acknowledged, leads to a desperate lucidity which excludes all distraction, renders vain the possession of every treasure, and finally effaces the night itself.

Here one senses the eloquent nihilism of Blanchot's maturity, but what interests me is its links to the retreat from Pétainist collaboration which I take the article on Sainte-Beuve's politics to be. There is, of course, good reason for adducing Sieyès as a prototype for Sainte-Beuve's behaviour. For the author of *Qu'est-ce que le tiers état?* was notorious for having both ushered in the Revolution and drawn it to a close: he was a principal co-conspirator with Bonaparte in the first 18 Brumaire. That, I assume, was Leroy's reason for linking him with Sainte-Beuve, who managed to be a man of both 1848 and 1851: Sainte-Beuve, or the second time as farce, if one likes. Blanchot, however, is less interested in the political manoeuvrer than in the long-lived survivor of political catastrophe. In the 1830s, it has been said, 'they thought him another Daniel delivered from the burning fiery furnace; the hair of his head had been singed, the smell of fire had passed upon him; and [people] drew back a little from his touch'.[60] At the end of 'La Politique de Sainte-Beuve', that is, we find ourselves somewhere between *The Work of Fire* (*La Part du feu*) and *The Writing of the Disaster*. The Sieyès of his retirement or 'philosophical silence', as he called it, was a man become, in his own words, 'entirely negative', committed to absolute silence on the subject of what he had been through. Sainte-Beuve, in his own *lundi* on Sieyès, evokes his silence, has him interrupting his every discourse: 'I no longer find the word. It's hiding in some dark corner.'[61] Translated into Blanchot's post-war idiom of 1948: 'A narrative (*récit*)?. . . . No, no more narratives, never again.'[62] The war is over; the *récit* is not forthcoming; and it remains perhaps for us to piece together the fragments of what it might have been.

NOTES

1 The relevant portion of the letter is excerpted in my *Legacies: Of Anti-Semitism in France* (Minneapolis: University of Minnesota Press, 1983), p. 117.

2 See my *Genealogies of the Text: Literature, Psychoanalysis, and Politics in Modern France* (Cambridge: Cambridge University Press, 1995), chapter 6, 'Iphigenia 38: deconstruction, history, and the case of *L'Arrêt de mort*'.

3 Philippe Ariès, *Un historien du dimanche* (Paris: Seuil, 1980), p. 184. Here, and elsewhere, all translations from the French, unless otherwise indicated, are mine.

4 Pascal Fouché, *L'Edition française sous l'Occupation, 1940–1944* (Paris: Bibliothèque de la Littérature Française de l'Université de Paris VII, 1987), vol. II, p. 80.

5 Pierre Hebey, *La NRF des années sombres: 1940–1941* (Paris: Gallimard, 1992), p. 136.

6 Pierre Andreu and Frédéric Grover, *Drieu la Rochelle* (Paris: Hachette, 1979), p. 489.

7 See my *Genealogies of the Text*, chapter 7, 'Writing and deference: the politics of literary adulation' for a discussion of the paradoxes of Paulhan's own insertion into the Resistance.

8 Jean Paulhan, *Choix de lettres*, Volume II (1937–1945) (Paris: Gallimard, 1992), p. 280.

9 Ibid.

10 For a discussion of Paul de Man's writings during the war, see my *Genealogies of the Text*, chapter 9, 'Perspectives: on Paul de Man and *Le Soir*'.

11 Maxime Leroy, *La Politique de Sainte-Beuve* (Paris: Gallimard, 1941).

12 Paul Guth, *Histoire de la littérature française* (Paris: Fayard, 1967), vol. II, p. 344.

13 'Compte rendu de la réception de Falloux à l'Académie Française', cited ibid., p. 345.

14 C.-A. Sainte-Beuve, 'Les Regrets', in *Causeries du lundi*, vol. VI (Paris: Garnier, 1853), p. 327.

15 Ibid., p. 336.

16 Ibid., p. 328.

17 Ibid., p. 335.

18 See Roger Williams, *The World of Napoleon II: 1851–1870* (New York: Collier, 1957), p. 127.

19 'Les Regrets', p. 335.

20 Ibid., p. 329.

21 Ibid., p. 337: 'The refutation, which was a long time in coming, in itself

would prove how accurate the article was.'
22 See Guth, *Histoire*, p. 346.
23 Ibid., p. 347.
24 Cited ibid., p. 348.
25 Ibid.
26 Hannah Arendt, *The Origins of Totalitarianism* (New York: Harcourt Brace Jovanovich, 1951), pp. 89–120.
27 Republished in Charles Maurras, *Œuvres capitales: essais politiques* (Paris: Flammarion, 1954), pp. 63–97.
28 Ibid., p. 84.
29 Ibid., p. 83.
30 See Zeev Sternhell, *Ni droite ni gauche: l'idéologie fasciste en France* (Paris: Seuil, 1983), p. 241.
31 Maurras, *Œuvres capitales: essais politiques*, p. 63.
32 Ibid., p. 71.
33 Ibid., p. 77.
34 Ibid., p. 78.
35 Ibid., p. 81.
36 Ibid.
37 Ibid.
38 In a review of Leroy's book in the April 1942 issue of the *NRF*, Ramon Fernandez could write (p. 485) that Sainte-Beuve 'foresaw a system of justice and a morality erected on new bases . . . a system of justice and a morality such as we find today anticipated all around us'.
39 Leroy, *La Politique*, p. 8.
40 Ibid., p. 95.
41 Ibid., p. 218.
42 Ibid., p. 194.
43 Ibid., p. 273.
44 Ibid., p. 212.
45 Ibid.
46 For a discussion of the Cercle Proudhon, see Zeev Sternhell, *La Droite révolutionnaire, 1885–1914: les origines françaises du fascisme* (Paris: Seuil, 1978), pp. 391–400.
47 Leroy, *La Politique*, p. 273.
48 Isaiah Berlin, 'Joseph de Maistre and the origins of fascism', in *The Crooked Timber of Humanity: Chapters in the History of Ideas* (New York: Vintage, 1992), p. 170.
49 Cited in Leroy, *La Politique*, p. 67.
50 The extended version of this chapter, which may be found in my *Genealogies of the Text*, chapter 12, includes at this juncture a discussion of Saint-Simonianism as a form of aestheticism (according to Leroy), the aspirations of the movement to constitute a *Gesamtkunstwerk* (according to Benjamin), and that Wagnerian ideal as the *political* model of National Socialism (according to Lacoue-Labarthe).
51 Gaetan Sanvoisin, 'La Médaille de Richelieu', in *Journal des débats*, 4 March 1942. The comment takes on a certain drollery when one recalls de Gaulle's pre-war role as Pétain's ghost writer for the book Pétain hoped would secure him his place in the Académie Française. See my

'De Gaulle with and against Pétain: the theme of the traitor and the hero' (forthcoming).

52 Marcel Bastier, 'Le Discours de M. Pierre Pucheu', *Journal des débats*, 10 March 1942.

53 Leroy, *La Politique*, p. 205.

54 Irving Babbitt, *Masters of Modern French Criticism* (Boston, Mass.: Houghton Mifflin, 1912), p. 106.

55 Thus Blanchot, plainly in retreat from his political past, refers in the article under discussion to 'the little profit which all true literary and critical minds derive from frequenting political groups, which are always more or less intolerant'.

56 Leroy, *La Politique*, p. 273.

57 Henri Brémond, *Le Roman et l'histoire d'une conversion: Ulrich Guttinguer et Sainte-Beuve d'après des correspondances inédites* (Paris: Plon, 1925).

58 Ibid., p. 117.

59 See Jacques Chouillet, *La Formation des idées esthétiques de Diderot* (Paris: Armand Colin, 1973), p. 501: 'Iphigenia is to all appearances the prototype of sister Suzanne. The nun, like Agamemnon's daughter, incarnates the victim borne to the foot of the altar; she is the image of human sacrifice.'

60 J. M. Thompson, *Leaders of the French Revolution* (Oxford: Blackwell, 1968), p. 3.

61 Sainte-Beuve, *Causeries du lundi* (Paris: Garnier, 1852), vol. V, p. 174.

62 Maurice Blanchot, *The Madness of the Day*, trans. Lydia Davis (Barrytown, N.Y.: Station Hill Press, 1981), p. 18. Translation amended.

Index